I·C·O·N·S

I·C·O·N·S

INTIMATE
PORTRAITS

DENISE
WORRELL

For my husband

Excerpt from "The Waste Land" in *Collected Poems 1909–1962*
by T. S. Eliot, copyright 1936 by Harcourt Brace Jovanovich, Inc.,
copyright 1963, 1964 by T. S. Eliot, reprinted by permission
of the publisher.

Published simultaneously in Canada
Printed in the United States of America
First edition

Book design by the Sarabande Press

Library of Congress Cataloging-in-Publication Data
Worrell, Denise.
Icons : intimate portraits, by Denise Worrell. — 1st ed.
ISBN 0-87113-306-7
1. Motion picture actors and actresses—United States—Interviews. 2. Motion
picture producers and directors—United States—Interviews. 3. Entertainers—
United States—Interviews.
I. Title.
PN1998.2.W68   1988   791.43′028′0922—dc19   88-32076

The Atlantic Monthly Press
19 Union Square West
New York, NY 10003

First printing

AUTHOR'S NOTE

*T*he profiles in this book were not originally written for publication. Traditionally, reporting stories and writing them are two different jobs at *Time* magazine. Correspondents in the field report stories. These reports are longer than a *Time* story and include eyewitness accounts of events, as well as commentary and detailed background information. The reports are not published but are used solely by the writer in New York as the basis for the story that will appear in the magazine. As *Time*'s Hollywood correspondent, I reported the following profiles for a small group of New York–based show business writers and editors. I wrote the reports—ten of them for cover stories—with the hope of giving my colleagues across the continent an immediate and intimate portrait of the person I interviewed. I wanted them to see what I saw and hear what I heard. This book is a revised and edited collection of those reports. I have tried to turn the original seven hundred pages into eleven short stories.

ACKNOWLEDGMENTS

*T*his book was Otto Friedrich's idea. He persuaded the Atlantic Monthly Press it was a viable one. It never occurred to me that the raw material for a book was in my file cabinet, nor did I splash through Manhattan's rain-drenched streets with rough manuscript in hand, as he did, in search of a publisher. I am honored and grateful to him beyond words.

Ray Cave and Martha Duffy, the most generous of editors, have ghost-touched all the profiles in the book. They guided me through the years the stories span, and I thought of them often as I wrote.

I especially want to thank Gerald Clarke, Jay Cocks, and Richard Corliss, the *Time* writers I always dreamed of being. I owe many thanks to Elaine Dutka and Elizabeth Bland, my longtime colleagues and collaborators; to Dick Thompson for his contribution to the George Lucas piece; to MaryAnne Golon for her perfect picture sense; to Leah Gordon and Sue Raffety; and to Dan Goodgame, Henry Muller, and Jason McManus, for their kindness and encouragement.

Liz Rosenberg, Glen Brunman, Maggie Unsworth, and Sidney Ganis gave me crucial help on individual stories, and I am indebted to them.

My love to my family who all have faith; to Alessandra Stanley for her long-distance reassurance; to Erik Vestville for his constant support; to David Thomson and Lucy Gray who urged me forward; and to Richard von KleinSmid, a passionate reader and dear friend.

I owe a great deal to Ann Godoff of the Atlantic Monthly Press for her initial instinct, sharp insights, understanding, and unwavering enthusiasm for the book.

I would also like to thank all the people I interviewed for giving me so much of their time and spirit.

Above all, I am grateful to Jeffrey Fiskin, who always listened to the voices in my head.

CONTENTS

INTRODUCTION

BY OTTO FRIEDRICH

What are the roots that clutch, what branches grow
Out of this stony rubbish? Son of man,
You cannot say, or guess, for you know only
A heap of broken images, where the sun beats . . .
                                                    —T. S. Eliot

*Y*ou are about to begin reading an extraordinary book of Hollywood portraits—intense,
perceptive, surprising, funny, rich—and yet these
portraits are also something more. There is superb reporting in this book because Denise Worrell is a superb reporter, and yet there is still
something more. The key to this something more
is in the title: *Icons*.

Icons are gods and yet not gods. An icon represents a god, which is not quite the same as being
one, or rather it represents the idea of a god. One
thinks of the fierce, hawk-headed deities un-

earthed in Egypt, or perhaps of the benignly egg-shaped stone figurines discovered in the Cyclades. It is the destiny of icons, one gathers, to be first worshipped, then buried and forgotten. Icons are thought to perform miracles, but they are also vulnerable, made of stone or clay, which can be smashed, of iron or bronze, which can be melted. Perhaps it is only the lucky icons that are buried and forgotten. The fate of the others is to be first worshipped and then destroyed. If icons were aware of being icons, would they not live in a state of dread?

Yet icons vary from culture to culture. As with so many things, the Greeks created gods that defied their own destinies. Not only do the figures of Zeus and Athena live on in marble but they outlive the ideas they once represented. They now represent not divinity but beauty. Even Venus de Milo is an icon, but not of anything sacred. The Romans, as usual, went to excess. They carved and molded icons to celebrate not only gods but monarchs and even regional governors. "The Roman magistrates very frequently were adored as provincial deities," Gibbon wrote with contempt, "with the pomp of altars and temples, of festivals and sacrifices. It was natural that the emperors should not refuse what the proconsuls had accepted. . . ." And so, throughout those long years of decadence, each emperor was proclaimed divine, and icons of him were erected and worshipped and rather often reduced to rubble.

The Old Testament sternly forbade such blasphemies. After the original declaration, "I am the Lord thy God and thou shalt have no other gods before me," the very next of the Ten Commandments is equally unequivocal: "Thou shalt not make unto thee any graven image, or any likeness of anything that is in heaven above. . . ." A fair number of the early Christian martyrs went to their martyrdom for having attacked and torn down what they called idols, the icons of Rome, but since the subsequent centuries of Christian growth were centuries of accommodation with forbidden traditions, theologians as early as the third century were explaining and justifying the iconography that would eventually bring us the glorious mosaics in St. Mark's in Venice, the Giotto frescoes in Assisi, the Michelangelo ceiling in the Sistine Chapel.

The worship of icons arouses deep and violent emotions. When the emperor known as Leo the Issaurian decreed the abolition of all graven images in the churches of Constantinople, the Vatican proclaimed his iconoclasm to be a foul heresy, and the ensuing clashes between church and empire caused bloodshed throughout much of the eighth century.

Nearly a millennium later, the Protestant Reformation raised the same arguments, which zealous reformers tried to resolve by smashing holy statues and stained-glass windows all across Central Europe. Nor would the violence end there. Walk today through the sacred corridors of Chartres and note that the saintly icons lining the walls still bear on their stone faces the wounds inflicted by the axes of the French Revolution. The burdens that we put on those we worship have always been heavy.

Religious strife is not an essential part of the American scene, perhaps because none of the traditional religions is overwhelmingly important to us. Having officially agreed to be tolerant and pluralistic ("Worship in the church of your choice," the posters say, implying that they are all more or less the same), having agreed not only to separate church and state but also to separate religion from education, religion from culture, and even religion from morality, we have agreed that everyone can more or less establish his own religion, and the only one to which we all (or most of us) pledge allegiance is the religion of success. We have even given it a popular name, particularly popular during election campaigns: The American Dream.

The religion of success is not a real honest-to-God religion—it explains neither our cosmological origins nor our destination in eternity—but it does provide those short-term answers that Americans seem to prefer. It does sound pragmatic and practical. It does provide a goal—success—and a methodology—success—and an ethos—success. Like any faith, the religion of success needs and therefore creates its own icons. Some of these are safely dead and enshrined, like the colored photographs of Jack Kennedy on the walls of tenements, but often even the dead are reported to be still among us (*"Elvis spotted in Bronx"*), for it seems to be an axiom of America's living religion that its icons should be alive.

We have three great sources for the creation of such icons. One is the national sport of moneymaking. Tell us, Lee Iacocca or Donald Trump, how we can become as rich as you. Another is the national sport of sport itself. Show us, Mike Tyson or Doctor J, how we can be stronger and faster than anybody else. Most of all, though, we like to create icons from that world of fantasy where Denise Worrell has found the figures she brings to life in this book, the world of song and dance and film and fame, the world where a carefully prepared script generally decrees that heroism is rewarded and love conquers all. We celebrate these quasi-supernatural icons of show business because we attribute magic powers to them, not only the power of being beautiful and triumphant but of knowing the answers that we do not know, the answers on how to live, how to be happy, how to be successful. For supposedly possessing these magic powers, we honor them with the highest rewards known to the religion of success: money, and publicity, and still more money, and still more publicity.

By some magical power all her own, Denise Worrell has been able to persuade some of these icons to talk, perhaps more fully than ever before, about how the religion of success really works. And it soon becomes clear that the deities whom we credit with knowing the answers to the mysteries really do not know those answers. On the contrary, as they try to talk about who they are and what they do, one of the most important elements that appears common to them all is one that we know all too well: pain, and behind that, fear—pain and fear suffered often and only occasionally overcome. Even the proud and cocky Madonna, speaking of her friend Prince, casually remarks: "He's frightened, but I'm frightened, too, for that matter. When I was a kid, I had a nervous stomach and I threw up every time I was frightened. Now I can't throw up. . . ."

"I had all the fears that a lot of kids usually have," Steven Spielberg tells Worrell, "of the netherworld living under my bed, of monsters living in the closet wanting to suck me in and do terrible things to me. . . . I was afraid of everything." When the contemporary master of childhood fantasy was first taken to see Walt Disney's *Snow White*, his reaction was almost inevitable: "I was absolutely terrified by the witch. . . . I burst into tears and started shaking and hiding my eyes." But come now to Disneyland as the far more controlled, the almost icy Steve Martin recalls returning to the magic store where he once learned conjuring tricks. He felt a need to assume a disguise. "I dyed my hair brown and wore a brown mustache," he tells Worrell of his own fight against fear. "It's not that people mob me on the streets, it's not like Michael Jackson came to town. It depends on where you are, but . . . I don't like being stared at or yelled at. . . ."

Worrell even tracked down the elusive Michael Jackson, past an array of security guards, and found him sitting in the darkness, unwilling or unable to say anything more than a faint "Hi." "He's sort of like a fawn in a burning forest," Steven Spielberg has told her, and Jane Fonda elaborated: "He creates around him a world that protects him." So does the remote and unapproachable Bob Dylan. "I feel like I fall short in just about everything," he tells Worrell. "I feel pretty calm most of the time, but then if I review my situation at all, it always seems like I'm up there walking the plank. I always feel like somebody's cracking the whip. Somebody or something."

One of the most fundamental fears is the fear that one may not really be what one thinks one is, or, worse, that one may not be able to find out who one is, or, still worse, that one may not be anybody at all. One may simply be empty, hollow, stuffed, nothing but somebody else's icon. All the money and all the flattery may be unearned, undeserved, not really one's own. This fear has always been acute in Hollywood, where the most celebrated icons have traditionally worn false names, false hair, false teeth, where the very nature of the common profession is to assume false identities and to live by the game of who am I. *Who am I?* "They didn't know what they had," as the screenwriter Daniel Fuchs wrote of the movie stars' insecurities in his novel *West of the Rockies*, "what it was in them that accounted for their good fortune. They didn't know how to present it, manipulate it, embellish it, portion it out — since they didn't know what it was or whether in fact they had anything at all."

Even so cool and experienced an actor as Paul Newman has difficulties with this question of his own identity. "You have got to separate what you are from what people think you are," he tells Worrell. "If you feel very ordinary inside your own skin then anything you achieve has to be fraudulent. I think my credentials as an actor, as a professional person, are fraudulent." A more emotional star like Bette Midler speaks of her evolving public personalities in a tone so disconnected as to sound almost schizophrenic. She remembers growing up with a cracked mirror, which helped her to believe that "in my mind's eye I'm beautiful and tall and thin and glamorous," and it was only when she began being photographed in public "that I realized my mental image of myself and my true image were not the same. I was very, very shocked." She remembers listening to old records of stars like Mae West and Ruby Keeler and "creating this idea, this persona. . . . The tortured torch singer in the middle of the fog with the fur piece around her neck sharing her sorrows with the world." She remembers that when she started playing nightclubs, "the big brassy broad beat the crap out of the little torch singer and took over." And finally she recognizes that "there's someone who lives inside of me who never shows up unless I'm drunk, and that person is a really hateful person. I don't like that person. . . ."

While such multiple personalities are not uncommon among Hollywood actors, it is interesting that many of Worrell's icons are not actors at all. Four are essentially directors, though several of these also write their scripts, and four are primarily singers, though they also act and write their own songs. What this mainly illustrates is how show business has changed since the days of the great studio empires, when salaried directors and salaried actors arrived on the assembly-line set every morning to shoot whatever the studio told them to shoot. Ever since the breakup of the studios and the development of the *auteur* theory in the fifties, the star director has become as much a celebrity as any of his actors, subject to all the fears and fantasies that traditionally accompany stardom. Filmmakers like Steven Spielberg or George Lucas are not only icons in themselves but icon-creators on an immense scale. Who but Spielberg could have drawn E.T. out of his own tormented childhood, and who but Lucas can even imagine all the details of all the inhabitants of his *Star Wars* trilogy? And who can feel more intensely than Lucas that ultimate destiny of the icon, to be cracked, smashed, buried alive? "I am burned out," he tells Worrell after the completion of his zillion-dollar dream. "I am burned out, period."

Throughout all this, there is always music, music in almost every film, music in the TV commercial, music in the shopping mall, music leaking from the jogger's earpieces and pouring from the ghetto box. And the music is different in every way from what it used to be. Bing Crosby used to sing songs written in Tin Pan Alley; Dylan sings Dylan, and Dylan's words are more important to the music than Tin Pan Alley's ever were. Not only are Madonna's words more important, but so are her clothes. The whole personality, in short, is more immediate, more grasping, more compelling—more that of an icon. And correspondingly more quickly discarded. What did ever become of the Fifth Dimension or Alice Cooper or for that matter the Sex Pistols or God knows all the others? For Michael Jackson to have lasted twenty years and still to make records that sell many millions is to become an icon of icons, so can anyone be surprised that he hides in the dark, among his video games and his swans, and that when Worrell finally finds him and shakes his hand, the hand "feels like a cloud"?

Still, these are not unique fears or anxieties. All of us have moments of wondering who we really are, or whether we are anything at all. And if one of the great strengths of Worrell's reporting is to show us that Hollywood's icons are not so different from us as the devotional publicity suggests, she also shows us how each of these icons achieved huge success through a kind of creative will. David Lean, for example, recalls that he was "an absolute dud" until an uncle gave him a camera that enabled him to begin a new life in the darkroom. Steve Martin made himself a master of the banjo by practicing for hours every night inside his parked car, then gave it up because he "wasn't getting any better." Madonna, who mostly taught herself to dance, then to sing, then to act, ascribes her triumphs to a moment of revelation that occurred when she realized that her mother was dying. "I knew I could be either sad and weak and not in control," she says, "or I could just take control and say it's going to get better."

Surrounded now by promoters and guardians and companions, paid attendants whose function is to provide just the right combination of publicity and privacy, each of Worrell's figures not only continues to explore the mysteries of who am I but seeks to create a temple where an icon can perhaps free himself from iconhood. For Spielberg, the temple is a fantasy movie studio filled with flowers and waterfalls and children's toys. Lucas, too, has built a private empire where films can be made amid riding stables and a lake specially stocked with fish. Steve Martin's temple is his own windowless house, where a push-button security system guards his personal museum of abstract paintings. Behind the walls of Michael Jackson's hidden palace, there are deer, a llama, peacocks.

And an old-fashioned red popcorn wagon, which Jackson uses not only to make popcorn for himself but to give it away to neighborhood children. It is surprising, or perhaps not so surprising, how often popcorn turns up in Worrell's book as the indulgence of today's gods. Popcorn is, after all, the warm and buttery food of vanished childhood, the food of childhood celebrations, of the circus and the baseball bleachers, of the birthday party and the Saturday matinee. "I just loved that smell of cheap perfume and the hot popcorn machine," Bette Midler says of the movie theaters of her youth. Madonna remembers that popcorn sustained her when she was poor. "I lived on popcorn, that's why I still love it. Popcorn is cheap and it fills you up." Paul Newman, with his practical turn of mind, not only relishes making popcorn but has put his version on the market.

"Popcorn, a can of beer, and a good book is just about as good a combination as there is in this lifetime," Newman says to Worrell. It is another small example of her remarkable gift for catching even the most reticent of icons in a moment of self-revelation, and of humanity.

GEORGE HOLZ / O

MADONNA

IS

HER

GIVEN

NAME

*O*n tour with Madonna and her band: a jagged week-long trek from Dallas to Houston, Houston to Austin, Austin to New Orleans. Just cities on the road. Concerts four out of six nights. A vast concrete airport big enough to house a starship. Lines of self-absorbed people and crowds hurrying under lights too bright. Miles of Texas flatland floating by a bus window. Empty auditoriums, acres and acres of empty seats. Cigarette smoke filling endless hours. Waiting. Silent, burly roadies in identical cut-off jeans methodically unloading trucks. Giant black boxes

1

of amplifiers, synthesizers, mixing boards, lighting boards, ramps, drums, basses, guitars. Night after night, packing them up, reloading. Hotel elevators with mirrored walls and digital numbers above the doors that chirp at each passing floor like captive, mechanical birds. A room-service tray in the hall with a silver coffeepot, broken potato chips, and glasses half full of watered-down Coke.

Then there's Madonna: She is standing in the aisle of a bus, her arms bridging two seats. She is wearing a long green knit skirt that is peeled down over her belly, and a green-and-red paisley shirt knotted above her waist; white anklets and red patent-leather oxfords; large tortoiseshell glasses. Her hair is piled on her head and held with a tilting red bow above her left ear. She has on no makeup, only red lipstick. Her complexion is pale, almost dewy, like the petal of a lily. She was born with the glamorous tiny mole above the right side of her lip.

Bill, the keyboardist in the band, tries to get past her to go to the bathroom at the back of the bus. She blocks the way.

Madonna: You can't get through.

Bill: I have to pee.

Madonna: Pee on the floor.

The same bus. Madonna is sitting by the window, leaning back. Her dancer's legs are straight up, with ankles crossed on the back of the seat in front of her. Her body is a perfect *V* silhouetted against Texas. She toys with the dial on her portable radio.

Question: Are you nearsighted?

Madonna: It's a secret.

Question: Can we talk later, maybe after the show tonight?

Madonna: I can't focus after a concert. I have to talk to my boyfriend for a long time before I go to sleep.

In Dallas, at dinner in a private room of a nearly empty restaurant, with Madonna's bodyguard, her publicist, her assistant, her brother, her guitar player. She is wearing a lot of paisley: brown-and-maroon paisley pants and a paisley vest over a white-and-brown paisley shirt. A sharkskin jacket with black trim is draped over her chair. She has on flat maroon velvet slippers decorated at the toes in swirls of gold braid. Her bangs are wispy, not even an inch long, and her heavy hair is streaked gold. Her jewelry is standard Madonna: a gold crucifix in her left ear; two heart-shaped rhinestone earrings in her right; rosaries and gold chains around her neck; on her wrists a charm bracelet and a gold antique watch. Her fingernails are painted fluorescent white to glow in the dark. She makes conversation:

"Arizona would be the worst place to grow up because there is no plant life."

"I had a dream last night that a black lady was throwing mint jelly all over me because I was telling her off."

"For weeks and weeks my boyfriend Sean kept telling me he was working on a present for me, and finally one day he brought me to his house in Los Angeles to see the present. He blindfolded me. I was really scared and I kept telling him to take the blindfold off, but he said no and then he led me to the backyard and put something cold and metal against my cheek. I started screaming and screaming and he said, 'Okay, you have to look.' He took the blindfold off and I saw that he had built a cross as big as a doorway out of metal. He had blowtorched the pieces together and made a chain. It was the chain he had touched my cheek with. He was proud of it. I hated it. After that I was in a really bad mood and so was he. Then he took the blowtorch and started cutting apart the cross."

"I've never had a Quaalude."

"I'm terrified of cockroaches. I can't even look at them. Whenever I saw them in my cupboard in New York, I screamed and ran away."

Backstage in the dressing room before the concert in Austin. Madonna has just completed a sound check of the stage. She has on her green long skirt and red paisley blouse, but now she is wearing cut-off red tights and lace-up black boots. Her brother Christopher, a New York artist who is helping out with costumes during the tour, brings in a white leather miniskirt layered with white fringe and decorated with silver crosses. She jumps up, takes the skirt from him, and vanishes. In five seconds she is back wearing the white mini over her red tights. She tries on the matching sleeveless fringed jacket and twirls round and round and round in front of a full-length mirror. The fringe flies and she sings out, "If I ever married a cowboy, this is what I'd wear."

Madonna takes off the white leather jacket but is still wearing the fringed skirt. She sits sideways on a cupboard laid out with food: cheese popcorn (her favorite), granola, Gator-Gum, soda. She nibbles at the granola and swings her leg as she talks.

"I saw the article in *National Enquirer* that said Prince and I were a couple. It was all wrong. Prince and I are friends. We talk on the phone sometimes. He told me he had finished another album. I couldn't believe it and I said to him, 'You just *released* a new album.' Music is everything to him. He is a tormented person. He almost never lets his guard down—even with me. And when he does, he is an eight-year-old who just wants to be held. His bodyguards go everywhere with him. At one restaurant the bodyguards sat at a table right near us. He doesn't talk to anybody. I have to order for him at restaurants. But I don't let him get away with not talking. I make him talk. Prince is isolated. He's frightened, but I'm frightened, too, for that matter. When I was a kid, I had a nervous stomach and I threw up every time I was frightened. Now I can't throw up. Once I ate a whole bag of Chee-tos and I wanted to throw up and I put my finger down my throat but I couldn't throw up."

The airport. The plane is late. Madonna has on a long, straight blue skirt rolled down at the waist, a cropped blue top, and flat black boots. Her hair is down and it curls over her shoulders. She sits on the arm of a chair, drapes her arms over the chair's back, and cradles her head in the crook of her elbow. Her hair falls and hides her completely. Her toes are pointing inward, pigeon-style.

At a ramshackle restaurant called Chez Helene that serves the best shrimp gumbo and jambalaya in New Orleans, Madonna and about fifteen members of her entourage are eating. It is a night off for the band. Madonna is splendid in a big-shouldered, gold brocade coat that once belonged to Prince. Someone offers her a bite of chicken and she says, 'No. I'm a vegetarian. I used to not eat anything that could take a shit. Now I eat fish. I changed it to not eating anything that walks on the earth." Madonna is bored at her end of the table, so she gets up and walks over to Lyndon, a freckled, handsome dancer, and sits on his lap. She plays tantalizing and coquettish. Someone asks her if she wants apple pie for dessert and she says, "I don't like crusts. I only like the insides." Then she adds, "I like the outsides of some things and the insides of others." The dessert is late in coming, and Madonna wants some excitement. "Freddy," she moans to her manager, "Do something. Kill yourself. Stab yourself."

Late one night Madonna has a post-concert party in her hotel suite. Rock music is playing loud. The dancers and the guys in her band are drinking champagne and eating cheese popcorn. Madonna wears a Keith Haring original: a green-and-yellow graffiti-print skirt and a cut-off yellow tank top. She is barefoot and her toenails are painted red. Someone says, "Madonna, that was a great show tonight. The audience was hot. You were great."

Madonna: I felt like a bomb exploding.

Question: Have you had flat audiences yet on tour?

Madonna: (to the members of the band): You guys, have we had flat audiences? (She burps.) Yeah. We've had flat audiences. Oregon was sleeping the whole time.

The same night, later. Madonna starts to leave the room to go finish writing a song with Pat Leonard, the musical director of the band. Madonna's brother, Christopher, agrees to an interview.

Madonna: (at the door) Don't tell her any lies.

Christopher: I never lie.

Madonna: Well, lie when you have to.

Smoke bombs are going off on the stage in Dallas. Madonna has just finished singing "Burning Up" and she says good night. The crowd stomps and shouts, begging for more. After a frantic five minutes Madonna reappears in a white embroidered wedding gown, lace gloves, and a mile-long veil of white tulle. She is carrying an armful of flowers. Shyly she says into the microphone, "Will you marry me?" Bedlam for a second, then "Yes," a prolonged screech, until one smitten adolescent howls, "I want to have your babies." She laughs and begins to sing "Like a Virgin."

These days everybody wants Madonna. Her first, or Virgin, concert tour, is sweeping the country. The twenty-eight-city, thirty-eight-date affair, of which she is lead singer, dancer, and driving force, sold out just moments after tickets went on sale: Los Angeles in seventeen minutes; San Francisco in twenty-four; New Orleans in forty-five. New York fans, many of whom huddled in line all night in the rain, bought up every seat for Madonna's three-night engagement at Radio City Music Hall in a record thirty-four minutes. Her first album, *Madonna*, has sold 2.8 million copies domestically. *Like a Virgin*, her follow-up, has already gone quadruple platinum (4.5 million sold) in the U.S. Fans have bought 6.3 million copies of her singles. Madonna's videos are among the most popular ever to run on MTV. And *Desperately Seeking Susan*, a wacky, low-budget farce starring Madonna as a freewheeling, flamboyant, East Village drifter, has so far grossed $16.3 million at the box office, largely thanks to Madonna's teen following.

Madonna is her given name. She is twenty-six, though she has lied about her age and said she is twenty-four. She is 5′4½″ with a strong and curvy body she pounds into perfection each day by running six miles. She dyes her naturally dark hair blond but leaves the roots brown. Offstage she wears almost no makeup. There is a space between her front teeth. Her voice is a little raw, a little husky, a little raspy. She is clear-eyed and bossy, the ringleader and the attention-getter. She has the most energy and works the hardest. She is the funniest, the boldest, the most loyal, the most generous. She is uninhibited, witty, sassy. She can be abrasive, impudent, and coy. She sometimes walks off like a sixth-grader who has just been sent to the principal's office—brave and defiant, but a little frightened too. Madonna was born on August 16, 1958, in Bay City, Michigan, to an engineer and his wife. They named her Madonna Louise Ciccone, after her mother. She grew up in Pontiac, Michigan, and moved to neighboring Rochester during high school. After graduating, Madonna received a four-year dance scholarship to the University of Michigan. She quit after a few semesters and moved to New York. There she earned a work-study scholarship with the Alvin Ailey dance company, and won and lost various small jobs. Two years later she met a musician named Dan Gilroy, who taught her how to play the guitar. She saw an ad in the newspaper for singers and dancers to go on a world tour with disco singer Patrick Hernandez. Madonna auditioned, and his managers told her they didn't want her to go on tour, but they wanted to take her to Paris where their record label was based. They thought she could be "the Edith Piaf of the eighties." They gave her money and a Paris apartment and a maid and clothes, but Madonna felt she wasn't going anywhere musically, so she headed back to New York. It was 1980, and she started playing drums in a group called the Breakfast Club. She also began to write songs. Then she formed her own bands with names like the Millionaires, the Modern Dance, Emmy, and finally Madonna. She played the local club circuit. She met a deejay at Danceteria in New York who was so impressed with her song "Everybody" that he helped get her signed with Sire Records in 1982.

MADONNA ON MADONNA:

Father

"My father is second-generation Italian. He was born in America. I think some of his brothers were born in Italy. He was the youngest of six boys. My grandparents came from Italy on the boat. They went to Pennsylvania, a town right outside of Pittsburgh, because the steel mills are there and there was a lot of work. They lived in sort of an Italian ghetto-type neighborhood, and my grandfather got a job in a steel mill. My grandmother and grandfather spoke no English at all. They are dead now, but when I was a little girl, I would see them all the time. They weren't very educated, and I think in a way they represented the Old Country and an old life-style that my father really didn't want to have anything to do with. It's not that he was ashamed, really, but he wanted to be better than that. I think he was the only one of all my grandparents' children who got a college education. My uncles stayed and worked in the steel mills. My father got an engineering degree and moved to Michigan because of the automotive industry. I think he wanted to be

7

upwardly mobile and move into the educated, prosperous America. I think he wanted us to have a better life than he did when he was growing up. That meant a lot to him.

"He was in the Air Force, and one of his best friends was my mother's oldest brother. This best friend got married down in Texas. I think my dad was his best man and my mother came to the wedding, and of course he met my mother and he fell in love with her immediately. She was very beautiful. I look like her. I have my father's eyes, but I have my mother's smile and a lot of her facial structure. She was French-Canadian but she was born in Bay City. The reason I was born in Bay City is that we were at my grandmother's house. I'm the third oldest child and the oldest girl. There were six of us. Then my mother died and my father remarried three years later, and he had children with my stepmother.

"My father was very strong. I don't agree with a lot of the ways he brought me up. I don't agree with a lot of his values, but he did have a lot of integrity, and if he told us not to do something, he didn't do it, either. A lot of parents tell their kids not to smoke cigarettes and they smoke cigarettes. Or they give you some idea of sexual modesty — but my father lived that way. He believed that making love to someone is a very sacred thing and it shouldn't happen until after you are married. He stuck by those beliefs, and that represented a very strong person to me. He was my role model.

"We weren't poor. We always had enough to eat. My father had a good job, but there were a lot of kids. We had a small house in Pontiac, and my two sisters and I shared one bed in one room. I didn't mind sleeping with my sisters at all. In fact, I liked holding on to them, especially when it was winter. Everything was always sensible, never indulgent. I remember we had the same black-and-white TV for ages and ages and ages. Of course, TV was not a big part of our growing up, anyway. My father didn't allow us to watch it very much. He didn't think it was good for us and he was very strict. He insisted that we cultivate ourselves with books and that we read the Bible and really spend time thinking about our spiritual side. We wanted to go out and play and go to sleep-over parties, but my father said no a lot.

"I was my father's favorite. I knew how to wrap him around my finger. I knew there was another way to go besides saying, 'No, I'm not going to do it,' and I employed those techniques. I was a very good student. I got all A's. My father rewarded us for good grades. That was the only time

8

we got money. From the time we were little kids, he gave us quarters and fifty cents for every A we got. I was really competitive in that way, and my brothers and sisters hated me for it. I wanted that money, and I got all A's. I made the most money off every report card.

"My father and I are still close. When I moved away to New York, we weren't really that close for a long time. He didn't understand what I was doing. First I was a dancer and I would call him and say, 'Well, I'm dancing.' He never, well, he's a sensible guy, and what's dancing to him? It's something you do in a nightclub. He can't imagine that you can make a living from it or that you could aspire to it or work at it or be proud of it or think of it as an accomplishment. He could never really be supportive about it. When I went to Paris and I went from dancing to singing, I would call him and say, 'Well, I'm in France.' And he would say, 'What are you doing there?' And I said, 'I'm going to be a singer.' And he said, 'What do you mean you're going to be a singer?' I would just say, 'Don't worry about it, Dad. I'm having a great time.' I would always tell him not to worry and that everything was okay, and he would say, 'How are you surviving? You're not making any money. Who pays for everything?' I would say, 'They pay for everything.' And he wanted to know what I had to do for that, and I didn't have to do anything, really.

"My father could never understand because I lived for so long without having a regular job. I lived a hand-to-mouth existence. I relied on friends and on money I could get here and there on short stints at jobs I could never keep. It was always amazing to my father. Once he visited me in New York and he kept the lights on when he slept so the cockroaches wouldn't crawl on him. He was horrified at the conditions I was living under. When I had my own band and started playing drums and guitar, I called him and he said, 'You're doing what?' I think I had been in New York for four years, and he was still asking me when I was going to come home and go to college. I said, 'Dad, just stop it.' It wasn't until my first album came out and he started hearing my songs on the radio that he stopped asking me.

"I think now he has some conception of my success. Now he reads about me and people bother him and he has to change his phone number all the time. All of a sudden he's popular, and my brothers and sisters are popular in school because of their association. If he didn't know then, he knows now. He still works for General Dynamics. He's an optics and defense engineer. He designs telescopes, lenses, and helicopters, and all sorts of secret government things that I don't really know about. He makes a lot more money now. I don't know if he's wealthy. I never considered my parents incredibly wealthy, but at least now they can travel. They go to Europe, and they have enough to have a good life."

Mother

"I was about six and a half or seven when my mother died. She had breast cancer. I remember her being a very forgiving, angelic person. I think my parents pissed a lot of people off because they had so many kids and they never screamed at us when we went to family gatherings or to my grandparents' house. My older brothers were very rambunctious, and they would start fires in the basement or throw rocks at windows and my mother and father would never spank them or yell at them. They never punished us. They would just hug us and put their arms around us and talk to us quietly.

"I have a memory of my mother in the kitchen scrubbing the floor. She did all the housecleaning, and she was always picking up after us. We were really messy, awful kids. She would be scrubbing the kitchen floor and we'd walk through and make mud tracks or spill cookie crumbs and she would never say a word. She would just go back and clean it up. I remember that. I remember having these mixed feelings. I have a lot of feelings of love and warmth for her, but sometimes I think I tortured her. I think little kids do that to people who are really good to them. They can't believe they're not getting yelled at or something, so they taunt you. I really taunted my mother. I remember also I knew she was sick for a long time, so she was very weak, but she would continue to go on and do the things she had to do. I knew she was very fragile and kept getting more fragile. I knew that because she would stop during the day and just sit down on the couch. I remember looking at her and thinking that she was very tired, and I didn't want her to be very tired. I wanted her to get up and play with me and do the things she did before.

"I know she tried to keep her feelings inside, her fear inside, and not let us know. She never complained. She was like a martyr, practically. I don't say that in a bragging way, but she never complained about the way she felt or her situation. I remember she was really sick and was sitting on the couch. I went up to her and I remember climbing on her back and saying, 'Play with me, play with me,' and she wouldn't. She couldn't,

10

and she started crying and I got really angry with her and I remember, like, pounding her back with my fist and saying, 'Why are you doing this?' Then I realized she was crying. [Madonna stops talking and covers her face with her hands and cries.] I remember feeling stronger than she was. I remember feeling her weakness. I was so little and I put my arms around her and I could feel her body underneath me sobbing, and I felt like she was the child. I wanted to take care of her. I stopped tormenting her after that. That was the turning point when I knew. I think that made me grow up fast. I knew I could be either sad and weak and not in control, or I could just take control and say it's going to get better.

"Then my mother spent about a year in the hospital, and I saw my father going through changes also. He was devastated. It is awful to see your father cry. One pillar of strength goes down, and then that's your other pillar. But he was very strong about it. He would take us to the hospital to see her, and I remember my mother was always cracking up and making jokes. She was really funny, so it wasn't so awful to go and visit her there. She was always smiling and radiant. Then my mother died. I remember that right before she died, she asked for a hamburger. She wanted to eat a hamburger because she couldn't eat anything for so long, and I thought that was very funny. I didn't actually watch her die. I left and then she died. Then everything changed. My family was always split up, and we had to go stay with relatives."

Stepmother

"As soon as my father started hiring housekeepers, we were all back together again. He just kept going through housekeepers one after the other because we never got along with them. Then he married one of our housekeepers. I don't really want to talk about my stepmother. I was the oldest girl, so I had a lot of adult responsibilities. I feel like all my adolescence was spent taking care of babies—my natural brothers and sisters and my stepbrothers and stepsister—changing diapers and baby-sitting. I have to say I resented it. When all my friends were out playing, I always had my list of chores awaiting me when I got home from school. I think that's when I really thought about how I wanted to do something else and get away from all that. I really saw myself as the quintessential Cinderella. You know, I have this stepmother and I have

11

all this work to do and it's awful and I never go out and I don't have pretty dresses. The thing I hated about my sisters most was my stepmother insisted on buying us the same dresses, or all the same outfits but in different colors. I hated that more than anything. I would do everything not to look like my sisters. I also went to Catholic schools, so I had to wear uniforms that were gray and boring and drab. I would wear weird-colored knee socks or two different-colored socks or put bows in my hair or anything. I guess that was the beginning of my style."

Kid Stuff

"My father made everyone in our family take a musical instrument and go to lessons every day. I took piano lessons but I hated them. I hated my teacher and I hated to practice. We had to practice for an hour every day when we came home from school. I would set the timer ahead when my parents left the room so I had only fifteen minutes and I'd do scales and I'd hate it. Finally I convinced my father to let me take dance lessons at one of those schools where you get ballet, jazz, tap, and baton twirling. It was really like a place for hyperactive young girls. I was pretty rambunctious. In grade school, boys didn't chase me on the playground, I chased them. I'd rip my blouse off and I had my T-shirt underneath and I'd start running after them. I didn't care.

"I wasn't really a tomboy. I was considered the sissy of the family because I relied on feminine wiles to get my way. My sister was a tomboy. She was really tough and hung out with my older brothers. They all picked on me. I always tattled on them to my father when they tortured me. My older brothers and sister would hang me on the clothesline by my underpants. I was little, and they put me up there with clothespins. Or they'd pin me down on the ground and spit in my mouth. All brothers do that, don't they? Or I'd beg them and beg them to let me go on bike rides with them and they'd take me into the woods and lose me. I'd be lost and crying and riding my bike into the trees. It was awful. Then I'd run home to Daddy.

"I wasn't quiet at all. I remember always being told to shut up. Everywhere, at home, at school. I always got in trouble for talking out of turn in school. I always blurted out answers before anyone called on me. I got tape over my mouth. I got my mouth washed out with soap, everything. Mouthing off comes naturally. Every time there was a musical in school I was always in it: *Cinderella* and *The Wizard of Oz* and *Godspell* and *My Fair Lady*—the ingenue role was always mine. And when there was a role for, like, a forward bad girl, everybody sort of unanimously looked over at me when they were casting it. Every time there was a talent show I was always involved in it. I would always do something outrageous. One year I wore a bikini and I had my girlfriend paint psychedelic designs all over my body with fluorescent paint and then I put a black strobe light on and danced to a song by the Who. *Baba O'Riley.* I was also a cheerleader for a while. I liked the pom-pom routine part of it but not the sports part of it. When we had cheerleading practice, I would always butt in and take over and make up routines. I never paid any attention to the games. I was too busy flirting with people in the stands or jumping up and down.

"I could never keep a job for very long. I always got fired. I just couldn't stand waiting on people. Or there was always some uniform code I couldn't adhere to. I always got fired from my baby-sitting jobs too. I worked for a janitor for a while in high school. The people down the street ran a janitorial company, and they employed my sister and me. We went to churches and schools after they were closed and cleaned toilets and floors. Dusted. It was slave labor. I got fired from every job I ever had. I never quit a job."

Music

"The first music I ever remember hearing was Chubby Checker and 'The Twist.' We used to do the limbo underneath a broom. Those are my first memories of music. I listened to the Archies and 'Sugar, Sugar' and 'Lay, Lady, Lay' by Bob Dylan. I loved that song. When I was about nine I gave dance lessons to neighborhood kids in my basement to 'Honky Tonk Woman' by the Rolling Stones. In my neighborhood there were mostly black kids and a few white kids. We used to dance in the driveway or in the garage. We had a record player in the garage, and we played 45s like 'Incense and Peppermint' and 'Give Me a Ticket for an Airplane' and 'Quinn the Eskimo' and a lot of Motown stuff."

Daydreams

"I used to have daydreams, really funny daydreams about growing up in an orphanage. My idea was that there would be no authority. I wanted to be an adult when I was five and not bossed around. I felt like I could always take care of myself. I also had dreams of being a ballerina and coming out on stage in my tutu, doing three hundred pirouettes and just defying gravity and amazing everybody. People would be clapping. I remember I used to have one dream over and over again: My father would come to my room and bring me a gift of a pair of satin toe shoes and put them at the end of my bed. When I woke up, I'd look and be so disappointed that they weren't there."

Virginity

"I remember when I was growing up I liked my body. I remember liking my body and not being ashamed of it. I remember liking boys and not feeling inhibited. I've always been really straightforward with boys and I never played little games; if I liked a boy, I'd confront him. I've always been that way. Maybe it comes from having older brothers and sharing the bathroom with them or whatever. I just wasn't afraid of boys. But when you're that aggressive in junior high, the boys get the wrong impression of you. They mistake your forwardness for sexual promiscuity. Then when they take you out on a date and they don't get what they think they're going to get, they turn on you. I was necking with boys like everybody else was. The first boy I ever slept with was my boyfriend and he had been my boyfriend for a long time and I was in love with him. So I didn't understand where this all came from. I would hear words like *slut* that I hear now. It's sort of repeating itself on me. Just for being free and open. I think I have always had a sensuality about me that the boys misunderstood. They mistook it and I felt like an outcast. I went through this whole period of time when the girls thought I was really loose and all the guys called me 'nympho.' The girls didn't want to hang out with me because I had a bad reputation and the guys didn't go out with me because you're not supposed to go out with the slut of the school. I was called those names when I was still a virgin. I didn't fit in and that's when I got into dancing. I shut off from all of that and I escaped."

Dancing

"When I was in the tenth grade, I knew a girl who was a serious ballet dancer. She was a studious, intellectual type and I was curious about her. She seemed really interesting. Her father was a college professor. She looked really smarter than your average girl but in an offbeat way. So I attached myself to her and she brought me to a ballet class and that's where I met Christopher Flynn, who saved me from my high-school turmoil and got me involved in dance. He had a ballet school in Rochester and I went to classes there. It was beautiful. The studios were so old, with really old wooden floors, old mirrors, and those old-fashioned fans on the ceilings with the blades that go around, and there were cats all over the place. I didn't know what I was doing, really. I was with these really professional ballet dancers, and I had only studied jazz up to then. My body was limber but I didn't have any ballet technique. I had to work twice as hard as anybody else, and I did, and I made vast improvements and Christopher Flynn was impressed with me. He saw my body changing and how hard I worked.

"I really loved him. He was my first taste of what I thought was an artistic person. He was a flamboyant homosexual, which I really didn't think of at the time. I just thought he was funny and animated. I remember once I wrapped a towel around my head like a turban because I was sweating. He came over to me and he said, 'You know, you're really beautiful.' I said, 'What?' Nobody had ever said that to me before. He said, 'You have an ancient-looking face, a face like an ancient Roman statue.' I was flabbergasted. I knew that I was interesting, and of course I was voluptuous for my age, so I knew guys looked at me, but I'd never had a sense of myself being beautiful until he told me. The way he said it, it was an internal thing, much deeper than superficial beauty. He educated me, he took me to museums and told me about art. He started taking me to gay nightclubs in downtown Detroit. It was all gay men and I loved it. Everybody was dancing and wild, and I'd just get on the dance floor and go crazy. Christopher Flynn was my mentor, my father, my imaginary lover, my brother, everything, because he understood me. He believed in me and encouraged everything that I wanted to do. He encouraged me to go to New York. He was the one who said I could do it if I wanted."

New York

"I saved up enough money for a one-way ticket and flew to New York. It was my first plane trip. When I got off the plane, I got in a taxi and told the driver to take me to the middle of everything. That turned out to be Times Square. I think the cab driver was saying, like, 'Okay, I'll show her something.' And he just dumped me there. I think he got a chuckle out of that. 'You don't know where you want to go?' 'No, just take me to the middle of everything.' I got out of the cab and I was overwhelmed because the buildings, you know, are really high. I walked east on Forty-second Street and then south on Lexington and there was a street fair. I started walking around. It was the summer, and I had on a winter coat and was carrying a suitcase. This guy started following me around and looking at me. He wasn't cute or anything, but he looked interesting. I said hi to him, and he said, 'Why are you walking around with a winter coat and a suitcase?' And I said, 'I just got off the plane.' And then he said, 'Why don't you go home and get rid of it?' And I said, 'I don't live anywhere.' He was dumbfounded. So he said, 'What are you going to do?' And I said, 'I don't know. I'll find a place. I'll go to the YWCA or something.' And he said, 'Well, you can stay at my apartment.' He had an apartment near the United Nations. So I stayed there for the first two weeks. He didn't try to rape me or anything. He was really nice. He gave me subway tokens. He showed me where everything was, and he fed me breakfast. It was perfect. [In a Blanche Dubois accent] I relied on the kindness of strangers. So then I got a scholarship to the Alvin Ailey school. When I started dancing, I met kids my age, dancers who lived in New York who were looking for roommates. I wasn't worried about not getting anywhere as a dancer. I knew I was a decent dancer.

"I moved from one dive to the next. I was poor. I lived on popcorn, that's why I still love it. Popcorn is cheap and it fills you up. One time I was living in this loft in the garment district. It was illegal. I was squatting. The guy who owned it wanted everybody to leave, and the way he did that was he turned off all the heat and hot water in the building. It was the middle of winter but I didn't leave. I spent all my days rehearsing music in a building a few blocks away. I just slept at this place at night. I had a mattress on the floor and I had electric heaters plugged in all around the mattress. There was a stereo system too. I had too many things plugged in at once, and in the middle of the night something blew. I woke up and the fucking stereo was on fire. Flames were leaping out of it. All the heaters were on fire. I was in the middle of this ring of fire. I jumped out and got a bucket and filled it with cold water and threw it on the fire. The worst thing you can do to an electrical fire is throw water on it. The flames got bigger. I took blankets and started beating it out. So it went out and everything was ruined. I put on one of my three select outfits, a turquoise sweater that I buttoned up and put on backward, and a pair of army fatigues, and I packed up a little bag and went to the music building and lived illegally in my rehearsal loft. Then I lived with my band."

Idols

"Growing up, I thought nuns were very beautiful. For several years I wanted to be a nun, and I got very close to some of them in grade school and junior high. I saw them as really pure, disciplined, sort of above-average people. I thought nuns were very beautiful. They never wore any makeup and they just had these really serene faces. Nuns are sexy. I would write little cards and poems to them in school. I just had a few favorite teachers, and they would invite me to the convent after school and I'd make cookies with them or have dinner there.

"I also loved Carole Lombard and Judy Holliday and Marilyn Monroe. They were all just incredibly funny, and they were silly and sweet and they were girls and they were feminine and sexy. I just saw myself in them, my funniness and my need to boss people around and at the same time be taken care of. My girlishness. My knowingness and my innocence. Both. I also had this idea that Marilyn Monroe had a glow or white light around her. I saw her in some old black-and-white movie on TV and I just thought I wanted to have that glow too. And I remember Nancy Sinatra singing 'These Boots Are Made for Walkin',' and that made one hell of an impression on me. And when she said, 'Are you ready, boots, start walkin',' it was like, yeah, give me some of those go-go boots. I want to walk on a few people."

Ambition

"I am ambitious, but if I weren't as talented as I am ambitious, I would be a gross monstrosity. I am not surprised by my success. I didn't plan it, but I'm not surprised because it feels natural. The only thing that is calculated in me is my desire to learn more and learn more and be better and keep moving on. When I was younger, I never said, 'Okay, this is the plan. I'm going to be a dancer and that's going to lead to singing and that's going to lead to acting and I'm going to move to New York and I'm going to move to Los Angeles.' You know, I never had a plan at all. My calculation was that I knew I had to apply myself and work. And that application—and that devotion and that desire and that ambition and that courage—was going to take me to the next step. So, that's my calculation.

"I don't see music and movies as being unrelated. I think when you are singing a song, you are making yourself very vulnerable. It's almost like crying in front of people. Acting is about that, too—communicating and being honest and just projecting a feeling or emotion. It's just a different way of doing it. I also love making videos. They're like little movies. After I made my first video it was just so great, I wanted to make a movie. The next thing I want to do is make a really, really big movie, but nothing is definite. I see myself directing eventually.

"I will make more albums. I will tour when my manager puts a gun to my head. I love performing, but the rock-star life on the road is a grueling thing for me. I don't think it's glamorous. At the moment, with the music and *Desperately Seeking Susan*, I think I'm affecting people in the same way either way. My personality is getting across. I really see myself as a comedian. In twenty years I know that I will be an actress. I aspire to be a great actress."

Image

"My image to people, I think, is that I'm this brazen, aggressive young woman who has an okay voice with some pretty exciting songs who wears what she wants to wear and says what she wants to say and who has potential as an actress. Sex symbol? That is such a weird question. I guess I would be perceived as that because I have a typically voluptuous body and because the way I dress accents my femininity, and because a lot of what I am about is just expressing sexual desire and not really caring what people think about it. Maybe that would make you a sex symbol, I don't know. There is a very modest side to me too. How far away is the image from me? It's about twenty steps away."

Fame

"I love being on stage, and I love reaching out to people and I love the expressions in people's eyes and just the ecstasy and the thrill. But I have to have a bodyguard around me for security reasons. When I finish a show, I can't stop on the street and sign a few autographs because the whole world would descend on me and I would be there three years. Sometimes when I go back to my hotel room, there are people hiding in the ice closet, waiting. That is scary. I feel intruded upon. I feel like I've given them something and that they're asking too much to expect me to be gracious to them and cordial and appreciative of their constant need to have more. I feel caged in hotel rooms wherever I go. After shows, everybody else goes out and I have to stay in.

"In New Orleans, after the show I took a cab to Bourbon Street with my bodyguard. I put a hat on and pulled it down low, but I stepped onto the curb and one person said, 'There's Madonna,' and then everybody said, 'There's Madonna.' We started walking down the street looking in windows and watching some jazz groups, and the more we walked, the more people started to follow us. It was like the Pied Piper of Hamlin. We turned around and there was a mob of people following us. The people don't want to hurt me. They just want to be near me. They want to touch me and they want to take my picture and they want an autograph. Actually it hasn't gotten to the point where I never go out. I still go running on the street and shopping. I don't send people out to do everything for me. I want to try to do as many things as I can in that regard, because I think if you keep yourself in captivity and really separate yourself from people, you start to have a scary opinion of the world. I don't want to feel that way. I've always felt fearless walking down the street. That's how I survived in New York. I never want to lose that.

"I don't sit around and contemplate my fame or how popular I am. I would rather be unaware of it because there is something about it that is sort of grotesque. Everything gets blown out of proportion; you lose your objectivity. I want to see myself the size that I am—you know what I mean—in relationship to the people around me. Before large crowds of people were listening to me, I was trying to get small crowds of people to listen to me. So I just want it all to be relative. I know my manager sometimes looks at me with dismay when he tells me I've sold six million records or sold out in seventeen minutes, and I just say, 'Okay.' I'm glad, but that's not what interests me, numbers. What interests me is what happens in my confrontations with people every day and in my performances every night.

"Yes, I wanted to be famous. I just wanted to have an effect on a large amount of people. I want to make them laugh. I want to make them feel courageous or brave or not afraid to express themselves. Everybody seems to feel like they have to beat around the bush and play games and not be straightforward. They're programmed to have layers. I don't think I ever had those layers. I knew when I was growing up I was never afraid, and I think I used to shock my parents. They used to take my straightforwardness for rudeness. I don't think I was special in behaving that way, though. It's just that most people when they grow up squelch that honesty that children have, that ability to come right to the point or be poignant. Every child is born with it. For some reason I didn't lose it."

Phenomenon

"I'm not really sure what is going on. My fans come from a wide age range. I think it goes beyond sexuality. Maybe my fearlessness and courage give people a good feeling. I think I have a real sweetness inside and love for life and a good sense of humor. Maybe people see that. I think a lot of people are afraid to express themselves that way, so maybe they feel they can attach themselves to an innocence and joy. I believe that dreams come true: that you can do what you want to do. I don't mean that in a *Rocky III* kind of way, either. I don't mean you have to go out and conquer the world and be a star. I mean, I came from a boring sort of middle-class life-style and a big family and I wasn't born with a perfect body.

"It all has to do with an attitude and loving yourself the way you are. Think of all the anorexics and suicides. Young people seem to be obsessed with not liking themselves. It's really awful. Before they even try, they have it in their minds they aren't good enough and start destroying themselves. I don't think that what I'm trying to say is hard to understand. I don't go overboard, really, in any direction. I don't shave the side of my head. My hair is not pink. There's a lot of playfulness and a lot of humor to the way I look and the way I dress. I don't feel that I'm putting on a costume. It's part of my personality and the mood that I'm in. Also I think that for the last ten or twenty years that part of a woman has been suppressed. There has been the feeling that it's not right to want to dress up and be feminine, because women think that if they indulge in that men won't respect them or take them seriously. Maybe kids now see someone in the public eye doing what I do. Maybe that's the phenomenon and why young girls are dressing up like me—because finally someone else is showing that it's okay."

Feminists

"To call me an antifeminist is ludicrous. That is a superficial observation. Some people have said that I'm setting women back thirty years. Well, I think in the fifties women weren't ashamed of their bodies. I think they luxuriated in their sexuality and being strong in their femininity. I think that is better than hiding it and saying, 'I'm strong, I'm just like a man.' Women aren't like men. They can do things that men can't do. If people don't get the humor in me or my act, then they don't want to get it. If ten-year-olds can get it and laugh, then an adult surely can."

Vanity

"Of course I'm vain. Every time I pass by a mirror I look. I like my body. I like the way I look most of the time. I have my ups and downs. I think everybody does. Maybe one of the reasons feminists speak out against me is that I represent girlish vanity and that is what they've been trying to get rid of because they think it belittles them or detracts from their intelligence or what they're trying to say."

Belly Buttons

"The picture inside the dust sleeve of my first album has me, like, in this Betty Boop pose with my belly button showing. Then when people reviewed the album, they kept talking about me having a cute belly button. I started thinking about it and I said, 'Yeah, well, I do like my belly button.' I think there are other unobvious places on the body that are sexy, and the stomach is kind of innocent. I don't have a really flat stomach. I sort of have a little girl's stomach. It's round and the skin is smooth and it's nice. I like it."

Boy Toy

"About four years ago I used to live in the East Village. I used to love hanging out at the Roxy with all the break dancers and graffiti artists and the deejays. We'd hang out in the streets. Everybody had a tag name they would write on the wall, like Whiz Kid or Hi-Fi. The thing was to see how much you could 'throw up,' get your name up, everywhere. It was a very territorial thing. One day I just thought of Boy Toy, and when I threw it up on a wall, everybody said they thought it was funny. They understood the humor of it. I can see how the rest of the world thinks I'm saying 'Play with me' and 'I'm available to anyone.' Once again it's a tongue-in-cheek statement, the opposite of what it says. I don't let anyone take advantage of me. That's obvious. And it was very obvious to those guys. I had Boy Toy made into a belt buckle. Then I started doing stuff outside New York City and I kept wearing the Boy Toy belt, forgetting that no one outside of the Roxy was going to get it. I don't wear it anymore because it's just become ridiculous. I think it's funny, but not too many other people do."

Clothes

"I like to combine things but in a humorous way, like a uniform skirt and fishnets. Sometimes I like really expensive things. I like Vivienne Westwood, Comme des Garçons, Jean Paul Gaultier, and Joseph Tricot. But I get a lot of stuff in thrift shops too. I don't like wearing constricting things, clothes I just can't hang out in, but I like to wear clothes that are sexy. I go to sportswear shops and get nylon shirts and things that kids on the street wear. I really love dresses like Marilyn Monroe wore, those fifties dresses that were tailored to fit a voluptuous body. A lot of stuff made now is for an androgynous figure, and it doesn't look good on me. I have always sort of elaborated with my dance clothes. I used to live in my dance clothes, my tights and leotards, but I always personalized them. I'd rip them all up and make sure the runs got really big and had a pattern to them. I started wearing bows in my hair one day when I was washing my face. My hair was long and I couldn't find anything to tie it back, so I took an old pair of tights and wound them around my head, and I liked the way that looked."

Material Girl

"I don't think money has changed my life. I never had money until now, and I never felt the lack of it. I buy more clothes. Right now I live out of a suitcase. I don't own a car. Just before the tour, I took driver's ed and got a license for the first time. I rented a car and it was a thrill. I'm not interested in buying things like furniture and dishes, but I know I will probably have to do it. My prized possessions are my ten-speed bike that's in New York and a rug I bought in L.A. that was imported from China. Someday they'll meet. I love bookstores. I read a lot of things. I read biographies of famous people and movie stars and people who have tragic lives. I like to know about other people. I love reading V. S. Naipaul and Milan Kundera and Lawrence Durrell. I love a great book. I love to escape into it. I can't wait until everybody gets out of my room and I can get back to my book. I like that feeling, it's very comforting."

The Name Madonna

"My mother is the only other person I have ever heard of named Madonna. I never had trouble with the name. Not in school or anything. Of course, I went to Catholic schools. And then when I got involved in the music industry, everybody thought I took it as a stage name. So I let them think that. . . . It's pretty glamorous."

Catholicism

"Catholicism gives you a strength, an inner strength, whether you end up believing it later or not. It's the backbone. I think maybe the essence of Catholicism I haven't rejected, but the theory of it I have—if that makes any sense. I don't go to church but I believe in God. I don't say my rosary but I think about things like that. I do pray. I think I always have whether I was conscious of it or not. The thing that has remained with me most, I guess, is the idea that you do unto others as you would have them do unto you. And the Ten Commandments. It's not right to steal or lie or cheat. I think it's pretty creepy when guys cheat on their wives and the other way around, stuff like that. When I was little, I had all the usual feelings of guilt. I was very conscious of God watching everything I did. Until I was eleven or twelve I believed the devil was in my basement. We had the kind of stairway where there were spaces between each step, and I would run up fast so he wouldn't grab my ankles."

Crucifixes and Rosaries

"I think I have always carried around a few rosaries with me. There was the turquoise-colored one that my grandmother had given to me a long time ago. I had it in a little box full of keepsakes and took it with me whenever I moved around. One day I decided to wear it as a necklace. I just thought it would look nice around my neck. I thought, 'This is kind of offbeat and interesting.' I mean, everything I do is sort of tongue-in-cheek. It's a strange blend—a beautiful sort of symbolism, the idea of someone suffering, which is what Jesus Christ on a crucifix stands for, and then not taking it seriously at all. Seeing it as an icon with no religiousness attached to it. It isn't a sacrilegious thing for me. I'm not saying, 'This is Jesus Christ' and I'm laughing. I'm not making fun of it. I like it. I think the crucifix is beautiful. It's sexy. When I went to Catholic schools, I thought the huge crucifixes nuns wore around their necks with their habits were absolutely gorgeous. I have one like that now. I wear it sometimes but not on stage. It's too big. It might fly up in the air and hit me in the face."

Marriage

"I do want to get married and have kids. I don't know when, but I think getting married is probably something very exciting and very challenging, and I would definitely like to have a child. I've only heard wonderful things about it from people I know who are near my age. I'm saying it like it's baking a cake or something."

Love

"I'm at the end of my patience with this interview. I want to run down the hallway and finish writing a song. I won't sing it, but I'll tell you the hook. 'Love makes the world go 'round.' It's really trite, but that's what it is. Love makes the world go 'round and straight and square and squiggly."

May 1985

Madonna married Sean Penn in August 1985. They made a movie together called Shanghai Surprise. *She recorded "True Blue," filmed* Who's That Girl?, *made a soundtrack album to go with it, and then toured the world in 1987. Madonna then starred on Broadway in David Mamet's* Speed-the-Plow, *a play about sleazy Hollywood producers, in a 1988 summer run. In January 1989 Madonna filed for divorce from Penn. A new album and her movie* Bloodhounds of Broadway *are scheduled for release in the spring.*

MARK SENNET / ON

THE ETERNAL CHILDHOOD OF STEVEN SPIELBERG

*O*n a far, far corner of Universal's concrete back lot stands a two-story pueblo-style office building. It is surrounded by a low, earth-colored wall marked with a boy on his bike balancing E.T. on the handlebars. Thousands of yellow daisies make a moat around the wall. Walk past the wooden, gridiron gate and suddenly the world turns Technicolor. The sunlight is pale straw. The sky is constant and blue. The grass is warm to the touch and cushiony. There are pear trees and palm trees and silvery-green olive trees and junipers and blue-green pines. Dainty wooden bridges arch over bright streams that curl into waterfalls. A clear pond is filled with fat fish, black and silver and gold Japanese koi that can live two hundred years. There are purple, red, and white blossoming bougainvillea and pink azaleas and orange and purple birds of paradise and spiky cactus plants of every kind. Butterflies cartwheel in the air. This is Amblin Entertainment, where Steven Spielberg dreams for a living.

Amblin has the roughhewn texture of a clay pot molded by hand. The walls and ceilings refuse to form sharp edges or straight lines, like a slightly skewed fun house. Native American artifacts are everywhere. Behind glass frames in the hallway on the main floor are the matching fawn-colored and fringed ceremonial garb of an Indian chief and his princess. The walls of the conference room are brick, each one made individually of mud and straw and fired in a specially built kiln. There is an antique Navajo rug on one wall, next to framed cartoons of E.T. from newspapers all over the country. At the push of a button, a panel in a massive oak chest pneumatically glides up to reveal electronic video equipment. The sleek screening room with forty red plush seats has a well-stocked candy counter, popcorn-maker, and freezer. Everything— M & Ms, Goobers, popcorn, ice cream sandwiches—is free. A day-care center for employees' children has a TV, piano, and six video games. The kitchen, professionally equipped, and for most of the year home to a staff chef, has copper pots and pans hanging from the ceiling over a butcher block island. Glass jars on the counter are filled with Oreos and pretzels and raisins and half a dozen other snacks. Large windows overlook a terrace with a sunken fireplace and barbecue pit.

Outside the kitchen is a gate that opens to a well-tended garden. Mario, the sun-drenched gardener, is proud to show his thriving to-matoes, strawberries, raspberries, grapefruit, oranges, lemons, can-taloupes, tangerines, corn, lettuce, zucchini, Japanese eggplant, cabbage, bell peppers, squash, artichokes, cucumbers, herbs, mint, and ruby grape arbor. The cook uses vegetables from the garden to make salads nearly every day. Out on the open grass is a circular Jacuzzi, cement patio, six lounge chairs, and a squeezed tube of Bain de Soleil. There is an enclosed dog run with indoor-outdoor carpeting next to a basketball hoop and cement court. Across from Amblin's front entrance a giant weeping willow tree shades a wishing well out of which Bruce, the *Jaws* shark, pokes his snout and white saw-teeth.

In the foyer a full-length glass-paned door opens onto a brown-tiled inner courtyard, a sort of Santa Fe atrium with palm trees, cactus plants, and flowers growing in corner gardens. A child's plastic tricycle, yellow, blue, and red, lies abandoned, turned on its side, next to a pink marble bust of an Indian madonna holding two children. A bounding golden retriever named Brandy wants to play fetch. A stairway to the second floor leads past a workout room filled with chrome-bright exercise machines. Behind another door is a cavelike sauna with primitive stick paintings on the carved rock walls. Two giant polished tree stumps hold Indian sculptures and decorate the hallway to Spielberg's office, which is big and cluttered and full of sunshine. High curved windows in two walls meet in a corner above built-in couches piled with pillows of many-colored Hopi, Navajo, and Apache blankets. The beamed ceiling is made of hundreds of dark red salt-cedar branches from Santa Fe. A bronze telescope on a wooden tripod points starward out the window. A Tiffany lamp and a plastic model of the Space Shuttle sit on Spielberg's plain wooden desk. Nearby is an IBM personal computer. Above the fireplace is a fancy TV, VCR, and stereo system. Opposite the desk on a wall that has low, coved recesses where Indian pots and other treasures are stowed, there is a portrait of the actress Amy Irving.

"I wanted Amblin to be a place where I could live and work," Spielberg says of the headquarters that Universal built for him in 1983 for a reported $5 million. "I wanted it to be a family setting, a residence. When Amy and I started seeing each other, I began to make frequent trips to Santa Fe, where she has a house. I fell in love with Amy and the architecture of Santa Fe at the same time and I brought them both back to California with me." Amblin is a household that revolves around Spielberg, but he doesn't have to clean up. There are eighteen full-time employees who work anywhere from ten to fourteen hours a day. "I like to hire people who have positive attitudes," Spielberg says, "who are funny, and who don't take themselves that seriously. It is a very uninhibited atmosphere, very free, a sort of campus hacienda. People here say what they feel, say what is on their minds. Amblin is our arsenal of democracy."

At thirty-seven, Spielberg, the slight, 5'8½", 151-pound permanent kid with shoulder-length dark curly hair pinstriped with gray, is the most powerful director in the history of movies. Six of the seventeen all-time biggest money-making films are his: *E.T.* (1982; $210 million in total rentals in the U.S. and Canada), *Jaws* (1975; $130 million),

Raiders of the Lost Ark (1981; $116 million), *Indiana Jones and the Temple of Doom* (1984; $109 million), *Close Encounters of the Third Kind* (1977/1980; $83 million), and *Gremlins* (produced by Spielberg, 1984; $79 million).

For the past few years Spielberg has devoted himself to building his company and a corps of professionals and friends to help him run it. Along with the five films Amblin will produce this year, including *Back to the Future* and *The Goonies*, there are about fifteen additional movie projects in various stages of development (one of them, almost inevitably, is *Peter Pan*). Spielberg the entrepreneur has been engaged in a tug-of-war with Spielberg the artist. And he is sick of the struggle. "You can't win a battle like this," he says. "All you do is trade priorities. You go from being an artist one week to an entrepreneur the next week. I'd much rather be an artist than an entrepreneur any day. But it has taken me two years to form my company, to design the building, and then to be there during the construction of it. Moving into the building and organizing Amblin has taken me away from directing. But in so doing, I found five films I wanted to make, and I've been spreading myself very thin among them. Next year I'm going to cut back to three films, one that I direct and two that I produce.

"I feel like a hard hat a lot of the time. I feel like I'm sixty floors up and people are dropping rivets on my head. I don't want to be a mogul. I want to be a director. When I grow up, I still want to be a director. I prefer directing to producing. And I don't want to work this hard ever again. It's no fun. I am a workaholic. Definitely. I've known that since I was twelve years old. Fortunately I love the work the way Patton loved the stink of battle. I do truly love it. But I have to stop. I regret not spending enough time with myself alone. I miss going on long walks. I miss coming home at two in the afternoon and watching soap operas and catching the news at four and then getting up and opening a closet and going through old photographs and old memorabilia and reminiscing about the old days. I miss the beach and going to national parks, having picnics and watching bears."

Spielberg's most successful movies all derive from his own childhood, a place he still visits. A flicker of his mind's eyelid and he is there: He sees it, he feels it, as vividly now as then. "I can always trace an idea back to my childhood," he says. Through his movies, Americans share Spielberg's childhood. "My first memory," he says, "is of being taken down steps in a very dark hallway that suddenly opened up into a bright room filled with old men with long beards and black hats. At the end of the room there was a bright red light on an upraised platform. The old men were handing me little crackers. I found out later from my parents that it was a synagogue in Cincinnati during a Shabbat with Hasidic Jews. I was in a stroller being pushed down the aisle by my father. The red light at the end of the room was the Eternal Light above the Ark. My parents later placed the memory at a time when I was about six months old.

"I was born in Cincinnati on December 18, 1947, and spent three years there. My father in those days was an electrical engineer and he got a job with RCA and we moved to Haddonfield, New Jersey. My father was part of the team at RCA that designed the first computers. In the late forties and early fifties the computer movement was migratory. Within thirteen years we moved from Cincinnati to Haddonfield, to Scottsdale, Arizona, to Saratoga, a suburb of San Jose. Just as I'd become accustomed to a school and a teacher and a best friend, the FOR SALE sign would dig into the front lawn and we'd be packing. I've always considered Arizona, where I was from nine to sixteen, my real home. For a kid, home is where you have your best friends and your first car, and your first kiss; it's where you do your worst stuff and get your best grades. Scottsdale was just like the neighborhood in *Poltergeist:* kitchen windows facing kitchen windows facing kitchen windows. People waved to each other out their windows. You always knew what your neighbors were cooking because you could see them preparing dinner and you could smell it. There were no fences, no big problems.

"My mom and dad were so opposite that that's probably why they were attracted to each other. The only vague similarity between my mom and dad is that they both love classical music and they both love all of us, my three younger sisters and me. Aside from that they had nothing in common. Nothing. My dad was a brilliant engineer. He had the fastest slide rule in Arizona. Everything with him was precision, accuracy, 'bead-on.' My father spoke two languages: English and Computer. When I was about eleven, he came home one night and gathered us together and made a very big point about getting our attention. He held up a tiny little transistor he had brought from work and said, 'This is the future.' I took the transistor from his hand and I put it in my mouth and I swallowed it. It was a defiant gesture and I'm not sure where it came from, but I swallowed the transistor. He laughed, then he didn't laugh. It got very tense. It was like the confrontation scene between Raymond Massey and James Dean in *East of Eden*. One of those moments when two worlds from diametrically opposed positions in the universe collide. It was a real point of departure. It was almost as if I were saying, 'That's your life and that's your future, but it doesn't have to be mine.'

"My mother had more energy than a hundred mothers her age. She was always feisty; she mixed it up. The main image I have of my mother is of this tiny woman climbing to the top of a mountain, standing there with her arms out, and spinning around. She was always just like a little girl who never grew out of her pinafore. The rest of us trailed after her—my dad, my younger sisters and me. She left a large wake.

"I was bombarded by classical music. My mother was a pianist. She would have chamber concerts in the living room with her friends who played the viola and the violin and the harp. While that was happening, in another room my father would be conferring with nine or ten men about computers, graphs and charts and oscilloscopes and transistors. They would be arguing and yelling about how to build a better mousetrap. Sometimes it was just a little too much to take in. These opposite lifestyles would give me circuit overload. My tweeters would burn out and my only insulation would be my bedroom door, which remained closed for most of my life. I had to put towels under the jamb so I couldn't hear the classical music and the foreign language of computer logic.

"My bedroom was like all the rooms of all the kids in all the movies I've been a part of. It was a compost heap of everything I never put away. It still is that way today. Gravity undresses me; gravity decides where all my things wind up. I don't think I've used a hanger in my entire life. I have always enjoyed living in my own debris. I like to be surrounded by all the things I am. So my room has gone from toys to paperwork and shop lists and sketches and storyboards and magazines and newspapers. I can mess a place up. Now, it takes me about twelve hours to really mess a place up. When I was a kid, I was a little bit faster. It took about thirty minutes.

"I used to keep parakeets in my room. They were my first pets. I was about ten or eleven. My parents figured the parakeets would be easy to take care of and they also figured that I would never let the parakeets out of their cage. They were wrong on both counts. I hated things trapped in small places, so I put the cage away and trained the parakeets to live on the curtain rod. At one time I had eight parakeets living on my curtain rod. Parakeets drip like candles in old Italian restaurants, so after a while the whole fabric of the curtains changed. They were living on the rod, living on my head, living on my shoulder. I used to teach them to talk and to perch on my finger and to land on my shoulder and eat out of my hand. I taught them how to say the standard things that kids teach birds to say, like 'Hello' and 'I'm hungry.' I'd find a name I'd like—say, Schmuck—and just give the other birds sequel names: Schmuck II, Schmuck III. No imagination. That's sort of all I did before I got into films.

"My parents wouldn't let me watch television. They really feared TV, especially violence on TV. They were concerned about how I would perceive life and how they wanted me to perceive life. I was only allowed to watch shows like *Jackie Gleason* or *Mickey Mouse Club* or *Lassie*. But when it came to shows like *Mod Squad* or *Dragnet* or any program having anything to do with the adult world, I had to leave the room and go upstairs or play. Part of the reason is that, when I was four or five years old, when I did see things on TV, I got scared. I would cry for three hours and my parents thought it was a very serious problem. I had a very grotesque, violent reaction to a documentary on snakes I saw when I was about four. There were very large shots of the snakes' hooded heads and their open mouths. I remember screaming and running upstairs and crying for hours and hours. That was the beginning of the end of TV for me.

"For six years my dad would rig the TV set with booby traps—like he'd cover it with a dust ruffle so he could tell if I snuck TV time while my parents were out to dinner. But I sneaked anyway. When the babysitters would inevitably fall asleep, I'd sneak downstairs and watch *Science Fiction Theater* and other taboo shows with the sound on very low. My folks were also very prudent about the movies I could see. They had taken me to see *Snow White and the Seven Dwarfs* when I was six, and when the wicked queen turned into a hag and a skeleton crumbled into pieces, I burst into tears and started shaking and hiding my eyes. For three or four nights I had to crawl into bed with my mom and dad. So my parents thought that all visual stimulus was dangerous and carefully began to censor my intake of TV and movies.

"I had all the fears that a lot of kids usually have: of a society of the netherworld living under my bed, of monsters living in the closet wanting to suck me in and do terrible things to me. I was afraid of furniture with feet. At night I was always afraid I would wake up and watch the furniture walking away. I had a fear of a crack in the wall. There was a crack in the wall by my bed that I stared at all the time, imagining little friendly people living in the crack and coming out to talk to me. One day while I was staring at the crack it suddenly widened. It opened about five inches and little pieces fell out of it. I screamed a silent scream. I couldn't get anything out. I was frozen. It's like what Elliot does when he sees E.T. in the yard. I will never forget that. It really happened.

"I was afraid of trees, clouds, the wind, the dark. There was a whole forest outside my window in New Jersey, and the trees at night had silhouettes of arms and heads and tentacles. My imagination was so active that I could lie in the backyard and stare up at the cumulonimbus clouds moving across the sky and absolutely terrify myself by just imagining shapes from the continuously changing cloud formations. I liked being scared. It was very stimulating. In my films I celebrate the imagination as a tool of great creation and a device for the ultimate scream. I liked pushing myself to the brink of terror and then pulling back. I would never go to the closet and open the door when it was dark, but I would always imagine myself going over to it, opening the door, and being sucked into it. In the morning I was the bravest guy—there was little seven-year-old Steven walking around the closet, saying, 'I'm not afraid of you.' Or talking to the trees and clouds, saying, 'I'm not afraid of you.' But once night fell, all bets were off.

"As I got older I was embarrassed by these fears because they were hanging on longer than I thought they should. I had no way to sublimate or channel them until I began telling stories to my younger sisters. This removed the fear from my own soul and transferred it right into theirs. They were a great audience for that kind of gentle manipulation. Not so gentle sometimes. I never made them cry. Scream, yes. Cry, no. I would come into their rooms at night before bed and tell them horrible stories. One story I told my sisters all the time was about the old World War II flier who had been rotting in our closet for twenty years. I took a plastic skull you buy in a model shop and put a flashlight inside so the eyes and face would glow, then I put my dad's World War II aviator cap over the skull and put goggles over the eyeholes. At night I would dare them, never force them, but dare them, to peek into the closet. My sisters were as curious as I was. They wanted to see it and they didn't want to see it. I would say, 'Listen, it's there if you want to see it.' One by one they would slowly open the door and go in. When they were inside, I put a plug in the wall and the skull would light up and they would start screaming. Eventually I would let them out. It's amazing that they even grew up. It's amazing that I grew up and they didn't kill me.

"Growing up, I wasn't religious, although I was Bar Mitzvahed in a real Orthodox synagogue. The first four rows were filled with Jewish men in their eighties who sang the Haftarah along with me, so that whenever I forgot something all I had to do was open my ears and listen — they were way ahead of me anyhow. It was like having a hundred prompters. Now, my mother is extremely orthodox and observes the dietary rules, but back then we were sort of storefront kosher. Whenever the rabbi left our house, it was, 'Strike the sets, remove the props.' My mom and I were sea food nuts, but of course lobster is not kosher. We'd bought three live lobsters for dinner one day, and sure enough, the rabbi pulled into our driveway. My mom panicked and threw these live crustaceans at me; I had to hide them in my room under my bed. And sure enough, the rabbi came into my room to see how I was doing. You could hear the lobsters clicking and clacking each other with their tails right under the bed. The rabbi just sort of stared. He sniffed the air and must have wondered what that *tref* scent was lingering in the kid's bedroom. The minute the rabbi left, my mom and I gleefully tossed the lobsters into a pot of boiling water and ate them.

"I just did a lot of things. My God, one day in Arizona three friends and I mixed up this batch of vomit, phony throw up, out of creamed corn and white bread marinated in water and baby food and parmesan cheese. I put the whole concoction into a brown paper bag and we went to a movie theater where they were showing a movie called *The Lost World*. I remember climbing up to the balcony of the movie theater, and on the count of three, my friends and I made these horrendous barfing sounds and I squeezed the stuff over the balcony onto all the people down below. A funny thing happened. It created a chain reaction and people began getting sick and they stopped the movie and the house-lights went up and ushers started running up and down the aisles to see who was sick. This scared us to death and we ran home. One of my friends was sixteen and was able to drive, but we were so afraid of getting into the car in the parking lot that we ran home. I walked six miles to get home. That's in *The Goonies*. That scene is actually in *The Goonies*. I actually put that in the movie.

"I also used to go up to Lovers' Lane with a still camera and a flash and creep up to the cars of the people who were necking. I would stick the camera up to the window and flash a picture and then I would jump back into our car and take off. I was like a commando kid. Hit and run, and then cackle with glee for hours afterward. Eventually I began putting some of these perversions on movie film.

"When I was twelve, my mother bought my father a movie camera for Father's Day. He'd take the camera out on family camping trips, and then we would have to endure his photography. The camera was always shaky, and he would stick it out the window of the moving car and photograph the road going by. So one day I said, 'Dad, can I be the family photographer?' and he gave me the camera. That summer I did all the family photography. I dramatized everything. My dad had to wait for me to say 'Action' before he carried the fish to the frying pan or even before he put the knife into the fish to clean it. My first PG-13 moment, I guess, was when I photographed my father gutting the fish.

"My first movie was of my Lionel trains crashing into each other. I was a train lover, and every Hanukkah I would get an addition to my train set. I used to love to stage little wrecks. I put my eye right to the tracks and watched the trains crashing. The trains would always break, and once my dad said, 'If you break your trains one more time I'll take them away.' So I took his camera and staged a great train wreck with shots of the trains coming in different directions and shots of the little plastic men reacting. Then I could look at my eight-millimeter film over and over and enjoy the demolition of my trains without the threat of losing my train set.

"I hated school. I just didn't think it applied to what I wanted to do. From age twelve or thirteen I knew I wanted to be a movie director, and I didn't think that science or math or foreign languages were going to help me turn out the little eight-millimeter sagas I was making to avoid homework. School was something I had to do, by law. During classes I would not listen to a word the teachers were saying; instead I would draw a little image on the margin of each page of the history or lit book and flip the pages to make animated cartoons. I used to draw forty-eight pictures—a two-second cartoon. I did just enough homework to move to the next grade every year with my friends and not fall to the wrath of my academically minded father. I give my dad credit for singlehandedly keeping my math grades high enough so I wouldn't be held back. My worst subject was physical education; I failed that three years in a row in high school. I couldn't do a chin-up or a fraction. I can do a chin-up now, but I still can't do a fraction.

"At school I felt like a real nerd, the nerd of the block. The skinny, acne-faced, wimpy kind of kid who gets pushed around by big football jocks and picked on all the way home from school. I was always running to hide in my bedroom where I was safe. I would often get home and say 'Safe.' I would actually call out 'Safe' to myself. I couldn't talk to girls or jocks. I never really dated. I remember I even flunked *The Dating Game*. I was in college and wasn't having much luck with girls so I wanted to go on *The Dating Game* to get a date. I thought that was the whole reason for the show. I was put in bleachers with twenty other men, and six girls asked potential questions. I couldn't answer one question. I was speechless, so they asked me to step down. I was essentially the first person they eliminated from the twenty. Anyway, I wasn't able to talk to girls and I wasn't able to speak out in class. I couldn't look people in the eye. The only time I ever raised my opinion about myself was when I began making little eight-millimeter movies and saw that I could do more than run from the local bully.

"When I was about thirteen, one local bully gave me nothing but grief all year long. He had a thing about Spielberg. I would be walking to class and I'd see him coming and go out of my way to avoid him, but he would knock me down on the grass. Or he would hold my head in the drinking fountain. Once he threw a cherry bomb between my legs in the school toilet; I got up before it exploded. He let the air out of the tires on my bicycle. When I was forced to play flag football in phys ed, this kid was always there to push my face into the dirt. He gave me three or four bloody noses. This was somebody I feared. I dreamed about this person more than anybody else in my life. He was my nemesis. Then I figured, if you can't beat him, get him to join you. So one day I went over to him in school and said, 'I'm making this movie about all these soldiers fighting the Nazis and I want you to play this war hero.' At first he laughed in my face and said his weekends were taken up by fixing cars and he had no time to be in movies. Then later he came back to me and said, 'Do you still make movies?' and I said yes. He said, 'I'll be in one of them.' I got him to come out on a weekend and I made a picture around him. I made him the squad leader, with helmet, fatigues, and backpack. He was this big fourteen-year-old who looked like John Wayne. After that he became my best friend.

"My first real film was a little three- to four-minute Western that I did when I was thirteen to get my photography merit badge in the Boy Scouts. The requirement for the badge was to tell a story with still photographs. Because we didn't have a still camera I asked my counselor if I could use my dad's eight-millimeter movie camera and he said yes. So I gathered my friends from the troop in the desert and we made the Western. We all wore cowboy hats and vests and our Halloween costumes and our little plastic Mattel guns. The movie was called *The Last Gun;* it was a story about a group of homesteaders who essentially are being crushed, driven off their land by evil land barons. A sheriff who is very brave forms a civilian posse and they make a last stand with gunplay against the greedy land barons. I killed off all the homesteaders and all the land barons. The last person alive after the gunfight was the sheriff. I asked some man nearby who was smoking to blow his smoke into the barrel of the sheriff's play gun, so the last shot of the movie is of the smoking gun. The sheriff turns and puts the smoking gun back into his holster and walks into the sunset.

"I screened the movie for the counselor and he insisted that I show it to the entire troop of seventy-five Boy Scouts before he would credit me and give me the merit badge. A lot of them were in the film, and when I started the picture and they saw themselves, they began whooping it up and cheering and having a great time. In that one moment I knew what I wanted to do for the rest of my life. When I heard those kids reacting to something I'd made inside my dad's camera, I just couldn't get enough of it. It became the strongest drug I've ever taken. Whenever I hear an audience liking any movie, mine or not, it reminds me of the noise and the peanut-gallery sounds those kids made that day in Phoenix, Arizona.

"I don't think my parents ever thought that movies would be something I'd succeed at. But they were both very accommodating. My dad would tolerate my movies if I kept my grades up. My mom let me off school at least once a week. I would fake being sick on Mondays so I could cut the movies I'd shot over the weekend. I'd put the thermometer up to the light bulb—Elliot does the same thing in *E.T.*—and call her in and moan and groan and say, 'I don't feel well.' She'd check my temperature and play along and say, 'My God, you're burning up. You're staying home today.' She knew of course that I was faking. She knew I used a heating pad to make myself hot. Later, when my mom came in to check on me, I would say, 'Mom, the fever broke.'

"I remember the time I was shooting a film called *Firelight*. I said, 'Mom, I need to film an explosion. Do you mind if I do it in the kitchen?' She said fine. I exploded about four pounds of baked beans and Cherries Jubilee on the ceiling, on the walls, on every piece of Formica and every piece of tile and all over the floor. For three years after that I remember my mother on her hands and knees with a sponge trying to scrape away what essentially had become as hard as Krazy Glue. This was something my mother tolerated. If I had just gone into the kitchen and done that, they would have sent me to reform school. But as long as I had the camera between myself and my own predilections toward juvenile delinquency, it was all right.

"I used to get away with a lot of shenanigans because the camera was always with me. Our family had a World War II army Jeep, but I was too young to drive it, so when I was making a lot of these films I would say, 'Mom, we're shooting a war movie behind Camelback Mountain and we need the Jeep for production value. Can you put on this tin helmet and this army-surplus uniform and drive the Jeep through my shot?' And my mom would drop everything, climb into the Jeep, and race out behind Camelback Mountain and helter-skelter barrel through the shot, hitting potholes, her blond hair sticking out from under this pith helmet that was barely hanging on by the strap. Then I would say, 'Thanks, Mom, that was a great shot.' She would drive home and I'd have my production value. Suddenly my seven-dollar film was looking like a twenty-four dollar film.

"I was about sixteen when our family moved from Phoenix to Northern California. That was not the happiest time in our lives. After a while my parents separated. My mom moved back to Phoenix. My dad stayed in Northern California. I moved to Southern California to go to college. I was seventeen when my parents divorced. They hung in there to protect us until we were a little older, but they knew they were going to separate years before they actually did it. I don't think they were aware of how acutely we were aware of their unhappiness—not violence, but just a pervading unhappiness you could cut with a fork, cut with a spoon, at dinner every night.

"For years, the word *divorce* for me was like a seven-letter word, the ugliest word in the English language. Sound traveled from bedroom to bedroom, and the word always came seeping through the heating ducts. My sisters and I would stay up at night, listening to our parents argue, hiding from that word. And when it traveled into our room and we heard it through our little heating grates, absolute abject panic set in. My sisters would burst into tears, and we would all hold one another. I feared that word. I feared the imminent separation of my family. I knew it was coming; I just didn't know when. And when the separation finally came, we were no better off for having waited six years for it to occur. We took it just as hard when it happened as we would have years earlier. I have two wonderful parents. They raised me really well. Sometimes parents can work together to raise a wonderful family and not have anything in common with each other. That happens a lot in America.

"During summer vacation when I was eighteen, I went to visit my uncle's family in Canoga Park. I wanted to see movies being made, so my cousin dropped me off at Universal for a tour of the studio. I got on the tram, but they weren't stopping at sound stages, so I wasn't able to see anything. Then, when everybody got off the tram for a bathroom break, I snuck away and never got back on again. I just wandered around, went to seven or eight sound stages, and was thrown off two of them. I met a man named Chuck Silvers, the head of the editorial department, and Chuck said to me, 'What are you doing on the lot?' I told him my story about sneaking off the tram. He thought it was hysterical and we talked for about an hour. He said he'd like to see some of the little films I had made, so he gave me a pass to get on the lot the next day. I showed him four of my eight-millimeter films. He was very impressed and he introduced me to a few associate producers who didn't have the time to say more than 'Hi. I'm on my way to lunch. Can't talk now.' Chuck said, 'Look, I don't have the authority to write you any more passes, but good luck.'

"By then I had been on the lot for two days in a row and had passed the guard. So on the third day I took a bus to North Hollywood. I had on my sort of Sunday-go-to-meetin' suit and I carried my father's briefcase. There was nothing in it except a sandwich and two candy bars. I walked past the guard and I waved, and he smiled and waved back at me and let me in. So every single day during that summer vacation I walked through the gate in my suit and hung out with writers and directors and editors and dubbers. I watched them dub *Send Me No Flowers* with Rock Hudson and Doris Day. I watched *Torn Curtain* being shot, but was thrown off the set by one of Alfred Hitchcock's assistant directors.

"I found an office that was not being used in an old building. I went to a camera store and I bought little titles, plastic letters and words used to do amateur titles for home movies, and I put my name in the building directory: Steven Spielberg, Room 23C. I came in every day. The people who knew I was squatting thought it was great and supported me. When I started college, at California State University, Long Beach, I arranged my schedule so that I only went to two days of classes. I stuffed fifteen and a half credits into two days of school just so I could keep three days open to go to Universal and hang out and watch. I met a lot of executives who told me that nobody was looking at eight-millimeter film anymore. They were embarrassed when I brought in my little projector and asked them to remove the pictures from their walls so I could show my little silent movies. They said, 'If you make your films in sixteen millimeter or even better, thirty-five millimeter, then they'll get seen.' So I immediately began working at the Universal commissary, scooping cottage cheese on people's plastic plates, cleaning tables, and washing dishes to earn the money to buy sixteen-millimeter film and rent a camera. I had to get those films seen.

"Eventually I met a man named Dennis Hoffman. He very much wanted to be a producer and I very much wanted to be a director. He had a lab, a special-effects optical house, and some money—at least enough money to afford $10,000 for one thirty-five-millimeter short film. So I ran home and wrote an eighteen-page script called *Amblin'*, about two kids, a boy and a girl, who meet in the Mojave Desert and hitchhike to the Pacific Ocean. It was a love story without dialogue, only music and sound effects. I shot it in ten days for $10,000. I showed the film twice to people at Universal. The day after I showed the film the second time, I got a call from a Sidney J. Sheinberg's secretary. I didn't know who Sidney J. Sheinberg was, so I said, 'Who is he?' There was a loud pause at the other end of the phone and then the secretary very calmly said, 'He is the head of TV at Universal.' I went in to meet him that day. He had seen my short film *Amblin'* and liked it. He offered me a seven-year contract to direct TV. I was twenty years old. I quit college so fast I didn't even clean out my locker. All these years later, I have this image today of that moldy chicken salad sandwich still in that locker.

"I was obsessed. I was obsessed from the time I was twelve years old. But I was really obsessed from the time I knew what a movie set was like and had felt that kind of excitement that you're on the outside of. You're on the outside of a wonderful hallucination that everybody is sharing and you want to get right in the center of it. I wanted to do more than just be a part of the hallucination. I wanted to have the hallucination. I wanted to control it. I wanted to be the director.

"Universal started by assigning me the pilot to *Night Gallery*, a three-part anthology starring Joan Crawford in my segment. I had never met Joan Crawford before. Actually I heard later that she had been promised a director like George Cukor and had no idea that they were going to assign an acne-ridden, sniffling-nosed, first-time-out director. I only knew years later that she had a temper tantrum when she found out that she had to work with me. She was regal. She was a tiny woman who stood tall and cast long shadows. It was a very traumatic experience for me. I was two days over schedule. On the last day, the producer took over and directed. When I showed him my first cut, he said words I'll never forget. He said, 'We're going to have to perform major surgery on your show.' And he went in and shifted the vision from my choices to his own choices. That's when I began to see the power of editing.

"I learned a lot of lessons with that show, but rather than say, 'Well, I'll let that roll off my back and go on to the next show,' I went to Sid Sheinberg and said, 'I can't do TV anymore. It's just too tough. I quit.' But he wouldn't let me. He gave me a year-long leave of absence. He said, 'I'll give you a year off. Do whatever you want.' So my salary was suspended and I went home and wrote for a year. All I did was write. I wrote a lot of stuff. I wrote *Sugarland Express* and a couple of other screenplays, one of which I sold to Fox. I made enough money from that sale so that I could eat. A year later I went back to Universal and I said, 'Sid, I'm ready to eat crow and pay my dues. Assign me something.'

"For the next two months Sid couldn't find one producer on the lot to work with me. Everybody thought I was 'Sheinberg's Folly.' But Sid finally got a guy to give me a shot at directing *Marcus Welby, M.D.* Then everything opened up. I got a chance to do two segments of *The Psychiatrist*. I used one of those to get me a *Name of the Game* that I'm real proud of called 'LA 2017.' That lead to the *Columbo* I directed, which was the opening show of the season. Then I read a short story called 'Duel,' about an innocent man being pursued by a mad truck. I found out it was being made at Universal, so I went to the producer and it took me a week to talk him into letting me direct it. I loved *Duel.* It was an exercise in suspense. It was like a chemistry experiment. I mixed all these chemicals together hoping it wouldn't blow up in my face. I did it in fourteen days.

"My first big success came when I swiped the galleys of Peter Benchley's *Jaws* from the offices of Richard Zanuck and David Brown. I read it over the weekend and went to Zanuck and Brown on Monday and I said, 'Let me make this movie.' They said, 'Darn it, we've got a director.' I said to them, 'Well, if anything falls out, I love this project. I especially love the sea hunt, the last hundred pages.' They came back to me in a week and said, 'The other director fell out and we'd like you to do it.' That's how it all started. I wanted to do *Jaws* because it was an experiment in terror. It is the behemoth against everyman. It is quite Gothic and quite on the nose. There is nothing subtle about *Jaws.* There are underpinnings that are subtle, but what it's about is pretty slam-bang.

"*Close Encounters of the Third Kind* was born when I was about five or six years old. My dad came into my room one night and he woke me up and he said, 'Come with me.' It was dark and it was right in the middle of the night and I was scared. My dad had never awakened me in the middle of the night and said come with me. He put me in the car and he had a big smile on his face and I was terrified. I kept saying, 'Where are you taking me?' He drove about twenty minutes and then we stopped, and there were a thousand people lying on their backs on picnic blankets in a big meadow, looking up at the sky. My dad spread out our blanket and we looked up and the whole sky was alive with what looked like hundreds of points of light darting here and there across the heavens. It was a meteor shower. My dad took me there as a surprise. I think *Close Encounters* was born right there. My whole fascination with alien beings coming to Earth to live and exchange cultures, ideas, and emotions—that was all born right there instantly.

"I thought the script for *1941* was off the wall. It was very much like *Hellzapoppin* meets the Marx Brothers meets *Saturday Night Live.* It was an insane mishmash of ideas. I really love that movie. I know all its faults and failures. It isn't funny enough. It is a noise riot. It has more noise pollution per square millimeter than any movie ever made, I think. It has too many characters to follow. There are too many story lines and not all of them pay off. The special effects overwhelm the characters. Part of the movie came from my love of model airplanes as a kid. I loved playing with toy airplanes and battleships and trains, toy B-17s, B-25s, Messerschmitts, Stukas, Mitsubishis, and Japanese Zeroes.

"*Raiders of the Lost Ark* is George Lucas's dream that I realized for him. This was an opportunity to make an action picture along the lines of all the serials that I had loved as a kid. I was very influenced by all the serials like *Tailspin Tommy* and *Sheena* and *Zorro* and *Batman*. All those serials they used to make, I just loved them. I used to see them all the time in the Kiva Theater in Scottsdale. They used to have old-fashioned double features with ten cartoons, previews of coming attractions, and a serial in between. I would spend an entire Saturday afternoon, five, six, seven hours in a movie theater watching all those things every week.

"*Poltergeist* is sort of gut-wrenching in its torture. It's about those things that kids imagine and the possibility that their imagining them is enough to make them real. It is a tortured film and is really all about what I did to my sisters when I was a child. It also came out of a ghost experience I had in Texas. I was looking for locations for a film I never made called *White Lightning*. We were staying at an old Gothic hotel and there was nobody there except the Texas film commissioner, the production manager, and me. It was about midnight, and we all went to our individual rooms. As I was getting undressed for bed I kept seeing something moving in my peripheral vision, and the minute I turned to see what was there, there was nothing. The minute I turned back I saw a figure moving out of the corners of my eyes. When I turned to see, no matter how slowly, it just wasn't there. This unnerved me. Suddenly the whole room got very cold, especially by this four-poster bed, and I panicked. First I took a series of photographs with my thirty-five-millimeter flash camera and then I got everybody out of bed and I ran downstairs to the car and I said, 'We've got to leave this place.' We checked out very quickly and we got into the film commissioner's brand-new Mercedes and it wouldn't start. A brand-new Mercedes would not start. Even old Mercedeses don't fail to start. It was about 1:30 A.M. and the nearest Holiday Inn was sixty miles away, but I wouldn't go back in. I said, 'We're leaving right now.' So we called up an old gas station attendant and woke him up. He came over and hot-wired the Mercedes and we drove the sixty miles to the Holiday Inn.

"I don't know if I believe in ghosts. I believe in the power of suggestion. I believe in mind over matter. I believe that there are people who are psychokinetic and telepathic. I've never seen a ghost in my life and I've never seen a UFO. I'm still waiting for those events in my life. It would be great if I got to see them together at the same time, especially if a ghost came out of a UFO. Then I could see a ghost and a UFO at the same time and I'd know they were both real. A ghost of an alien would be interesting. I'd like to see that.

"*E.T.* was always there. It came from as deep a place inside me as any person can probe, but I don't think I had to reach very deep to make this movie. It just took thirty-four years to float up to the surface. It took a long time for me to get ready to make a movie like that. I had to get to a certain place in my development as a person to be emotionally ready to make *E.T.* Having purged myself of a lot of things in making *Poltergeist,* I was ready for *E.T.,* which was a beautiful thing to direct and work on. It was the best experience I've ever had making a film. It was like being a family man before I actually was one and tasting what it would be like to be a daddy and really opening my heart up for the first time to the possibilities of being a father to my own kids. It was the first time I ever wanted to have kids of my own. I think if *E.T.* was inspired by anything, it wasn't by the science fiction of the fifties and sixties but by my own upbringing in a divorced family. *E.T.* is about a family that mends itself in an extraordinary way.

"*Indiana Jones and the Temple of Doom* is an over-accelerated adventure. It's a film that needed speed brakes and we just didn't design them into the overall model. It just went too damn fast. But it's a movie I'm really proud of. I think people misunderstood our intentions. It was intended to be scary. *Temple of Doom* is not going to be a festival of comedy and a treasure of delights. People wanted so badly for the film to be exactly like *Raiders,* and they weren't prepared for a film a little bit harder in spirit, darker in tone.

"The television anthology series, *Amazing Stories,* is a repository for all these little ideas that have taken a long time in my own life to deal with but will never be movies because they aren't strong enough to stretch beyond twenty-three minutes. It is a place for lost little boys and ideas that have nowhere else to go, a sort of foster home for ideas that will never grow up into adulthood but will always be lost little boys."

"I consider myself a powerful director and a fortunate director, but I do not consider myself the best director making films. I do not feel that way about myself. I never really have. There are too many people who are making movies now that I admire more than I admire my own skills. I admire Michael Cimino and Francis Coppola and Martin Scorsese and George Miller. I admire a lot of people. I actually admire anybody who has the guts to go out and make a movie, because it ain't easy. There are a lot of people around me I still learn from. I never want to stop learning. The minute you think you're the best you stop watching other people's movies and you stop learning. That's a real trap. When I watch a movie I feel rewarded when it is very good and depressed when I don't like it. I still feel envious when I see something that someone else has accomplished that I wish I'd done. I think envy is a very healthy drive because it makes you want to improve yourself and your work.

"I don't dream at night that much because I dream all day. I dream for a living. Once a month, the sky falls on my head. I come to, and I see another movie I want to make. I'm always thinking of new ideas and new movies and new forms. I usually just keep my ideas in my head for a long time. Sometimes I write them down. If an idea is not developed enough, I sometimes just keep it in my head. If an idea is perfectly developed, I might still keep it in my head. I'm a real incubator. I'm not a microwave, I'm a slow oven. It takes me a long time to forge an idea into something that I'm ready to go out and put my name on and spend time with. Sometimes I think I've got ball bearings for brains. These ideas are all slipping and sliding across each other all the time. My problem is that my imagination won't turn off. Every morning I wake up so excited I can't eat breakfast. I have never run out of energy. It's not like OPEC oil. I don't worry about a premium going on my energy. It's just always been there. I got that from my mom.

"I use an imaginary audience as a sounding board for some of my ideas. I become the audience. I say, 'Well, that makes me laugh.' I want people to love the movies I make and I'll be a whore to get them into the theaters. I'll pick concepts that I think are easily digestible. I care what audiences think; I'm obsessed by it. As a filmmaker, I try to think for the audience before the film is shot. I've been labeled manipulative because of that, but I think film is a manipulative medium. Any time you get somebody to laugh or cry you're manipulating emotions. And you don't know those people well enough to manipulate their emotions. You're going into their lives, you're reaching into their hearts, or you're tickling their funny bone, and that's awful rude for a stranger to do, isn't it? It's nice to be able to violate the privacy of someone's home with TV or confound people because they have chosen to see your movie. You've got the chance to be intimate with strangers you'll never meet. That's what entertainment is all about. I love that. I ingest that like Goobers. I can't get enough.

"My aim for every picture isn't to have the widest audience possible. Though, I've scared myself with the audiences I've reached with some of my films—that I don't even understand. My aim is to make the best possible film. I'm not greedy. If I were really greedy I wouldn't be making five films this year because I know all five films aren't going to top *E.T.* I keep making movies because I love making movies. I'm not trying to be some world record holder or trying to get an Olympic Gold Medal every time I make a film. The bronze medal will do.

"Once the script is done and I'm casting, I like to cook. I get the actors to cook pies and bread and cookies and pastries and exotic desserts because I have found that actors are very nervous when they come to meet you for the first time, especially when it is across a couple of lounge chairs in a very cold hotel room. I find that if you're wearing an apron and you're covered with flour, an actor comes in and immediately puts down his portfolio and ten thousand résumés and starts breaking the eggs and mixing the batter. I can discover more about that person over homemade-from-scratch pasta than I can over a little walnut coffee table in a New York hotel room.

"The toughest part about making movies is the deal. My least favorite part is the deal. Conceiving and exploring, casting and cutting— cutting is my favorite part. The most fun I have is when I'm in the editing room. It becomes very personal and rather wonderful. I love that isolation, especially after the cacophony, the sheer white noise of a movie crew on location or on a sound stage. Just the relief from the din is rewarding. Directing is not my happiest time. Directing is very hard. It's very, very hard. It's very draining. It's very conflicting. Every day you're full of self-doubt, sometimes self-pity. On a Monday you think you've got the best movie ever made and on a Tuesday you feel your film is unreleasable. Those two feelings with me are interchangeable throughout the entire production of a motion picture. I get discouraged. I feel abject discouragement. 'Who talked me into this? Why did I do this picture? What's wrong with me? People are going to laugh us out of the theater.' And the next day, 'This is really good. This is going to be wonderful. It's going to last for a thousand years.' And the next day, 'It's not fair. I should be back home. I should be at the beach right now. What in the hell am I doing to myself?'

"When you are directing you have to keep a lot of things in your head and in your heart and in your whole system. When I start to make a movie, the movie is already made. It is already directed, photographed, and edited in my mind, and now I have to go through the laborious task of making the picture a second time. I plan my movies enough so that I'm satisfied that I know what the movie is going to look like. I storyboard everything. It's like you have a wonderful dream about what you're supposed to do today and when you wake up in the morning you've already had the dream and been satisfied with it and now you have to go off and really do it. It takes a lot of work to turn something invisible into something substantial.

"When I first start to direct a movie I feel kind of like a deep-sea diver out of water. I've got the tanks on and the flippers on and I can't walk very well. I've got the mask on and I can't see very well because it's all fogged up. I'm loaded down with weight belts and I'm four times heavier than my normal weight. It's only after the movie is over that I achieve some kind of negative buoyancy because all that stuff has come off. I've shed the tanks and the flippers and the mask and finally thank goodness that's all over and all the ideas, I hope, are in the lab being processed. I come onto the set waterlogged with all these ideas and information and I have to communicate with the crew and the actors to unload. Making movies for me is somewhat a process of unloading, unburdening, unwinding, from a really unnatural pregnancy."

During the summer of 1985, Spielberg is back on a sound stage at Universal, this time shooting *The Color Purple*, but he is also much preoccupied by the prospect of Amy Irving giving birth to their first child. "This is going to be a $180,000 baby," he says. "I'm taking two days off when the baby is born. I've put two days at $90,000 a day into the budget of this film. It's going to be great. I'm looking forward to this baby more than anything else. The baby is going to be my biggest and best production of the year. I don't care if it's a boy or girl as long as it's healthy and isn't born speaking right away. I've been having these persistent dreams that the baby comes out talking—being very articulate and opinionated and telling me where it wants to have dinner tonight. A child that talks at birth—I've been having dreams about it. I won't know quite how to handle that. When I go to North Carolina to finish *The Color Purple*, I'm taking Amy and the baby with me. I have this image of me directing the movie with the baby in my arms, just rocking the baby and directing. That's just a fantasy. The sound man won't let it happen, but that's a real fantasy I have."

The Color Purple, based on Alice Walker's epistolary novel about a poor and abused black woman, is a departure for Spielberg, away from the magic or the thrill or the wide-eyed wonder of his previous films. "*The Color Purple* is the biggest challenge of my career," Spielberg says. "It's the biggest challenge I've ever put myself through. It is a radical U-turn in my movie directing. I am doing it because I love the book. When I read it, I cried and cried. I said to myself, 'I've got to do this for me. I have to do this for me. Otherwise I'm just going to be a baker giving people doughnuts and bagels and French bread and croissants, all their favorites. I want to make something that might not be everybody's favorite, but at least this year is my favorite.' *The Color Purple* is the kind of character piece that a director like Sidney Lumet could do brilliantly with one hand tied behind his back. I began to wonder if perhaps all I could do was make pictures about my own childhood, my dreams and wonders, 'wouldn't-it-be-neat-if' stories. I've never made a confrontive drama like this. It unnerves me, but I'm going into it with both eyes wide open, my heart beating a thousand miles an hour, my heart beating at Mach 2.

"I was starting to be afraid of doing something off my beaten path. I was getting a little too cocky and a little too arrogant about my own style. I said, 'Gee, I can do that kind of film, that's easy for me. I can make a hit out of that.' I found my leg stuck in the trap I built. That sort of arrogance really began to bug the hell out of me. When you cut a trail in the wilderness and you look back and you see where you've been, that's always fun. You say, 'Gee, ain't I great. Look how far that trail goes, across mountains, around lakes, through forests.' But suddenly after *E.T.*, when I began to look ahead in my life, I saw this trail that was being cut in front of me, partly because of me and partly because it is very easy to be led by success, popular demand, and ovation. I don't want to be led. When I could already see the trail, I got scared. I don't want to see where I'm going. The whole titillation of fear and excitement I've always felt about the unknown—of putting my sisters in the closet and shutting the door, of seeing that tree outside my bedroom window and shutting the drapes till morning—all that was taken away from me. I'm trying to rediscover my own frontiers, to know where the boundaries are. That's my human adventure; it's both terrifying and exciting. I want to strike out into new territory. That's the unknown I've created for myself."

Spielberg's baby, Max Samuel Spielberg, is born Thursday, June 13, 1985, at 1:52 P.M., weighing in at seven pounds, seven and a half ounces. Spielberg is ecstatic. "I'll spoil the baby," he says. "My mom spoiled me. I think Amy will be the disciplinarian in the family. She'll be strong with our child and I'll be the pushover. Until now Amy and I together have looked elsewhere for our 400 cc of real life—spell that r-e-e-l. I'm great with a movie camera between me and reality, but the baby is just the excuse I need to look real life in the eye and not be afraid of what I discover. It's been so hard for me to grow up. If my kids take me seriously as a father they're going to have a tough time growing up too. I feel a lot like Peter Pan. I have always felt like Peter Pan. I think a lot of us get real smart about ourselves and we impose a kind of intellectual aura about ourselves. I think that's what growing up is. It's thinking too much and it's not reacting enough. I will always want to make films for children of all ages. I think you can stay a kid all your life and still be a responsible member of the community. I don't think staying a kid and irresponsibility go hand in hand. I think it's a blessing when you can grow gray and still be a boy at heart. It's wonderful."

June 1985

Steven Spielberg and Amy Irving were married in Sante Fe in November 1985. The Color Purple was released at Christmas 1985. The Motion Picture Academy of Arts and Sciences honored Spielberg as "a creative producer" in 1987 with a special Oscar. His Empire of the Sun came out in December 1987. Spielberg "presented" Who Framed Roger Rabbit?, *the top-grossing summer film of 1988.* Indiana Jones—The Last Crusade, *Spielberg's third* Raiders *film, came out in May 1989. Max Samuel Spielberg hosted his first premiere for the release of the animated feature* An American Tail *when he was eighteen months old.*

TED T

STEVE MARTIN IN COLOR

*S*teve Martin's hair, his face, his lips are all one color. Gray. His expression is tight, set in concrete. He has small eyes, blue, deeply inset under thin black brows. He looks like Steve Martin only when he laughs. He is early for an interview at Sant Ambroeus, an elegant Old World *pasticceria* in Manhattan on Madison at Seventy-seventh. He doesn't stand when we shake hands. As I sit down, he puts aside the *New York Post* and the *New Yorker* he had been reading. "I bought the *New York Post* and then I had to buy the *New Yorker* for balance," he says without a smile. He is meticulously groomed. His fingernails look manicured. He is wearing what is certainly a custom-made white shirt, with immaculate stiff cuffs and collar. It is open at the neck. His jacket is hip, loose, coppery, and iridescent. He has on white trousers and black athletic shoes. His talk is dry, thoughtful, methodical, with no flow, no drama, no comedy. He is nice, bland, unpretentious, subdued, matter-of-fact, polite, reserved, very private. There is no silliness, no giddiness, no spontaneity, no play, no fun. Every detail must be suctioned from him. Because of his coloring and his colorless responses, he seems tired out, bleached out, desiccated to the roots of his hair. No antic energy. No act. When we talk about magic, his childhood obsession, I ask him to do a trick, and very hesitantly, reluctantly, he pulls a quarter out of his pocket and makes it disappear. He orders a salad, mineral water, two iced teas. Several times during the meal he takes a little black-and-white tube of ChapStick from his pants pocket and puts it on. "Do you have chapped lips?" I ask. "No," he says. "I have a habit." Later, when it is clear I am not going to eat much of my chocolate mousse cake, he takes a spoonful of it, though only after he rubs the bowl of his spoon vigorously in his napkin. He is compulsive, precise, detached, deadpan. A masked man.

Casually Martin says, "I'm not 'on' all the time. Not at all. The concept of a comedian being 'on' all the time is very depressing to me." He is protective of his privacy. "I don't want the way I live to get out to the world," he says. "Once private things get into print, your private life is over. Everybody knows exactly who you are, and it makes you dull." Talking about his comedy is also anathema to Martin, the icon-comedian of the seventies in the white suit, doing his arrow-through-the-head routine, getting attacks of "Happy Feet." For the most gifted comic actor of the eighties—*The Jerk, Dead Men Don't Wear Plaid, The Man With Two Brains, All of Me, Little Shop of Horrors*—interviews are work. He submits to this one only because of his film *Roxanne*, the sleeper hit based on Edmond Rostand's *Cyrano de Bergerac*, that he wrote, stars in, and loves. "The purest way to do something is to do it and then let the work speak for itself," Martin says. "However, in show business you have to rely on audiences, and the way to get an audience to attend is to let them be aware that a movie is out. You end up compromising your art by talking about it and explaining it when it really should speak for itself. But that's the price you pay. I'm loath to analyze my comedy because I really can't. I can sort of make something up and guess, but I'd rather do it than analyze it. You really rob it of any kind of mystery when you analyze it. I don't find myself that interesting, but I find comedy interesting."

Steve Martin, forty-two, is a superb five-string banjo player. The story of Steve and his banjo is the story of his life: "I was eighteen and I heard Earl Scruggs play the banjo on a record and I went crazy and I said, 'I'm going to try and learn that.' During the day I would put Earl Scruggs, Jim Rooney, the Stanley Brothers, all these records on the turntable, and slow down the speed from 33⅓ to 16, and I'd pick out each note, note by note. It was very methodical. I learned to play the banjo practicing in my '57 white Chevy parked out in front of my parents' house in the middle of the night so I wouldn't wake anybody up. Now I've quit playing the banjo. I quit because I wasn't getting any better. It's like I reached the end of it. I'd given what I had to it. Not that I perfected it or learned it completely, because there are certain things I can't play, but I wrote my five songs, you know, and I wasn't going to get any better without taking lessons or going on the road with a bluegrass band. So I lost interest in it."

Same with stand-up comedy: "I felt like I had achieved it. I felt like there was nothing new to do, only new material to do. I don't mean that stand-up was over because I had perfected it, not at all. I'm saying it was over because I had given what I had to give to it. It's like I did it, I know I can do it, and when I was doing it, I was doing it as well as anyone."

Same with collecting art and studying philosophy: "I started collecting nineteenth-century American paintings fifteen years ago, then sold all of them about seven years ago and began collecting twentieth-century American art. You study a period and then you start looking at the next period. You just keep moving up. What happened was very much the same thing that happened to me when I studied philosophy. You study the early philosophers like Thales, the earth-air-fire-and-water guy, and you go, 'Gee, I see, this is it.' Then you read Socrates and you go, 'Ah, this is the real thing.' Then Plato: 'Oh, yeah.' Then you read Aristotle: 'Oh, yes, I see.' So with each one you're saying, 'This is the best, this is the best.' So now you proceed right up through history and go through Descartes, Hume, Kant, Sartre, Wittgenstein. The end."

Martin's current fascination is with computers. He says, "For a guy like me, computers are really fun. They are endlessly complicated, so you never really have that I-know-that kind of feeling." Martin is also nowhere near saying he has "done" movie acting. He does say, "I want to explore comedy in films until I can finally say to myself, 'Yes, you did comedy.' I think there might come a point when that will happen. Then I might find myself going into more dramatic roles or directing. I don't feel I have to prove I can do a Broadway play or be a romantic leading man. I certainly don't want to play Hamlet. I would love deep in my heart to do some great dramatic role, but whether I could pull it off or whether it would be valuable is another matter. I don't want to do drama just for the heck of it. My orientation is comedy, and that's what I know best. My films will always be about comedy. I'm interested in comedy no matter what form it takes, whether it's slapstick, or smart, or character, or sketch. I like a big broad dumb joke as much as I like a very smart joke. A lot of people disrespect low comedy. I have great respect for the big joke. People are afraid to like slapstick. Dead word. The movie *Airplane*, for example, it's got great jokes and it's all about jokes and it doesn't have anything else in it but jokes. I loved it."

For now Martin says he is going to stick to writing and acting in comedies: "Starting out in movies, I felt very confident that I could act because I was too dumb to know any better. The more I looked, the more ground I got to stand on. I feel now I have a frame of reference with the movies. Having made all these movies, having seen a lot of movies, having turned my eye toward movies, now I feel I can approach a new picture and actually have a response to it, not just be confused. I feel I understand movie acting more, so now I can begin to explore it. I have not learned it. It is rich enough so you can find something new to mine each time. And you can get older in acting. You won't always be forty. There will be a new type of performance when you're fifty, sixty. With movies you have a long way to go before you have actually proved something to yourself or to the world. Down the line, I'll direct. It's the hardest job, directing. I think I will.

"I was aiming for show business from early on," Martin says. "A girl I met actually sidetracked me. I was about eighteen. [Martin gets animated for a minute. He talks faster.] This is interesting, unbelievable. This girl I met when I was working at Knott's Berry Farm was my first love. Her name was Stormie Sherk. She was a very big influence in my life in that she got me interested in college. I had no interest at all in college, and she got me interested. She made me read *The Razor's Edge*, things like that. That's when I got interested in learning. I thought it was very, very important to learn as much as I possibly could. She went on to marry a famous Christian record producer. She became a Christian singer and recently published a book about her life. At the time I didn't have a clue about it. Her mother was schizophrenic. She had drug problems. She was an abused child. She mentions me in the book. She said her relationship with me was the only relationship she ever had with a man she didn't end up hating. Stormie got me interested in college.

"When I was eighteen, I started going to California State University, Long Beach. At the same time I worked at Knott's Berry Farm at a place called the Bird Cage Theater. The Bird Cage is still there. They do melodramas. We did four shows a day. First the play, the melodrama, would go on, and then I would come out and do my magic act or a banjo thing or some little skit. It was really basic training. I'd work five days a week, maybe including the weekends. At school I studied philosophy. Sartre was probably my favorite philosopher. I studied Kant and Hume and Socrates and Plato. I was just fascinated by it. Wittgenstein is sort of technical existentialism, very hard to comprehend. His philosophy really comes down to sayings that are very startling. I appreciated Wittgenstein because it analyzed all the philosophy that came before it. Remember, I was a college student and I was romanticized by philosophy. I thought it was the highest thing you could study. It seemed to be about truth and life and all those clichés I don't necessarily believe in anymore. At a certain point in my life I wanted to teach philosophy. I wanted to be a professor.

"Philosophy took me through this natural arc of being incredibly interested in what truth is, and then, as I studied the history of philosophy, it became less and less important to me, and by the time I got to Wittgenstein it seemed meaningless, so I changed my major to the arts. That idealistic, youthful quest for certainty or so-called truth became pointless to me and it didn't matter what the truth was anymore. The study of philosophy itself triggered my feeling that the quest for truth was pointless. Clear definitions no longer meant anything to me and were not important to have. The study of metaphysics—I didn't believe anymore that there was this magic unity. Ethics—I didn't believe anymore that there was bounded certainty. Everything pointed to the arts, that you define your life, you define yourself, you define what you think by what you do. Pure existentialism. You create meaning with the arts. You don't have to discover meaning. There is no certain way to do things in the arts. The rules are completely made up. There is no right or wrong in the arts. You can do whatever works. It is the difference that makes something great in the arts, not the sameness. It became clear to me that creativity is unbounded by rules and regulations. True and false don't apply to the arts. True and false apply to the world and to facts. The arts have another standard. These are the musings of a twenty-one-year-old kid.

"That's one side of it, the intellectual, theoretical side. But there was this other side of me that was doing magic acts at the Bird Cage Theater and getting on stage whenever I could. There was my natural propensity to be a performer and entertainer and show-off. So maybe part of this was just rationalization for what I really wanted to do. It was a conscious decision to go into show business. I said I will hate myself if I never try show business. It had been a part of my life ever since I'd been a kid. To suddenly give it up . . . I always would have wondered what might have happened in show business. I realized I couldn't be happy wondering. That's another reason I didn't continue with philosophy. I never did get a degree in it. I went to school for four years, but in my last year I switched to UCLA and changed my major to theater. I wasn't concerned with getting a degree at all. I just didn't care about it. I had enough credits, but I didn't have all the required courses in that department. I quit in my fourth year of college to write for the Smothers Brothers' TV show.

"In my life I remember a very sort of depressing and important discovery I made. I was about nineteen or twenty years old, sitting in a college class at Cal State, and I was playing the banjo and doing my magic act and getting jokes out of joke books, and I realized that in order to be original I had to write all my material myself. This discovery was so painful because I didn't know how to write and never had written and never even had thought about it. But it was like an apparent truth. I had to do it. It also was a bit of a gimmick, like, 'Here's the way to be original.' It was so obvious that it was bound to come out different. I had no experience at writing, or even thinking up things. I didn't know where to begin. It was depressing. So I started to listen in my life, to hear where I laughed and where other people laughed. When I laughed, I would take that situation in life and try to work it into a line or routine or something. I began noting moments in the day where I would laugh. That is how I began writing. At the time I was working at a nightclub called the Prison of Socrates in Balboa, and at a club in Pasadena called the Ice House. I was also still working at Knott's Berry Farm. I tried things out at these clubs. A lot of things I tried didn't work. I thought it would be funny to get very serious. I wanted to do a dramatic reading of some of my college material, so I chose the periodic table of the elements. It was all abbreviations, so I would just go 'phuh, mem, fe.' It didn't work.

"Being in philosophy, I had these theories. You have to understand the context this was coming out of; comedy up to that time was pretty much Bob Hope monologues with jokes. I thought with a joke the audience either laughs or it doesn't. If people laugh, you're a hit; if they don't, you're a miss. But I thought if you gave your audience no place to laugh, they would find a place to laugh by creating their own tension. In other words I wouldn't tell them—by doing jokes and giving them a punch line—'Here, now you're supposed to laugh.' Traditionally jokes build up tension in an audience, and the punch line releases tension. I would let the audience itself find what was funny, and therefore it would be truly funny to them. So I eliminated all jokes from my routine. I did everything off-the-wall, completely strange. One of my first bits was the nose-on-the-microphone routine. I made a big announcement, 'I am going to do the nose-on-the-microphone routine.' And I would lean forward and put my nose on the microphone and then take a bow.

"One of the things I observed when I started to write my own material was that the strongest kind of laughter is when you laugh and you don't know why. The nose-on-the-microphone routine, for example; you can't say why that is funny. That to me was the strongest kind of comedy I could do. When the audience was laughing and didn't know why. That is the kind of laugh I was going for. It's not like, 'He said this joke and here's the punch line and you're falling on the floor.' It's not going to a club and hearing a comedian say fifty jokes. It comes down to, 'I just look at him and laugh.' I think that is a very infectious, enduring kind of laughter. It's like being giddy. It's almost like being high, not chemically, but euphoric. At that point when you're laughing so hard you seem to truly lose your ego.

"Another theory was that I would never acknowledge to the audience that I was not going over. I was completely confident all the time. That created a character on stage, a gung-ho guy who was too involved in himself to know he was not going over. So I had these two elements: never give them a joke they can recognize, and also pretend this character thought he was the greatest comedian in the world. This was early on. Those were the theoretical beginnings of a comedy act. At the time I needed theory. I used to believe that people who paint, write, whatever, work from theories for their own head. The theories don't relate to what actually comes out, but it helps you think fresh. Mind you, I don't necessarily believe these theories anymore. At the time I believed them. I needed some kind of theory from which to operate, to believe in, while I was out there bombing. Theory is for when you're young and creating and like to think that what you're doing is important. As you get more confident you just let it come. But your enthusiasm and your youth and your theories and thinking you were doing something good and wonderful and distinguished would carry you through.

"I think my study of philosophy had a lot of impact on my comedy because I have a real strong sense of absurdity. And that's really what it is about, what's absurd and what isn't. I started out from a rebel position in comedy, a rebel position from show business in general. In the early seventies, show business was very much rat-pack Vegas phony. The act had a little bit of showbiz satire in it. I did an entire Las Vegas act in one minute. I would come out and completely talk real fast, sing a song really fast, and get off. 'Hey, how ya doin' tonight, welcome to Las Vegas blvvblvbblbvb, and I'm going to sing 'Gotta Be Me,' Gotta blbblvlvb-blvbl, okay, thank you very much, good night.' I had whole routines on cool, suave guys trying to meet girls. I did lounge-singer parodies. I used to look at the comedy around, and it was all the same.

"My act was an act that evolved by doing it every night, and changing little tiny bits. I would write it and rewrite it and change a little element, not enough so you'd notice, but increment by increment. And sometimes it changed consciously. Sometimes I sat down and actually thought about what I wanted to say, what I wanted to mean. I used to have long hair and wear hippie clothes, and then I said, it's over. I felt like I was the first person to cut his hair. I was probably responding to a mood, anyway, but it was a conscious decision. Coming out of the Vietnam War, the country hadn't laughed for a long time. Every comedian was political at the time. I felt then it was really time to be so stupid and sort of forget your troubles and let someone else be so idiotic and egocentric. The act was completely about something other than everything that was going on at the time, which was extremely serious, extremely political and self-conscious. That is what I wanted to do around 1973.

"My act was intentionally apolitical. It was a conscious decision I've never been able to describe accurately. To me, political satire doesn't result in anything. I have always felt estranged from the government. They're big, we're little. I wanted the act to be about an individual. The small world. How distorted your thoughts could get just being alive in the world. I didn't want it to be about me commenting on this big world that was inaccessible, unresponsive, bureaucratic. The government starts rolling, you can't stop 'em. You know, this was that time of political turmoil and disrespect for political people. Like, how could they pardon President Nixon? You just give up. I believed that whoever is president, it doesn't matter. They're all the same. Little variations here and there. Meaningless. My belief was that the government wasn't really what affects you and me, and this person and that person. What really affects us are our little lives. Our lives and our friends affect us more than any government bill ever would. That's why I felt almost proud not even talking about the government. It wasn't really worth talking about."

A second interview, in a suite at the Ritz-Carlton overlooking Central Park, is smoother. Martin's got some juice in him. He has walked about twenty blocks from uptown. He says he feels flabby, needs the exercise. He is wearing an eggshell-colored long-sleeved shirt, blue cotton casual pants, black athletic shoes, and a blue baseball cap ("My disguise," he calls it) that is embroidered with "Gourmet Poker Club" and a King of Clubs. He and a few of his pals play every once in a while, although Martin admits he doesn't like it much now. He says, "I used to love to play poker. I wanted to win money. But as soon as I got some money, poker held no interest for me anymore." He sees some folders of newspaper and magazine articles about himself on a table and he goes over and looks through them. He examines my portable computer with great interest. He laughs more today, and his face crinkles up into his signature smile. For lunch he orders vichyssoise and fruit salad ("I'm a vegetarian," he says. "I don't know why"), a pitcher of iced tea, and mineral water. When the bill comes, he maneuvers to see it and remarks, "What a tab." He does the ChapStick thing again. Later, when his wife, British actress Victoria Tennant, who starred in TV's *The Winds of War* and appeared in *All of Me,* visits as scheduled, Martin relaxes. He slumps back in his chair and lets her carry the conversation. He even starts yawning. Tennant, a tart-tongued beauty with long limbs and fairy-blond hair, is protective of Martin. She refuses to make a date for an interview about him. She says she wouldn't ever reveal "intimate insights into Steve Martin." She thinks it is "repulsive" to talk about one's art. She will only say Steve is "interesting to live with and he makes me laugh."

"I was born in Waco, Texas, on August 14, 1945," Martin says. "When I was five, we moved to Inglewood, California. I have an older sister, Melinda, who is a California housewife. My parents are alive. I think I look like my father, but everyone says I look like my mother. My father has pure white hair. My mother too. I started going gray when I was fifteen. It's an inherited trait, I think. It never bothered me. I never thought about it. My father's name is Glenn. My mother's name is Mary Lee. They live in Orange County. They're retired. My mother tells me that wherever she goes she introduces into the conversation that she is my mother. I mean restaurants, department stores, everyplace. I don't know how she does it. I find it very embarrassing. I think my dad is pretty proud. I don't want them interviewed. I always try to keep them low-profile. I'm very worried about threats. My father was involved in real estate as a salesman, as a broker, and he was eventually president of the Newport Board of Realtors in Orange County. He had been an actor in his spare time. I went to see him once when I was very young, about four, at a little theater in Los Angeles on Melrose. That was the only place I ever remember seeing him. I was so young. I don't remember much about it. I didn't understand it. It was over by the time I was growing up. He was in the USO during the war. My mother is generous. She was a housewife.

"We come from sort of a typical WASP family, I would say. It's not real close-knit, not a lot of hugging and kissing, not real vocal or loud, the opposite of that. We were middle-class. When I was ten, suburbia developed and we moved to Garden Grove. All the orange groves were going down, and all the tracts were going up. We moved into a tract house. It was two miles from Disneyland. This was about 1955. We lived in a little wood-frame tract house, painted green. Lime green. My parents were concerned with bringing up a child in the proper way. And I was concerned with having a ball. I was raised as a Baptist, not a Southern Baptist. It's a very easygoing Protestant religion. It's not fire and brimstone, not strict at all. I'm not a Baptist now. Four years of philosophy takes care of all that. My childhood was typical. I can't think of anything more typical than my childhood. No beatings, nothing bizarre. I didn't grow up in a whorehouse [as Richard Pryor did]. I had a very happy childhood. My mother cooked. I don't know if she baked. All I remember, when frozen food came in, we were right there buying frozen food. There is nobody I know of in the family who was in show business. I have my whole family history. My uncle did one of those roots things. He published it in two volumes. It goes back to the Revolutionary War. Soldiers, Indian blood, criminals, train robbers. Mostly out of the South, Texas. English, Scottish, Irish.

"When I was ten, I got a job at Disneyland selling guidebooks. I just loved the idea of Disneyland. I heard that they were going to have openings, and I went there immediately. I rode my bicycle there every day. I made two cents a book. If I sold 100 books, what's that, two dollars? I wanted to be the best salesman. The norm was about 50 a day. One day I sold 625 books. I think that was a record. The guidebooks had pictures of Disneyland, a map, little stories. I don't know, I never read it. I wore a straw boater hat, garters on my sleeves, and a bow tie. I stood at the front, at the gate. The guidebooks cost 25 cents. I did that in the summer and on weekends. I did that until I was twelve or thirteen, and then I spent a year at Frontierland doing trick roping like cowboys do with the lasso. Frontierland is a part of Disneyland where the theme is the frontier days. There is a fort, a steamboat, the mine ride. I stood out in this corral and sold these little ropes that you could swivel like a lasso. I would demonstrate them and sell them. It wasn't really a step up from guidebooks. A step sideways. I didn't do very well. They were hard to sell. I had to wear a Western costume, cowboy shirt, hat. I did a little bit of that in ¡Three Amigos! Then I went to Adventureland, to Tiki's Tropical Traders, and I became a warehouse boy. It was a hat store, and I opened boxes of hats and put them on the shelves.

"Then, when I was fifteen, I got a job in the magic shop, which was my dream come true because I got to perform magic for people. This shop was in Fantasyland. It was called Merlin's Magic Shop, and it had a sword in a stone. There was a trick to pulling the sword out. It was like a funny shop. We'd make jokes with the people who came in, and we'd spray them with snake cans. We sold magic tricks, rubber vomit, things like that. Stuffed toys; magic sets; nails through the head; gum that was supposed to make you pucker; pepper gum; invisible, disappearing ink; funny plaques with funny sayings like, 'There's no place like this place anywhere near this place, so this must be the place'; shrunken heads; skulls that glow in the dark; peanut brittle candy (you open it up and snakes come out); linking rings; a finger chopper—like a little guillotine, you put your finger in and the blade looks like it passes through your finger. We had thousands of gags we would pull on people. And I used to write them all down so I would have all our gags on three-by-five cards. I catalogued all the material of the magic shop. I still have those cards.

"I also have incredibly detailed notes on magic shows I did when I was fifteen or sixteen. Notes on what I did, how it went over. I worked for the Kiwanis Club. They'd hire a kid for five dollars. I'd go down and entertain them at their meetings. I loved magic as a kid. I bought books, took books on magic out of the library. I remember my uncle buying me a magic trick when I was six or seven at the Farmers' Market and I was just fascinated. I did magic acts for my parents, and if somebody came over, I did my magic act for them. Magic was the poor man's way of getting into showbiz. You buy a trick for five dollars or two dollars or fifty cents and you've got an act. It told you what to say on the instructions. I worked at Merlin's Magic Shop for about three years, from when I was fifteen to eighteen. The shop is not there anymore. Now there is a magic shop on Main Street.

"It is very eerie to go back now. I went back with Victoria recently in a disguise. I dyed my hair brown and wore a brown mustache. It's not that people mob me on the streets, it's not like Michael Jackson came to town. It depends on where you are, but Disneyland can be very tough, and I don't like being stared at or yelled at. I went and stood in the store where the Magic Shop was, and it was like it was yesterday, and it was really twenty-five years ago. It was extremely bizarre because I knew every nook and cranny of the shop."

Much of Martin's stand-up act was inspired by his Disneyland days, although he developed "Happy Feet" in his living room. "I wanted to do something that looked like I was being controlled by someone else," he says. "I think I started out moving like I was out of control, and I would start looking up at the sky like I was being controlled by somebody, and that eventually fell away and I just started doing, 'Uh-oh, I'm getting happy feet.' 'Happy Feet' is a thing you just get and you can't control it and you are just in trouble.

"When I was at Disneyland, there was a woman from the South working there. She had a phrase she used to use: 'Well, excuse me for living.' I always thought arrogant entertainers were hysterically funny, so one night at a club in San Francisco I decided I was going to get mad at the spotlight operator. I ask for a blue spot for my mood—I was going to play the banjo and be very moody—and the spotlight doesn't turn blue, and I just get so incensed so incensed so incensed, and I call him every name, and I say, 'I'm out here giving and giving and giving, and you can't even give me a blue spot.' Then I couldn't think of a way to get out of it and wanted to say, 'Well, excuse me for living' but it was too long, so I abbreviated it to 'Well, ex*cuuuuuse me.*' So that was an actual bit that I did. The phrase caught on with people and became independent of the bit that went before it. I used to love to do that routine.

"I learned juggling when I was a kid. I met the court jester at Disneyland. He is still around. His name is Christopher Fair. He rode a unicycle, he juggled, he did magic, he did everything. He taught me how to juggle. I went home and practiced with croquet balls, that's all we had at home to use, and I bruised my fingers badly because the croquet

balls were so heavy. I was fourteen, fifteen. I had incredible per-
severance with stuff like that, just would not give up. You learn how to
juggle in three months or two months or two weeks, but getting extremely graceful at it takes years. I always learned everything on stage.
I wasn't afraid to be bad on stage juggling, or bad playing the banjo.
And eventually you get smooth at it because you've done it so much. I'm
not a very good juggler, I can do three balls, that's it.

"I loved making balloon animals. I never learned how to make them. I
just watched magicians and comedians do it. It was part of the show
business parody—I would make bad balloon animals. I didn't even
know how to tie them or twist them or anything. They were just bad
balloon animals. The arrow through the head was a thing we used to sell
at Disneyland. To me it goes back to the theory. It's like, God, these gags
are so dumb. I used to put it on and leave it on. It was one of those
things, like, I'd put it on and ten minutes later the audience was saying,
'He still has the arrow on.' It was just so silly. I wanted to end the act
looking as ridiculous as possible. So I had the balloons on my head, the
arrow through the head, the nose glasses, and the bunny ears. I liked
the idea of doing something so dumb. It was like anti-comedy."

At first Martin would take his act just about anywhere. He recalls,
"At California's Russian River Resort, I stood on a stage outdoors and
played to a parking lot of cars and campers like at a drive-in. People
didn't get out of their cars. If they liked something, they would honk.
And I used to go to San Francisco and work a club up there. There was a
window open to the street and I performed in front of the window, and
people would walk by and look in and see something going on and then
they'd come in. So I had to start my act with nobody in the audience, and
when people would come in, they'd be shocked because there was nobody there. At Harrah's in Nevada I followed an elephant act. Sometimes nobody cleaned up and there'd be elephant shit on the stage.
Vegas could be very tough, especially when you're a nobody and you're
opening for Helen Reddy or somebody. Backstage at a dinner show,
you'd hear the sound of people eating and silverware tinkling and they'd
introduce you and there would be no change. They'd have their face right
in their food and nobody was looking at you and, oh, it was so horrible. If
I had material that lasted thirty minutes at a regular nightclub, it lasted
twelve minutes in Vegas because there'd be no laughs.

"In 1968, I was in college at UCLA taking TV writing classes and working at a club in Westwood called Ledbetters. At that time my interest in college was waning. Then I was hired to write for *The Smothers Brothers Comedy Hour*, their summer show starring Glen Campbell. I quit school and took the job. It was called *The Summer Brothers Smothers Show*. I got hired by a fluke. An artist-songwriter named Mason Williams was very instrumental in getting me on that show. Mason Williams was dating my ex-girlfriend, who told Mason he should read my material. I sent him my college creative-writing stuff and I was hired and I don't know why because my stuff wasn't very good. In fact, Mason hired me to come in and paid me out of his own pocket. Then I continued over into the *The Smothers Brothers Comedy Hour* as a writer working with Bob Einstein. I think I was getting paid five hundred dollars a show, which was great money. To me that was enormous. I felt like I was very rich because I had no savings, I never had had any savings. I worked there for a year and the show was canceled.

"I went over to write for *The Glen Campbell Show*, and it was not me. I just didn't feel up to it and I wanted to perform. It was a very momentous decision, it was like, dare I leave this high-paying job? I was getting up to $1,250 a show. But I decided to go back to performing full time. I had continued to do some performing at night, at the Ice House in Pasadena and other nightclubs. Then Bob Einstein called me up and asked me to write with him for *The Pat Paulsen show*. And I said okay, and that was something like $1,500 a week. So I did that for half a season. I guess I went on the road a little bit, and then I went to write for *The Sonny and Cher Show*. Part of my deal, though, was I would be a writer if they let me perform on the show in sketches. But I didn't really get to do anything on that show. I ended up playing a head on a plate. They'd lift up the cover of the plate and I'd have a one-liner. Then I quit.

"At this time, when I was in my early twenties, I had my first anxiety attack. I thought it was a nervous breakdown, but it wasn't. An anxiety attack is terrifying. The symptoms are an increased heartbeat, like two hundred beats a minute, your mouth goes dry, and you don't know what is happening to you. The attacks last ten minutes to an hour. It took me about three years to get over them. Through investigation I found this was a fairly common thing. Once I found out what they were, they started to subside. I conquered them through education. What happened to me was I felt insecure—I was writing for national television, I felt like I didn't know what I was doing. I didn't know what to write, I didn't know anything. I didn't know if I was capable of handling it. Also, I was not eligible to go to Vietnam. First I had a college deferment and then I had migraine headaches. I had them for two or three years. I had a note from a shrink and a doctor, and then the war was over.

"Meanwhile I decided to go on the road with the Nitty Gritty Dirt Band. Bill McEuen was my manager. I had met him in high school, and he became my manager while I was writing for Glen Campbell. His brother John was in the Dirt Band. Bill was managing them, too, and the band very generously hired me as an opening act. They gave me part of their money and it was extremely generous of them. So I went around opening for them and for other rock bands, and it was the worst kind of humiliation. I'm talking about the audience at the time. They'd watch *Midnight Express* and *Rock Concert* on TV, and be crazy at a show. Their behavior was antithetical to good comedy. You need audience attention for good comedy, and I got a lot of 'Get Off' and that kind of thing.

"I had to make the decision that I wasn't going to be an opening act. I was always broke, in the hole. I called up David Brenner, who was getting very successful at the time, and I said, 'How do you make a living?' He said, 'I go into a club and I take what comes in at the door and the club owner takes the bar. I have someone stand at the door with a counter.' So I decided that that's what I was going to do. The first time I ever headlined was in Coconut Grove, Florida. It was very frightening. I did my act and then this review came out in the *Miami Herald*. It was a rave. It said, 'This is it, this is the act, the place, the time, everything.' The club started selling out. I started to do TV shows like *The Steve Allen Show*, *The Joey Bishop Show*, and I just sensed something was happening. In San Francisco there is a club called The Boarding House. I had opened there many, many times. So I went back as a headliner. The club started selling out. I suddenly started making $3,000 to $4,000 a week. I went from nothing to that—just on the decision to headline, to make them come to see me. This was around 1973 or 1974.

"Another important job for me was in Nashville. I guess every comedian has this experience when the place is packed and it is hot and the audience is just there and they are seeing something that is so new to them that it is exciting. It was just thrilling to go on and have these shows with the audience just dying. The first time I took the audience outside into the street with me when the show was over was at a college in North Carolina, I think. I was onstage. It was one of those stages where, in order to get off the stage, you had to leave the building. So I said, 'That's the act and thank you very much,' but I didn't have anyplace to go, and they were still sitting there. So I walked out and I realized they were following me, so I just kept going, and there was an empty swimming pool. I asked everyone to get in the swimming pool, and then I swam across the top of them. They all held me up and I swam and swam. It happened again, I think it was in the South, and I took the audience outside and we went to McDonald's and asked for five hundred Big Macs to go. Word started to spread that there was something happening in the world of comedy.

"I had enough experience and enough material and the confidence. It was all starting to work. I also developed a lot of material because everything was working so well that I could really be free to ad-lib. Most of my material was written on stage. I'd ad-lib and then remember it and start to develop it. I started to go on *The Tonight Show* around 1973. At first I got on with a guest host, and then I got on with Johnny. There was an energy. Extremely powerful. The energy just happens. I can't really explain that. It's something I never think about, really. On stage the energy is really from the audience. You can't let them down. There is a powerful feeling, but it is not related to good and evil.

"Meanwhile Bill McEuen, who was a great supporter and was always back there laughing when the audience wasn't, had been recording everything and was hustling around for record deals. He was responsible for bringing David Picker [then head of Paramount] to see me perform in San Francisco. Eventually that led to a movie deal. My first album, *Let's Get Small,* was released. It went platinum and nobody had expected it to do anything. There hadn't been a comedy album in years. By then there was a momentum. I went on *Saturday Night Live* in 1976 and it was all over. I went on the road the next night, and there was this incredible response. Places started selling out. I was playing 500-seat theaters, then 1,000 seaters, then 1,500, then 3,000, 7,000,

10,000, 20,000. It was happening so fast. We made a movie deal at Paramount with David Picker to do *The Jerk* and a short called *The Absent-Minded Waiter*, which was nominated for an Academy Award. Then David Picker left Paramount. Paramount hated my deal and gave me back *The Absent-Minded Waiter*, which I now own, and the screenplay for *The Jerk*. They let me keep the $50,000 advance. I made *The Jerk* at Universal. The rest is history. It was about 1980 when I stopped doing my stand-up act. I was tired of it. I don't miss it. I didn't have anything else to say. It was a labor to come up with the material. Material I had by 1976 had been cultivated for ten, fifteen years. Then suddenly, because the media was eating up this material so fast, to come up with another hour or two of what had to be great stuff, was just . . . it was over."

The Jerk was the third biggest hit of 1980. It brought in $43.3 million in rentals, but Martin's next five pictures, *Pennies from Heaven, Dead Men Don't Wear Plaid, The Man With Two Brains, The Lonely Guy,* and *All of Me* earned a total $38.2 million. The hottest comedian of the seventies was bombing at the eighties box office. It hurt. Martin says, "It is very painful when you have a failure. When you start to have the number-one record or be number one at the box office and everything is calculated in terms of numbers, it is very easy to fall into the trap of seeing yourself as a number. You start to play the numbers game. 'I'm number four, why aren't I number three?' You know a decline is inevitable. My problem is, I don't get the same exhilaration from success as I get depression from failure. In all the arts, failure is just around the corner. It's the nature of what we do, to make up something and then go try it. You can't predict what's going to happen. You can work two years on a movie that comes out and lasts one week, then goes away. You're always vulnerable to failure. Anyone who is arrogant in the arts is just plain ludicrous. Just wait.

"I'm not always pleased with the way my movies come out. You have different feelings about a movie. Usually you feel good about a movie because you're in the middle of it and you've spent a couple of years on it, and later you start to realize what it actually is, whether the critics tell you or the audience tells you or you just start to think about it. I don't like to judge these things. I do think *The Jerk* is a great first film. I know I yelled all the way through it. I saw it the other day and said, 'Jesus, why did I yell?' But there was nothing to be ashamed of. It was my first film. You are allowed to go nuts, go over the line, under the line, big jokes, little jokes. *The Jerk* was essentially about my act and the kind of comedy I was doing. I had the idea based on a joke in my act, which was, 'I was born a poor black child.' I just thought the movie should be filled with jokes.

"*Pennies from Heaven* came right after *The Jerk*. My stand-up days were coming to an end. I was working in Las Vegas. I was very depressed. Not clinically depressed, but I didn't know what to do next. I didn't want to make *Jerk II*, you know. I was lost, lost, lost. I didn't want to do stand-up anymore. I had no idea what kind of film I wanted to make. Then my agent called me one day and said, 'There is a script called *Pennies from Heaven*. It's a remake of this old Bing Crosby movie.' He had it confused. The way he described it, I knew it was the movie version of the BBC series *Pennies from Heaven*. I was immediately interested. The script was magnificent. I felt I was lucky to be saying those words because I thought they were beautiful. I thought the emotions in it were beautiful. I thought the element of hope in it was so magnificent, so moving, that I wanted to do it no matter what it cost me in terms of my career. I didn't know if the audience was going to understand my making such a radical movie. I was pretty much advised against it. But I wanted to. And it was a great period in my life. The music was a discovery to me. I had this music to listen to, these sounds from fifty years ago. They were quite beautiful. It was very moving. I learned to dance. I was only going to learn to tap dance, but the choreographer kept piling it on. I was very dedicated, rehearsing hours every day. Starting out it was an hour or two, then four and five, and then eight hours a day trying to learn the choreography. I learned all kinds of stuff—tap, waltz, all kinds of steps.

"I thought *Dead Men Don't Wear Plaid* could be very funny and classy. And it seemed original. This was a movie constructed from film clips, so we had to go along with whatever story the clips dictated. We had to make up a cheesebomb ending. There was never a natural ending that paid off. Although I liked the movie going in, I knew we weren't going to have a satisfying ending. We had made such a complicated story, the only way to wrap it up was through cheating, through cheesebombs. Carl Reiner and I finished *Dead Men*, and we thought it was great and wanted to work together again. I said, 'Let's make a brain movie.' So we made *The Man with Two Brains*. I went from the thirties in *Pennies from Heaven* to the forties in *Dead Men* and I thought, 'fifties brain movie.' I wanted to do it in black and white with those really skinny ties. Carl convinced me to make it modern. A regular movie. It was completely made up. It was written very quickly. That was a movie strictly about ludicrousness. To me it was one of those movies where you make jokes all along the way and then it sort of unravels. It's not quite a whole thing, although when I saw it again on TV, I did think it was funny in that sort of basic, dumb spirit I like.

"I wanted to do *The Lonely Guy* because I thought it was filled with heart. Then, when *All of Me* came along, I was really confused. I was so low because the last three pictures had failed. I didn't know what to do, what kind of movie to make, or if I was even going to make a movie. I read the script for *All of Me* and thought it was very funny. Then I started having doubts. Carl Reiner was begging me to do it, so I said, 'I'm flying to New York tomorrow. I'll reread the script on the plane and I'll call you when I land.' I read it again; I thought it was hysterical. I said I can't turn down something funny. That would be the dumbest thing of all. That movie was when I met my wife, Victoria. Ultimately, *¡Three Amigos!* could have been better. It didn't fulfill what I wanted it to be. I wanted it to be a big, dumb comedy. A lot of laughs, a lot of big, dumb situations. It became more of an action picture than a comedy. I might be prejudging it.

"To make *Roxanne* was always a folly, according to conventional wisdom. It's not a splashy summer film. It's not about cops and robbers, nobody gets killed. It's about romance, and there have been few genuinely romantic movies. I liked its emotion, its heart, its strong story, and that it was funny along the way. It is a very personal film to me because it is the first film I wrote entirely by myself. I remember mentioning the idea to David Goodman, a screenwriter friend of mine. I told him I wanted to update *Cyrano de Bergerac* and I said I needed a reason. You just can't do the play again in modern clothes. I didn't feel you could or should. I said to David, 'I need something different about it.' And he looked at me and said, 'Cyrano gets the girl.' And I said, 'Ah, that's perfect. Gets the girl.' So I started attacking it. I had my own translation from the French made. It was done verbatim, no interpretation by the translator. If there was a word or phrase for which there was no translation, she said 'no translation.' I slowly started distilling, sticking very close to the play at first. I wrote it virtually scene for scene from the play. It didn't quite come off. It is just my way of writing. I like to get the whole thing down and then start changing the interior of it. That way the structure is always sound. It changed incrementally over several years of writing. I wrote many, many drafts. I'm guessing twenty to twenty-five drafts. I'm guessing I wrote it in two or two and a half years.

"I thought about using some feature other than a nose, but then it became futile because I couldn't think of anything else. I felt it would become '*Cyrano*, and they changed the nose to an ear.' Nothing had the sweetness of a nose. A nose is real and yet it is fantasy. It is not quite a real handicap like a missing leg. It is a friendly handicap. It doesn't imply some horrible accident. It is not like the Elephant Man. It is sort of a metaphor for all disfigurements or handicaps that people have, real or imagined.

"Some of the *Roxanne* reviews said I was like Charlie Chaplin. Well, that's embarrassing to me. I would never presume that. I don't think about the physical moves. It's just like making a movie. You don't think about it. It's like if I was twenty-five years old and I was in some nightclub in Winston-Salem, North Carolina, and I thought about how hard it was, I'd quit. I think many people have this physical coordination. I think of my coordination—it's like compensated coordination. I don't have the coordination of a real dancer. Once Carl Reiner told me this story about when he was doing *Your Show of Shows*. He did some German double talk and his mother called him up and said, 'I didn't know you spoke German.' And he said, 'No, no, they pay me because I can't.' That is the way I view myself when it comes to all this dancing and so-called coordination. I'm not really coordinated. I look like I'm slightly clumsy at it, but I'm able to compensate so that the clumsiness is graceful. That is the way I interpret what I do. It's acting, kind of. It's a feeling. There is a feeling—that feeling that goes through your entire body where even your little finger is working. Very exhilarating."

There are no windows in the front of Steve Martin's gray, one-story Beverly Hills house. In the sunlight you have to look carefully before you can make out the lines of a garage and a front door. A car, draped with an off-white tarp and sitting on the concrete horseshoe driveway, could be mistaken for a contemporary sculpture. The front yard is a small, landscaped hump of green grass. At the door there isn't even a peephole; just a lot of push buttons, a grate, and other earmarks of a high-tech security system.

The front door opens and closes quickly behind me. I step onto a lush sea-green wall-to-wall carpet. Immediately I look up to high skylights. Sunlight is falling on a Robert Graham bronze sculpture of a nude girl, placed at eye level on a pedestal of two cubes, one white, one black. Then, for a second, it feels as if I have accidentally walked into the observation deck of Captain Nemo's *Nautilus* when panels slide back and reveal a rich, strange world that is rearranging itself in countless patterns. Immense paintings hang from ceiling to floor on the walls. There are colors—swirling, swarming colors. Chrome yellow, chartreuse, olive, viridian, gray, shades of rose fading to white, mauve, ultramarine, halos of blue, green, pink, white, ocher, opalescent pinks and yellows, raging blacks and whites, charcoal wisps, fleshy pink and blood red, muddy blue, brown, maroon, Mycenaean gold, peacock blue. Reverently, modestly, Martin guides me through the room. As we stand in front of each painting, he talks about it. Slowly the colors coalesce into one of this country's finest private collections of twentieth-century American painting: Charles Sheeler, Georgia O'Keeffe, Richard Diebenkorn, Willem de Kooning ("He's the greatest American painter," Martin says), Franz Kline, Cy Twombly, Helen Frankenthaler, Kenneth Noland, Nathan Oliveira, Edward Hopper, Stanton Macdonald-Wright, David Hockney, Roy Lichtenstein, Grant Wood, Arthur Dove, Charles Demuth, Alfred Leslie, Jennifer Bartlett. There is also a Picasso.

There are no doors in the house. All the rooms flow into each other. Paintings hang throughout. There is elaborate track lighting in the main rooms, oversized oatmeal-colored couches and chairs, a basket of pink, spiky seashells from Africa and Australia. Martin has a distinguished art library that covers one wall of a room and overflows onto the floor and tables. In the dining room there is a low, dark brown table. Martin's three banjos and dulcimer lean against a wall. One long desk in the office holds two identical Hewlett-Packard Vectra personal computers. Steve and Victoria both work there. (She is writing a screenplay and a book.) The house is L-shaped, and the bedroom and kitchen, at right angles to each other, open onto an atrium with a rectangular, colonnaded swimming pool. Martin has lived in the house for seven years. He worked with the architect in redesigning it.

Martin is a trustee of the Los Angeles County Museum of Art, where he has endowed a gallery. He will not pose with any of his paintings for photographers. "That is a bit of a cliché," he says. "It's like what they do at cocktail parties for art openings. Collectors stand in front of their paintings and the picture becomes a minor point. It's like the person standing there is somehow taking credit for the painting. I don't want to use the paintings to promote me. I don't think there is any great virtue in collecting art. It's a myth that if you collect art you're an intellectual or something or that it makes you a smart person. Art is a visceral pleasure. It is not exactly an intellectual pleasure, although it can be. So it is hard to take any credit for something that is like physical pleasure."

Martin is sitting in one of his overstuffed chairs, his private gallery surrounding him. Mary, his flossy, white Persian cat, is on his lap. He strokes her gently. An alley cat named Betty is somewhere out of sight patrolling the rooms. "I love cats," Martin says. "I have two cats, one an incredibly smart, affectionate alley cat saved from the pound, the other this incredibly stupid, beautiful cat." Martin talks with his characteristic detachment about collecting art. "When I was in college," he says, "I bought a big Roy Lichtenstein reproduction on canvas. It cost seventy-five dollars. It was called *Little Big Painting*. It was a perfect reproduction, only bigger than the original canvas. It's funny, I just had dinner with Roy Lichtenstein about three nights ago. Isn't that funny? I started collecting nineteenth-century American painting when I got some money, around 1974. I used to really read about nineteenth-century art. When I was playing colleges, I would head right for the library and check out the books and start studying the painters' lives. Now I find studying the lives of contemporary artists less important. The histories have yet to be written, first of all. And also, I feel like I'm reading about myself when I read about some artist who grew up in Texas, went to New York, met a dealer. It's completely uninteresting to me. I just see it as my life, like, 'They went to California to work.'

"Collecting art is my biggest hobby. It takes a lot of time, fun time. I find that the actual literature on contemporary art is indecipherable, with the exception of Robert Hughes. I also find it important to have an art library. If you can pull out a book published in 1931 that has your Edward Hopper in it, then you know the painting is real. I just bought a painting by Stanton Macdonald-Wright. It was painted in 1916. It would be among the first modern paintings painted in America. So last night I hauled out all my books on Synchronism in early modern painting and I found out the story of the painting, where it was painted, everything. I really don't go to art auctions very often because I'm usually in California. I have nothing against auctions. I'd have to say I'm outside the art scene. I have a couple of artist friends I find really fascinating, but it is because of their personalities, not because I'm a collector who wants to meet artists.

"I don't love paintings like I love my wife," Martin says. "I mean, I love them in a different way. I have thought about this because the question comes up. People seem to want to get into it. At first I thought, 'I don't need a reason to love paintings because paintings have been loved forever.' I couldn't really explain to myself why I love paintings or like them or am interested in them or intrigued by either them or their trappings — meaning the dealers, the auctions, the museums, the traveling, everything from the highest form of loving them to the lowest form of loving them. But I tried to observe something about it, and it is that painting is opposite from performing or show business. I have no talent for painting at all. I've tried enough to know I'm terrible. I have no interest in doing it. Paintings are different from show business in that they exist in space, and show business exists in time. A movie lasts an hour and a half, but the painting lasts two minutes or however long you're going to look at it. I think painting is so different from what I do that it's an escape for me. I like to sit down and look at the paintings; or Victoria and I will sit down and look at them and talk. You just sort of look around you at these things. Sometimes I feel so lucky to own them. It's like, good grief, these things are beautiful. Like, how did this happen?"

When Martin walks me to the door and out to the tiny porch, we say good-bye, and I ask him, "What do you like about a house with no windows in front?" He answers, without a pause, "It's the house that says, 'Go away.'"

August 1987

Planes, Trains and Automobiles, *Martin's Thanksgiving 1987 hit, grossed more than $50 million. Martin played Vladimir to Robin Williams' Estragon in Mike Nichol's production of Samuel Beckett's tragicomedy* Waiting for Godot. *The play ran for seven weeks at Lincoln Center last fall. Martin's comedy* Dirty Rotten Scoundrels *was released at Christmas 1988.*

PLAIN-WRAP SUPERSTAR PAUL NEWMAN

*D*uring dinner at the posh Fournou's Ovens restaurant in San Francisco, Paul Newman orders a salad. "Is endive in season?" The waiter says yes. "Could you do me a favor and chop up some endive, real fine [he makes chopping motions with his hands] and bring it in a bowl?" The waiter nods. "Tomatoes?" Another nod. "Could you cut them up for me?" Yes. Does Mr. Newman want salad dressing? "Oil and water. Could you bring me a little bowl? I'll mix it myself. Do you have mustard?" Dijon. "Good. Lemon? How about some lemon slices? And I'll need some

chopped bacon bits. Nine slices. No, eight will be enough." Newman
sniffs the oil unself-consciously, pours it into a bowl, adds a drop of
water "to cut it," a little mustard, salt and pepper, and squeezes a slice
of lemon into it. He mixes it, tastes it, ceremoniously pours it over the
endive and tomato, and with a final comic flourish, dishes on the bacon
bits. The waiter standing in the background is enthralled.

Paul Newman makes great salad dressing. So great that for a lark he
and a few friends have started manufacturing the stuff—Newman's Own
Olive Oil and Vinegar Dressing (*Appellation Newman Contrôlée*). His
self-mocking grin is on the bottle, you can get it at your local grocer, and
all profits go to charity. Newman, fifty-seven, has an abiding appeal.
His grin and breezy charm may be artful camouflage for brooding
moods and a life of personal and professional ups and downs, but as he
would say, that's his business. He looks better than ever. At 5'10" and
145 pounds, he is vigorous and slim. His hair is silver and his forehead
has three deep creases, but his laugh is easy. He has driven a 170-
mph, turbo-charged Datsun 280ZX into middle age, has been married
to actress Joanne Woodward for twenty-four years, has helped raise five
daughters, has lost his only son, has made plenty of lousy movies, and is
deep in the middle of writing his first screenplay.

Risking ridicule, he has burdened himself with the fight to end the
nuclear arms race. He has long since admitted that he has neither
extraordinary talent nor genius. But that hasn't embittered him or kept
him from trying new things. He has culled a kind of excellence in his
life from a fear of mediocrity. "I don't have a lot of regrets," Newman
says. "Whatever is there is simply there. I just think I did the best I
could with whatever equipment I had. I don't think I'd do anything
different. If you changed something about yourself, then you wouldn't
be yourself, would you? You'd be something else, something more over
here, something less over there. I suppose I wish I were Mario Andretti
or Laurence Olivier, but I guess I don't wish it hard enough or fiercely
enough."

Newman, a movie star to end all movie stars, debunks superstardom
right off. In his latest movie, *The Verdict*, he plays a boozing lawyer on
the skids, not a part for a vain man or an actor concerned with his image.
"I liked that character, Frank Galvin, the humanity of the guy, all of his
failures, his self-doubt, self-revulsion. There is no way for an actor to
protect himself in that part." Newman has a near compulsion not to take

himself seriously. "Why do you think I started selling salad dressing?" Newman asks. "To remind me not to take myself too seriously." Newman's favorite line out of all his movies is from *Slap Shot*, a film he thinks is hilarious: "What a fuckin' nightmare." "Look," Newman says, "you have got to separate what you are from what people think you are. If you feel very ordinary inside your own skin, then anything you achieve has to be fraudulent. I think my credentials as an actor, as a professional person, are fraudulent. I have never done or learned anything quickly in my life. My experience as an actor in the beginning was certainly ordinary. You can't take a little lad from Shaker Heights and have him assume any gigantic proportion.

"I was a slow starter as a racer. I came very late to politics and to literary curiosity. I always wanted to be an academician and wasn't. When I played football at Kenyon College, my ambition was always greater than my talent. So I can't take myself seriously. I suppose the salad dressing is a manifestation of that. The movie *Buffalo Bill* is about the kind of person who believes that he is the legend he has created. When he is confronted by a primitive who draws his power from simple, plain reality, of the two, obviously the hollow one will fold and collapse like an accordion." William Goldman, who wrote the screenplay for *Butch Cassidy and the Sundance Kid*, says, "I don't think Paul Newman really thinks he is Paul Newman in his head."

Because he is so detached from the image, Newman is amused by the notion that he became a sex symbol. "It surprised me," he says. "When I did William Inge's *Picnic*, in New York, I was an understudy to the leading man, Ralph Meeker. He had about him the quality of a sexual animal. Josh Logan directed the play. When I replaced Ralph for a week, I asked Josh if there was a chance I could play Ralph's part on the road, and Josh said, 'I don't think so, because you don't carry any sexual threat.' I've been chewing on that one for the last twenty years. The sex-symbol thing has nothing to do with me. It has something to do with the way I choose to play the way the character is written." Newman says he doesn't wish he had been born ugly, but he doesn't put much stock in his good looks, either. "If you get your first shot at something because your appearance is acceptable or desirable, then it is pretty hard to knock it," he says. "If that simply becomes the thing that people measure your worth by, then it is fair for the recipient to take some kind of umbrage at that. I have such an extraordinary envy of the gorgeous people who preen as they come through the door, measure their success by the number of eyes they manage to attract. It is a great gift, and it must make their lives very simple."

Newman is very private. When you ask him a question, it is like knocking on a door. A long pause and maybe the door will open and maybe it won't. His answers are deliberate and well thought out. He hates personal questions. "I am very uncomfortable in this age of candor," he says. "Personal convictions are open to examination, but not personal relationships. I've gone through bad stages in my life and in my career, but those are private for me. Whether I've been face-down in a urinal is simply nobody's business. It has more to do with gossip and prying and snooping than it does with curiosity, the motive of which is to learn and better oneself. There is voyeurism in it rather than just an honest interest, so you can say to yourself, 'Oh, now I see, I'll try to remember so I won't do that myself.'"

Newman makes it a policy not to give autographs (the grandness of the gesture offends him), although there are exceptions. As he steps out of a car on his way to do a radio interview about a nuclear weapons freeze, an old man in a polyester suit, leaning on a cane, hobbles up to him and says, "Mr. Newman, please may I have your autograph for my wife?" Newman looks at him, hesitates, says in a low voice, "I don't give autographs. . . . Well, okay." On the way out of the same radio station a young guy stops him for his autograph and this time Newman says, cheerfully, "I don't sign them things. Psychological warfare." Newman resents strangers' rudeness or attempted intrusions into his life. He says, "It infuriates me when people say, 'Take off your dark glasses so I can see your baby blues' or 'Stand over there so I can get a picture of you with my dog.' It is irrelevant to them what you're doing, having dinner with your kids or whatever; they feel the right to stop you. I resent that. I react the same way to that as if they had stuck me in the middle of the forehead. If there is anything designed to make you feel like an object or a piece of meat, it's that. They would be offended if I said, 'I'd be happy to take off my shades, ma'am, if you'd let me examine your gums.'"

After forty-five films in twenty-eight years, which harvested five Oscar nominations for Best Actor—*Cat on a Hot Tin Roof* (1958), *The Hustler* (1961), *Hud* (1963), *Cool Hand Luke* (1967), and *Absence of Malice* (1981)—and his fair share of critical acclaim, Paul Newman gives his acting ability an "okay" rating. "I've become a much better actor as I've gotten older," he says. "I'm probably more comfortable with the parts I've done recently. When I first started out, I was terrible. I look back on the early things I did and chastise myself for working so hard. It is what we call in acting 'demonstrating.' Instead of having the courage simply to do it, I was worried about telegraphing attitudes and emotions to the audience to make sure they understood. Now in my thirtieth professional year, I think I have finally learned to simply do it." Newman laughs. "Before I'd start a scene in *The Verdict* I would go off to the corner and whisper to myself, 'Less is more, small is beautiful.'"

Newman started acting with a local children's group in Cleveland and pursued it at Shaker Heights High School. Later, at Kenyon College in Gambier, Ohio, where his former drama professor, James Michael, remembers "having trouble not casting Paul as the lead in every play," Newman acted because he liked it. He never dreamed he would make it a career. When he was a child watching matinees like *The Perils of Pauline* at the local theater, he says he never "looked up at the screen and thought anything as perceptive as 'I wish.'" But after graduating from Kenyon in 1949, Newman spent a season doing summer stock in Williams Bay, Wisconsin, and the following year joined the Woodstock Players in Illinois. There he met actress Jacqueline Witte and married her. He had just finished his seventeenth production when news came in May 1950 that his father had died. Newman went back to Cleveland to help manage the family sporting-goods store. Restless, he ran a driving range and did some commercials for a local bank at the same time. Newman was set free when the family decided to sell the store. Seven months later, at the age of twenty-six, he packed his wife and their infant son, Scott, into a 1946 Chevrolet his mother had given him (she was afraid he wouldn't make it all the way to Connecticut in his 1937 Packard), withdrew the nine hundred dollars he had in the bank, and drove to New Haven to begin work on a master's degree at the Yale University School of Drama.

"Acting was the only thing I had ever done that I had any success at," Newman says. "I wasn't driven to acting by any inner compulsion. I was running away from the sporting-goods business. I realized that there was a tremendous romance to the business world, but I simply was not captivated by it. I went into acting even though I was terrorized by the emotional requirements of being an actor. It was always so difficult for me in my early years, my adolescent years, to show a lot of emotion. I could be badly hurt, physically, and never cry. I had an incredible threshold for pain. I had to have a lot of dental surgery when I was a teenager, and I remember I used to get through a whole issue of *Time* magazine during seventy-five stitches. The doctors were amazed.

"I was always very small for my age. I never really physically grew up until I was eighteen, and then I grew five and a half inches in one year. I went through the entirety of World War II on two razor blades. I used to get the bejesus kicked out of me very regularly in grammar school, junior high school, and high school, simply because I wasn't anywhere near as big as anyone else. I suppose you anesthetize yourself from the pain. But that isn't a very valuable quality for an actor. If you can't get to your emotions, you can end up with a very placid, uninvolved kind of personality that isn't very magnetic on the screen.

"At Yale I was a directing major, but even directing majors had to act in plays. I remember when I first got there, a guy who was directing George Bernard Shaw's *Saint Joan* came up to me and said, 'I want you to do this,' and I said, 'Sure.' And I looked at the script and the first thing I saw was that my character, the priest, was supposed to be heard weeping off stage. The muscles contracted in my stomach, and immediately I tried to figure out some way to play the whole thing facing upstage. And then I thought, 'What an asshole. I drag my family with only nine hundred bucks all the way to Connecticut and then think of all the ways I can cop out.' At the time I was living in a boardinghouse, and I took that script downstairs to the boiler room and I said, 'Okay, buddy, you are going to sit here until you find out where it is going to come from or you get out of this business right now.' So I discovered it was available somewhere."

After a year at Yale (he never received a degree), Newman went to New York and played small parts in several live television shows and tried out for the theater. In 1953, when he got the job as understudy in *Picnic* on Broadway, his wife was pregnant again, and he had only fifty dollars left in the bank. Then he graduated to a supporting role and received good reviews. Newman says, "I was lucky. If the play had not been a success, I don't know what would have happened. I had responsibilities. With a play, what are your chances? But it won the Pulitzer Prize and it provided fourteen months of work. And that is when I learned to act, during the run of that play while I was going to Lee Strasberg's Actors Studio." During *Picnic* Newman signed a long-term

$1,000-a-week contract with Warner Brothers (which he bought back in 1959 for $500,000) and made an inauspicious film debut as a Greek slave named Basil in *The Silver Chalice* in 1954.

Asked to assess his career, Newman offers a wry, sometimes caustic, sometimes cryptic, critique of a remarkable series of hits and not so memorable misses:

The Silver Chalice (1954): "Junk. When this movie was shown on television in 1963, I took out a two-column ad with a wreath around it, like an obituary notice, in the *Los Angeles Times,* that said: 'Paul Newman apologizes every night this week.'"

Somebody Up There Likes Me (1956): "Had some fun with that."

The Rack (1956): "Really aspired to something, and nobody went to see it. I had such great hopes for it. It got very respectful reviews. A perfect example of me working too hard, trying too hard."

Until They Sail (1957): "Not much to play there."

The Helen Morgan Story (1957): "Uggghhh."

The Long Hot Summer (1958): "Pretty good, I think. Again, constantly aware of how hard I was working."

The Left-handed Gun (1958): "Spotty, a little bit ahead of its time, a classic in Europe. To this day I still get eight hundred dollars at the end of the year. Go to Paris right now and I bet you it is playing in some tiny theater."

Cat on a Hot Tin Roof (1958): "Pretty good film. Still aware of how hard I was working."

Rally 'Round the Flag, Boys (1958): "A situation comedy. I was probably very weak."

The Young Philadelphians (1959): "Just kind of a cosmopolitan story that didn't demand very much."

From the Terrace (1960): "Pretty good soap opera. Didn't ask for an awful lot."

Exodus (1960): "Chilly."

The Hustler (1961): "I had occasion to see some segments of it recently. Again, very conscious of working too hard, which comes partly from lack of faith in your own talent and lack of faith that just doing it in itself is all the audience requires."

Paris Blues (1961): "I had some fun with that. Not that it is a great film."

Sweet Bird of Youth (1962): "Pretty good."

Hemingway's *Adventures of a Young Man* (1962): "I tried to do what I did in the TV show, and that wasn't the way to go at it."

Hud (1963): "Pretty good. Again, working hard, working hard."

A New Kind of Love (1963): "Joanne read it and said, 'Hey, this would be fun to do together. Read it.' I read it and said, 'Joanne, it's just a bunch of one-liners.' And she said, 'You son of a bitch, I've been carting your children around, taking care of them at the expense of my career, taking care of you and your house.' And I said, 'That's what I said. It's a terrific script. I can't think of anything I'd rather do.' This is what is known as a reciprocal trade agreement."

The Prize (1963): "A lark."

What a Way to Go! (1964): "Done out of whimsy."

The Outrage (1964): "I liked that a lot."

Lady L (1966): "I woke up every morning and knew I wasn't cutting the mustard."

Harper (1966): "Yes, an original, original character and most marvelous because he would simply accommodate any kind of actor's invention. There was no way you could violate the character; he was so loose and funky and whimsical."

Torn Curtain (1966): "Not so good."

Hombre (1967): "I kind of liked that. By then I was doing it less and enjoying it more."

Cool Hand Luke (1967): "I had great fun with that part. I liked that man."

The Secret War of Harry Frigg (1968): "A lurch at comedy. I didn't accomplish it very well."

Rachel, Rachel (directed, 1968): "Great fondness, great fondness. That is a good film."

Winning (1969): "Pretty good story about racing. The people were not integrated well into the racing, but pretty good."

Butch Cassidy and the Sundance Kid (1969): "A delight. It's too bad they got killed in the end, 'cause those two guys could have gone on in films forever."

WUSA (1970): "A film of incredible potential which the producer, the director, and I loused up. We tried to make the thing political and it wasn't."

Sometimes a Great Notion (starred and directed, 1971): "A much better film than its popularity would signify."

Pocket Money (1972): "Loved the character. The script never came together, though."

The Effect of Gamma Rays on Man-in-the-Moon Marigolds (directed, 1972): "I may not have been able to make the transition from stage to film. Too much theater and not enough cinema. I screwed up there."

The Life and Times of Judge Roy Bean (1972): "Marvelous. The first three quarters of the picture are classic. We never seemed to be able to come to grips with the ending, though. I loved that character."

The Mackintosh Man (1973): "Thought we could make a pretty effective melodrama out of that, and I was wrong."

The Sting (1973): "Oh, great fun, good film."

The Towering Inferno (1974): "Of its kind, rather good. Get the actors off and the stuntmen on as quick as you can."

The Drowning Pool (1975): "Only time I ever played the same character twice [Harper], and it didn't work."

Silent Movie (1976): "Just a cameo."

Buffalo Bill and the Indians (1976): "Don't know what happened to that one. Made a mistake somewhere along the line. Great potential."

Slap Shot (1977): "One of my favorite movies. Pretty funny. Unfortunately that character is a lot closer to me than I would care to admit — vulgar, on the skids."

Quintet (1979): "Again, made a mistake somewhere. Great potential. Director Robert Altman is very interesting, a real explorer."

When Time Ran Out (1980): "I'm trying desperately to look the other way."

The Shadow Box (directed for television, 1980): "Great fondness. Great fondness. I take some pride in that one."

Fort Apache, the Bronx (1981): "Some pretty good moments, I guess."

Absence of Malice (1981): "A relatively easy part for me, and compatible with the image."

The Verdict (1982): "It was such a relief to let it all hang out in the movie—blemishes and all."

Newman loves to rehearse a part. He loves to get the script home at night to pick away at it, but he does not like to get up in front of a camera the next day during the actual shooting. He says, "Working at it and rehearsing it are very private. But the second you are in front of the camera, in front of the crew and all those people, it is like dropping your pants. You have to expose yourself. It makes me uncomfortable." To prepare for a role, Newman usually locks himself in a room for a week before rehearsals. Although he feels after doing it for thirty years that he can now pull a character out of his own life experiences, he used to have to travel for inspiration. Before shooting *Cool Hand Luke*, Newman went to West Virginia, and there he found Luke in the person of a dusty tomato farmer whose name he can't remember.

Newman makes no apologies for his many mediocre films. Some of those movies he had to make when he was under obligation to Warner Brothers, and Newman does believe that "an actor should act." He has managed to make an average of one and a half films per year since *The Silver Chalice*, though he considers that "nothing" compared to the output of contract actors like Spencer Tracy or Clark Gable. Newman says: "If I worked on only those scripts that I would weep with remorse for if I couldn't do them, then I would work only once every three years. Then your instrument gets screwed up and rusty." He admits that he is not very good at one-line comedy but thinks he is "very good at character comedy." George Roy Hill, director of *The Sting* and *Butch Cassidy*, says, "The way Paul played the card scene in *The Sting* is one of the best pieces of comedic acting I've ever seen. I defy any actor to play that scene better." Adds screenwriter Goldman, "Newman is a victim of the Cary Grant syndrome. He makes it look so easy, he looks so wonderful, that everybody assumes he isn't acting."

At the moment, Newman plans to cowrite, coproduce, direct, and star in *Harry and Son*, about that moment in the relationship between a father and his twenty-two-year-old son when the father hasn't released his control but the son is about to break away. Newman insists the story was not suggested by the death of his twenty-eight-year-old son, Scott, four years ago, even though he says he "definitely" will make a film about Scott one day. *Harry* is Newman's first attempt at writing a screenplay. "I like writing it," is all he says. "It will be interesting to work on something I had a hand in creating."

The Newman philosophy of choosing a script is, "part conviction, part whimsy, part why not?" But these days, he claims, there's not much from which to choose. He used to spend two percent of his reading time on scripts; now it is eighty percent, which amounts to about one script a day. Newman, Robert Redford, and George Roy Hill have been looking for a script to do together since they made *The Sting*. Newman says, "You would think that since the three of us manage to see sixty to seventy percent of the good stuff that goes through this town, we would be able to find something we could do together. We can't." Newman thinks that this is because television eats writers alive and that as society becomes more complex, it becomes harder for a writer to come to conclusions about anything. Audience tastes have changed too. Newman remembers a couple of summers ago when someone came up to him and said, "You must take great pride in your craft." He answered, "It is hard to do that when the three biggest stars in the business are two robots and a shark."

"My childhood," says Newman, "was tragically ordinary. I see it in print: 'Paul Leonard Newman was born January 26, 1925, the son of Arthur S. . . . .' and I say, 'That isn't exactly riveting, is it?' I was very comfortable. I never went to bed hungry. I didn't leave my imprint on anything." Newman says he never played a character in a movie that he thinks closely resembles him. But he does see himself in Thomas Mann's Tonio Kröger. "That's me. That story was probably Mann's examination of how he felt about himself. Never seemed to fit in. Always had a gentle envy of the blue-eyed people. Thought he never gave anything of himself."

Newman grew up moderately wealthy in a three-bedroom home in

Shaker Heights. His father, a German Jew, had a share in the family's prosperous sporting-goods store. His mother, Theresa Fetzer, whom Newman remembers as "an absolutely gorgeous woman with a volcanic emotional makeup," was a Hungarian-descended Catholic. She died in September 1982. Theresa raised Paul and his only brother, Arthur, now fifty-eight, a film production manager living in Lake Arrowhead, California, as Christian Scientists. "I didn't come away with any beliefs," Newman says. "But being brought up with a religion gave me a chance to examine my feelings, and I found that my religion is a very personal thing, and if there is a capital Thou, it exists somewhere between the collarbone and the navel. It is no more or less moral or ethical if it is not a formal statement." He calls himself a Jew, "because it's more of a challenge."

After high school Newman spent four months at Ohio University and then, at the age of eighteen, enlisted in the Navy. He was about to begin training as a pilot when he found out his brilliant blue eyes were color-blind. He served in the Air Corps for three years as a radioman on torpedo bombers in the Pacific. In June 1946, he entered Kenyon College, where he majored in drama and managed an overall B-to-C grade-point average, spending most of his time at the school's theater and consuming a lot of beer in the process. He also started a student laundry in 1947, on the theory that it is more efficient for a lot of people to bring dirty laundry to a central place than for one person to go around picking it up. He rented a little shop and every Saturday brought in a fifteen-gallon keg. Beer was free to customers, and that was the end of the competition. He made seventy-five to a hundred dollars a week, and with the GI bill put himself through school. Newman's drama professor, James Michael, says Newman was "a harum-scarum kid, extremely intelligent, energetic, and charismatic, but who lacked self-discipline." Michael adds, "He might have gone on being a fun kid without ever making it, but he pulled it all together, probably because of his intelligence."

Newman's transition from harum-scarum kid to serious, disciplined, even driven, actor may have occurred around the time of his father's death. "My father," Newman says, "was quiet, erudite, brilliant. He was the youngest reporter ever hired by the *Cleveland Press*. He should have been a writer, but he went into the family's sporting-goods business. He wrote me letters six days a week when I was away at the war and at school. I have every letter. He had a voracious appetite for literature, was very knowledgeable about politics and world events, and he had a marvelous, whimsical sense of humor. I think he always thought of me as pretty much of a lightweight. He treated me like he was disappointed in me a lot of the time. And he had every right to be. One of my recurrent living nightmares was that I would never be able to provide for my children the way my father provided for me. It has been one of the great agonies of my life that he could never know. It was the one thing I desperately wanted to show him, that somehow, somewhere along the line, I could cut the mustard. And I never got a chance, never got a chance."

Newman stands guard over feelings about his family. At the moment, his wife and daughters remain in the East while Newman is in California to campaign for a nuclear weapons freeze, but one senses there is a wistfulness, an idealism, a concept of family that he never quite knew how to realize. Once, in the middle of talking about how far-flung his family is (his daughters are in different states, his brother is on the West Coast, his cousins in the Midwest), he stops and says, "One of the most touching things I ever saw was at the Shelburne Museum in Vermont. I was coming around the corner and there it was — it looked like a child's cradle but it was six feet long. I said to the attendant, 'But what is this?' and she said to me, 'In the eighteenth century the extended families were very close and they used cradles like that to rock their grandparents to death in.' As the old people were dying, everybody, grandchildren and everybody, would literally come up and rock them to death. It broadcast to me such an incredible picture of family warmth and closeness."

Newman and his first wife, Jacqueline Witte, divorced in 1956 after six years of marriage and three children: Scott; Susan, twenty-nine; and Stephanie, twenty-seven. When asked about the marriage's failure, he says cryptically, "I wasn't very helpful, I don't suppose. But then, I guess in the final analysis, you do the best you can with the information you've got. If you don't always have the right information, you might not do so well."

From what he says, Newman greatly admires and is devoted to his second wife, Joanne Woodward, whom he met in 1953 when he was in *Picnic* and she was the understudy for the female lead. The two were married in January 1958. They have three children: Nell, twenty-three;

Lissy, twenty-one; and Clea, seventeen. Newman calls Woodward a "voluptuary" and says she is like a "piece of litmus paper, capable of turning into any color, really, depending on what liquid drops onto it. It ain't ever boring, I'll tell you that." Newman thinks he and Woodward have a "marvelous marriage, but it has had its ups and downs, certainly. It is not a fairy tale. There have been painful and difficult moments and intransigence and stubbornness, but there is a thickness that comes from that which has allowed us to survive. I guess at the core of it there must be a great measure of respect, a recognition that somehow there is effort and motion involved. But it does work. Even with violently opposite tastes. We do both have a continuing interest in the theater, but Joanne's appetite for ballet and the opera is much bigger than mine. So I trade her two auto races for *The Nutcracker* and *Giselle*. After twenty-four years, the marriage is still filled with discovery."

Newman speaks almost reverently about his wife's acting abilities. "Given the right parts, she is a great actress. I love directing her. She can find so many different facets of herself to play. Those are two different people in *Rachel, Rachel* and *The Shadow Box*. That is magic." Newman also likes acting with her. "Just instinctively, when we work together, we both know we can't get away with any old tricks because the other one is sitting there, nodding his head knowingly, saying, 'Yes, I seem to remember your doing that one on the twenty-eighth page of *The Helen Morgan Story*.' Nailed."

When he talks about his children, Newman tenses a bit. "I'm a good father in flashes," he says. "I don't think I'm very consistent. I send out too many conflicting signals. Every time they come into the room, they have to say a password to find out if they're friend or foe. I'm not good with babies. I'm pretty good when they're between the ages of about three and fourteen. After that I would feel more comfortable if you would simply refrigerate them until maybe twenty-four. I don't know. There aren't any easy answers. Joanne and I could have been more consistent in terms of discipline and productivity and behavior generally. I suppose we could have functioned more as parents and less as friends, given them a very structured and impartial set of rules. My family means an awful lot to me, and sometimes I'm afraid I don't show that."

In 1978, Newman's only son died from an accidental overdose of alcohol mixed with painkillers. He had been in a motorcycle accident and was taking the pills for injuries he had suffered in it. Newman and

Woodward created the Scott Newman Foundation in 1980 to grant annual awards of $150,000 to individual motion picture or television writers, directors, and producers who most eloquently and forcefully convey to the public the problems of drug abuse. Newman still sounds a bit lost and bewildered when he talks about his son. "We were like rubber bands. One minute we were very close, the next minute I didn't know what was happening. The distance was just enormous. I don't think I'll ever escape from the guilt. Whether it is real or imagined is irrelevant. I'll be packing that around for quite a long while, I guess."

Newman is now touring California to campaign for Proposition 12, which requires that the governor of California write a letter to the president of the United States asking him to propose a nuclear weapons freeze to the Soviet Union. The argument about Proposition 12, however, goes far beyond the limited scope of the initiative and into the specifics of U.S. and Soviet nuclear capability and the rationality of a limited nuclear war. Newman knows his stuff. He is diligent. He spends hours poring over government documents and newspaper clippings. He has memorized facts and figures and quotes everybody from Eisenhower to Einstein.

The trouble is that although he has his lines down, he hasn't really created a Paul Newman political persona. He is just Paul Newman, the liberal man with a lot of convictions relying on a repertoire of facts to make his case. He gets nervous in interviews, sometimes becomes inarticulate, and sometimes won't answer a direct question, dismissing it as "irrelevant" if he has made up his mind to change the subject. Newman likes to be in control, and in politics you can't control all the variables. He isn't quick on his feet and often sounds wooden, or programmed. He lays out little white cards with bits of information on them when he is doing a radio or television interview and will scribble notes to himself during a commercial or when a questioner is talking.

Newman says he has been interested in the arms race since the early 1950s when Herman Kahn's book on thermonuclear war came out. He has been an activist since the mid-1970s. In 1978, President Carter appointed him Special Ambassador to the UN Conference on Nuclear Disarmament. But his concern has flared since the Reagan administration resurrected the possibility of limited nuclear war. Over the past two decades Newman has campaigned for a number of liberal causes. In 1963, he marched for civil rights in Washington and Alabama. He supported Senator Eugene McCarthy's presidential bid in 1968. ("That was a one-issue thing. He was opposed to the Vietnam War and so was I.") That same year Newman served as a delegate to the Democratic National Convention. He made it onto Nixon's "Enemies List" in the early 1970s, which, he says, is "the greatest single honor I have ever received." He was one of the founders of Energy Action, a group organized to provide information about energy from a source outside the oil companies to congressmen and citizens. He also has spoken out for gay rights. But in the final analysis, Newman says, the nuclear weapons buildup "is *the* political issue today. The other issues could be, and therefore are, irrelevant, aren't they?"

Newman, who otherwise is not outwardly emotional—is usually a polite, distant, even detached, person—has taken this issue into his gut. "I hope I am emotional about it," he says. "That is one thing I hate about the strategic analysts who get up and in really cool, calculating, academic voices talk about accepting losses of thirty-four million Americans in a nuclear exchange. They are so removed from any sense of blood or agony. The victims are simply figures they put through the computer. I am involved the way every citizen ought to be involved on the issues. I don't know how you can be part of your times or extract the benefits of a democracy without participating in it."

One day, looking crisp and clean-cut in gray slacks, navy blazer, white shirt, and maroon tie, Newman participates with his usual vigor. At a *News at 4* live television interview in Los Angeles, he says, "I really don't trust Russians. I don't think what they're doing in Poland and Afghanistan is conscionable. But outside of those issues, I think they are willing to protect their people. You don't have to trust the Russians. You simply have to verify them. A freeze is verifiable. Even the Reagan administration says so. Their plan is to build up, then reduce, then freeze. So why not freeze our advantage now?"

The next morning, Newman, who travels with no entourage but today is in the company of a nuclear freeze public-relations person, seems agitated. Dressed in brown slacks and a white short-sleeved shirt with an alligator emblem (he carries with him a white broadcloth long-sleeved shirt and brown wool plaid sport coat), he is smarting from a remark his conservative counterpart, Charlton Heston, made on *The*

Merv Griffin Show earlier in the week. Newman has just heard about it: "Newman should get his head in gear before he talks." Newman is especially angry because he had been a guest on *The Merv Griffin Show* before Heston and would not now have a chance to defend his point of view. So Newman is ready to do battle. First stop is an interview with talk-show host Michael Jackson on KABC radio. During a commercial Newman learns that Heston is going to be Michael Jackson's guest the next day. He is indignant: "Heston is riding piggyback on me; really sabotaging us. He's refuting my points, but I'm not getting any rebuttal." Jackson agrees to ask Heston some of Newman's specific questions.

Later in the day, during taping of a segment to be aired on *The Last Word*, ABC's new late-night news program after *Nightline*, Newman finds out that Heston is going to be live on the show and will be able to see Newman's taped interview and then comment on it. Newman is angry. He starts saying things like, "Hi, Charlton. It's me, Paul. I've got a terrific part for you, a hysterical Army officer, or how about a machine gun?" Newman finally appeals to the Los Angeles producers of the week-old show, who agree that it isn't fair. If Newman can arrange to be in a room with two separate phones and two separate phone lines, the producers will fix it so Newman can hear what Heston says on one line, and then ask him questions on the other. Newman makes the phone call from a friend's Malibu home. It is a success. Newman and Heston exchange opinions, and Heston doesn't resort to the personal attack Newman anticipates.

Now Newman wants to debate Heston the next night on *The Last Word*. One of the show's producers calls ABC in New York and gets the go-ahead to arrange it. Newman cancels a scheduled day-long San Diego tour and spends six or seven hours preparing for the confrontation with Heston that night. He confers with scientists at the Jet Propulsion Laboratory in Pasadena, reads, writes his opening remarks, and is briefed by a couple of nuclear freeze advocates.

Newman is nervous before the debate. He taps his fingers against his lips and talks through them. His mouth is dry and he keeps licking his lips. He is wearing his brown pants and brown plaid blazer, and brown argyle socks. When the debate begins, it is Paul Newman the man talking, and he is up against Charlton Heston the actor. Heston is smooth and condescending, starting virtually every sentence with

"Paul," or "Now, Paul." In his opening speech Heston makes the surprising claim that it is the nuclear freeze advocates, not the opponents, who are the fearmongers and who approach the issue by way of passion and not reason. Newman becomes in turn emotional, frustrated, and shrill. At one point he brusquely cuts off a caller named Irene by telling her that her question is not "relevant." Heston is taunting and provocative. Newman scores when he quotes Einstein as saying, "The Atomic Age has changed everything but the way we think," and then points out that "You guys are thinking the old way." But Newman sits stunned for a second when Heston makes his final remark: "Paul, if this were the summer of '34 instead of the fall of '82, would you vote for a nuclear freeze?" A dramatic, if cheap, thrust, which Newman cannot parry.

Afterward Newman is crestfallen, and his handshake is damp with perspiration. The next day, cheerful again, he says, "I've done better and I've done worse. But in the final analysis, it was better than not doing anything at all."

Newman thinks his personality is "splattered." His favorite and often repeated expression has to do with balance. "Well, it's like anything else. You pick it up on one end and you lose it on another." "He has so many different pieces," says his friend Arthur Loew, who produced *The Rack*, "that he would be very hard to do an imitation of. Anybody could do an imitation of John Wayne. I don't see how anyone could do Paul. He is too complex."

Arriving at the San Francisco airport after a transcontinental flight, Newman could be mistaken for a somewhat skinny but athletic forty-year-old gone prematurely gray. He is wearing faded, pressed blue jeans, light brown suede boots with no heels, and a brown Army-style jacket with a lot of pockets. He has on dark sunglasses and is carrying a brown leather travel case. When we reach the car, he gingerly unzips the case, takes out a black garbage bag, opens it, triumphantly holds up two cans of cold Budweiser, and grins. He wears a beer tab on a silver chain around his neck.

Newman takes his shoes off in limousines. At 11:00 A.M. one day he spots a Baskin-Robbins from the window and says, "Oh, let's stop and get ice cream. Is there time?" The driver stops. Newman puts his shoes back on, and everyone hops out. He stares at the list of flavors, and, after an intense, silent scrutiny that lasts about a minute, asks for a one-scoop mint-chocolate-chip cone. "I guess I just hate formality of any kind," he says. "A formal kind of education, a formal religion, a formal way of behaving."

He loves practical jokes and will spare no expense and go to virtually any length to pull one off. Newman says, "George Roy Hill told me once that beneath every practical joke there is a large or small element of malice. That remark caught me up short and I had to think about it, but I suppose the smaller the amount of malice involved, the more valid the joke is. I do them for fun." He recalls his pranks with great glee.

Once Newman cut George Roy Hill's desk in half with a chain saw. "I couldn't seem to get his attention," says Newman. "But he always answered my phone calls after that." Newman had told Hill's secretary that he would give her a job if George fired her for letting him in. Later the secretary told Newman that when Hill came in and saw the desk, he just stood there for a minute staring, without saying anything. Then he strode to the piano and pounded out Bach furiously for a full ten minutes. Hill then went to the desk and laughed. He nailed it together with a two-by-four and pretended it hadn't been sawed in half. About four months later, Newman got a bill in the mail from Universal for the price of a new desk. Newman then sent the studio a two-page, single-spaced letter from his lawyer saying, "It is true I damaged the desk and that I should pay for a new one, but since I am paying for a new one, the old one is mine and I am renting it to Hill for sixty dollars a week, which makes Universal in arrears by almost three hundred dollars." Letters went back and forth for several months.

Newman says he was conscience-stricken because of a joke he played on director John Huston during the shooting of *The Mackintosh Man* on Malta. Newman had to play a scene up on a parapet of a tower that had a tiny porch circling it. He arranged with his wardrobe man to make it look as though they were having an argument before filming started. The camera was a hundred yards away, and when "Roll 'em" was called, Newman ignored it and stormed onto the parapet shouting, "What did you say?" to make it look to the people behind the camera as if he and the wardrobe man were still arguing. They threw a dummy dressed in Newman's clothes over the railing of the porch. The dummy caught the railing, and to those below, it looked like a man struggling to keep from falling. Newman says Huston nearly had a heart attack.

Newman always complained about Robert Altman's cheap white wine. He called it "goat piss." When the two worked together on *Quintet*, Newman walked up to Altman one day and presented him with a live baby goat. He put the goat in Altman's arms and said, "Here, now you have your own vineyard." On the set of *Buffalo Bill*, Newman had three hundred baby chicks put into Altman's trailer. They were there from about seven in the morning until six at night. Altman never did get the smell out. Another day during filming, Newman told Altman that he was having a special lunch prepared for him. He had Altman's kid leather big-cuffed gloves deep-fried and served to him on a platter.

For Newman's birthday one year, Robert Redford sent him a Porsche and had it delivered to the driveway of Newman's Connecticut home. Unfortunately, the Porsche looked as though it had rammed into a tree sideways at about four hundred miles an hour. No engine. No transmission. Newman promptly had the car compacted into a tidy cube, put a ribbon around it, and arranged through Redford's real-estate agent to get it through the security of Redford's house and have it placed in the foyer. Another time Newman had about one hundred and fifty cartons of toilet paper made up with Robert Redford's face on every sheet. But when he saw the toilet paper, even Newman realized how absolutely tasteless the joke was. He didn't send it, because the two are merely "close acquaintances," as he puts it.

During an interview in the blooming backyard of Newman's Beverly Hills home, a bee falls out of the sky onto the table. Newman jumps up, bends over the ailing insect, and touches its wing with his finger: "C'mon, fella. Something happened to its wing. He's a goner. He has a definite motor problem. Well, he may be a very old bee. Maybe we should get him something sweet." Newman goes into the kitchen, brings out some honey in a bowl, and dabs a drop with a wooden stick near the bee's feeble antennae. When the bee collapses dead in the honey, Newman picks it up and sets it down on a nearby flower. He no sooner sits down again then a fly falls dead on the table. Newman says, "My God, are you a killer? What's in the tape recorder?" And he lays the fly to rest next to the bee. "Maybe they'll mate and breathe the breath of life back into each other."

Newman hates forgetting anything. On the way home from a nuclear freeze appearance on a TV news show, he tries and tries to remember a figure he had read in that morning's *Los Angeles Times* about nuclear warheads. He frets until the driver offers to pull over and get the paper out of the trunk. The next day, standing around with a group of people drinking beer after a TV broadcast, Newman can't think of the name of the author of *The Right Stuff.* He asks four people, and when the fifth person says "Tom Wolfe," he is elated. He goes back to the people he had asked and tells them, "Tom Wolfe. It was Tom Wolfe." Newman says, "I'm like a terrier. When I want something bad enough, I grab on to it and won't let it go. I just worry it and worry it until I am either criminally unsuccessful with it, or I lick it or I absorb it."

"Paul's genius," says his friend, lawyer and restaurateur Ron Buck, "is his ability to concentrate. When he purses his lips, I just go lie down and wait." Newman's concentration is the reason he is one of the best amateur race-car drivers in the country, although he hadn't even tried the sport until he was in his late forties. He has won two Sports Car Club of America Amateur National Championships. "Racing is all concentration," says Maggie Smith, sixty-three, the salty general manager of Newman Racing. (Newman calls her "Magoo.") She has known Newman since 1954, when she worked with him as production manager on *The Silver Chalice.* Smith says, "Paul has total inner concentration, whether he is acting or directing or racing. You think he is looking at you, but he isn't really. He's inside his head. You know that he is probably out at turns five, six, or seven, figuring out where he can pick up a tenth of a second here or a thousandth of a second there. He's thinking of the possibilities, running the course in his head."

Without hesitation, Newman says that "competition" is the thing he gets from racing that he doesn't get out of acting. "I enjoy the precision of racing," he says. "It is remarkable to be able to harness something as huge and as powerful as a car and put it as close to where you want it as you can. Besides, it's a kick in the ass." During a tour of the living room of his Beverly Hills home, Newman points out framed pictures of Woodward and his children on top of the grand piano, but when he comes to a photo of his champion race car he sighs. "Ah, there is the real beauty." His family supports Newman's racing "wholeheartedly," with the one reservation that it is very time-consuming. Newman doesn't make movies in the summer because he doesn't want anything to interfere with his sport. He races on weekends during the season, which stretches from the end of April to late October. "Paul is a lot more alive than most of us," says George Roy Hill. "He likes to take chances. He doesn't want to play it safe. He doesn't want his talent or his excitement about life to atrophy."

When Newman sees a broken red candle that someone has Scotch-taped back together, he gets up from the couch and says, "Why is that poor candle like that?" He then gently instructs the housekeeper to melt the candle together. His standard for barbecues is high: The hamburger meat must be freshly ground chuck, ground twice with a twenty percent to twenty-two percent fat content. He loves details. He loves learning new things. He happily points out, for example, that a tomato can get sunburned, that popcorn can indeed be cooked with lard. He can't sit still until he looks up the word *imprimatur* in a dictionary. In a limo, he constantly backseat-drives and wonders aloud if there is a way out of traffic, or if we should perhaps turn left there. He hates being late. He thinks American drivers are "not courteous and basically unconscious" behind the wheel. He is always asking how things work.

Newman drinks anywhere from three to six cans of Budweiser a day. Budweiser sponsors the Newman racing team and he drinks only Bud. He never gets a beer belly and says, "Well, that's the luck of the draw, isn't it?" He does, however, get up early every morning and run three miles. When he has the time and a good newspaper, he sits in a two-hundred-degree sauna for an hour every day. He brings a portable four-by-four sauna with him when he is on location making a movie. "Nobody can get me in there," Newman says. "I can just go in there with my newspaper and get rid of all the gravy and Budweiser. It is as much a sanctuary as a steam."

Although Newman's salary is reportedly three million dollars a film, he doesn't live extravagantly by Hollywood standards. His clothes are plain. He lives in an old, converted farmhouse on a sprawling property in Westport, Connecticut, owns an apartment in an East Side Manhattan hotel, and a one-story blue stucco house in Beverly Hills. The Beverly Hills place is small but comfortable. The yard is filled with flower gardens. There is a pool and a Jacuzzi in the enclosed back. The living room has a celery-green Oriental rug with a red floral pattern in it, and a flowery chintz couch with matching curtains. The house is no set piece; it looks lived in. Newman also owns a couple of souped-up

VWs and a silver Porsche 928. He apparently spends his free time with only a few close friends, who are often business associates. Newman's brother, Arthur, says, "Paul was always a very private person. He hasn't changed." "I don't have a legion of friends," Newman says. "I guess I am something of a loner."

In recent years he has acquired a taste for literature. He loves Bach. He learned how to play the piano when he was a boy and goes back to it occasionally. He takes early-morning swims in the summer in the creek behind his Connecticut house. He can drive a long golf ball, thanks to the time in 1950 when he managed a driving range in Cleveland. But thanks to the same circumstance, he can't putt. He loves to "bet you a nickel, bet you thirty-nine cents, or bet you eighteen and a half cents," and he collects gleefully. He draws caricatures, gets by in French, and has this recurring dream, the actor's nightmare: "You aren't ready to go on stage, you don't know the play, yet you're putting on a very good show of bravado. Then the curtain goes up and you go out on stage and nothing happens. Or you're sitting on the grid just before a race and saying to the crew chief: 'Give me the key. I've got to start the car.' Of course, race cars don't have keys. But it is infuriating." Newman plays a little bridge and poker. He remembers going to a disco some years ago and shooting a few games of pool. When he finished, he walked over to the bar and got a beer. A young kid came up to him and said, "Mr. Newman, I just want you to know that I saw *The Hustler* four times and I watched you play pool tonight and it was one of the biggest disappointments of my life." Newman laughed.

One of Newman's greatest, if lesser known, talents is popcorn making. This is how he does it: He shakes just so much salt into a bowl of freshly popped corn, and after every shake of the salt he gives a little toss to the bowl to spread it around. He pours melted butter over a knife that is perpendicular to the bottom of the bowl and flicks the knife as he pours the butter over it so that the butter falls evenly, like water from a rotating sprinkler. Newman's commitment to excellence in popcorn is so great that, as with the salad dressing "caper," he plans to go into the business. All proceeds will go to charity. "Popcorn, a can of beer, and a good book is just about as good a combination as there is in this lifetime," Newman says as he sits down in front of the TV to watch the news, grabbing handfuls of popcorn from a full bowl and sipping a can of Bud.

November 1982

Newman's Own salad dressing caper is now a multinational business selling Newman's Own "Oldstyle Picture Show Popcorn," "Industrial Strength Venetian Spaghetti Sauce," and "Old-Fashioned Roadside Virgin Lemonade." The company has donated more than $15 million in profits to charity. In 1987, Newman directed Joanne Woodward in The Glass Menagerie *and also won an Oscar for reprising his role as pool hustler Fast Eddie Felson in* The Color of Money. *He stars as General Leslie R. Groves of the Manhattan Project in the film* Fat Man and Little Boy, *and will play Louisiana Governor Earl K. Long in a movie about the stripper Blaze Starr. He now races a Nissan Turbo 300ZX for Planter's Peanuts and has captured two more Sports Car Club of America championship titles. Newman met Gorbachev at the Reagan-Gorbachev summit in Washington in December 1987 at the Soviet leader's request.*

FABIAN / SYGMA

NASTASSIA KINSKI: WILD CHILD

*N*astassia Kinski's brown hair is long and un-
kempt. Stray strands fall unheeded into her
cappuccino. Her gray-green eyes are changeable;
her dreamy face is full of shadows. There is a tiny
scar on her left cheek, the imprint of some wild
thing. She is always hungry. "I used to eat my
eyebrows," she says. "Until I was eleven or twelve I
sucked my thumb and pulled at my eyebrows with
my fingers. Sometimes I would put honey or something sweet on them, then pluck them and play
with them in my mouth." Her lips are full, sen-
suous, arched exactly like her eyebrows. She eats

as if she were famished, sometimes wiping her wet mouth with the back of her hand, or mopping up the last particle of lamb chop with a piece of bread. At lunch one day, excited to be biting into a giant strawberry dipped in chocolate, she makes a drumroll noise with her tongue: "Dum de dum dum." Her voice is thick and foggy, coming from deep in her throat. Her favorite hello and good-bye are "Did you sleep well?" and "Sleep well." She is pure, with a waiflike, mysterious, fearsome beauty. Her teeth are perfect and white, and when she draws near to whisper a secret, her breath is like a baby's, like whipped cream.

Nastassia, twenty-two, is German-born, an internationally known model and movie actress who rose to prominence three years ago as the victimized heroine of Roman Polanski's *Tess*, and previously as his teenage nymphet-mistress. In Francis Ford Coppola's *One from the Heart*, she played a high-wire walker in a circus; in *Cat People*, directed by Paul Schrader, she was a descendant of panthers, torn between animal lust and human love. Perhaps the image with which Nastassia is most closely associated, however, is Richard Avedon's 1981 photograph of her naked in an undulating pose with a python wrapped around her. Now she is in the middle of filming her first Hollywood comedy, *Unfaithfully Yours*, directed by Howard Zieff. Kinski's costar, Dudley Moore, says: "There is something so ready to run about her. She almost looks like a young deer with those big eyes and the sturdy stance she's got. She is always vigilant, receiving these signals, always ready to move away and hide. She is not quite comfortable with herself, but that, again, is a lot of the charm of her, the fact that she really doesn't quite see it, then does, then doesn't. It's like strobe lighting. She goes back and forth with ambivalence about herself."

Nastassia is always chewing gum on the movie set. Once the director shouts out: "Should we try to match the tempo of Nastassia's gum chewing?" She tosses her head back and forth, paws the ground impatiently as she waits to film a scene on the movie set at Twentieth Century–Fox. She flutters with white electric curlers framing her face like a plastic mane, or she lopes around Sound Stage 16. She stoops to pick up a handful of sawdust and sniffs it, then lets it slide through her fingers. She and Dudley Moore play games on the set, chasing each other around and meowing like cats. "It is a joke, it's funny," Nastassia explains. "But at the same time it's more than just a joke to me. It's an understanding. When I'm in a bad mood or upset about something, Dudley makes me laugh with a cat's language. He meows in every color. With expressions we can understand what the other is saying."

One day Henry Kissinger, a member of the Fox board of directors, visits the set of *Unfaithfully Yours*. He walks up to Nastassia and says, "I saw you turn into a panther." Her pale face is startled and she stammers, "Oh, good." She then asks him how he is and how the world is going. At every stop, lunch, dinner, party, Nastassia disappears for about five minutes to call her mother, Brigitte, who is staying with her for a while in Los Angeles. Once she has to borrow a dime to do it. One day she skips an interview with a London *Times* reporter because her month-and-a-half-old Mexican Chihuahua has distemper. She spends twenty minutes on the phone with her mother, who thinks Nastassia should take the dog with her to New York, another ten minutes with a veterinarian who talks her out of it. After work she pulls on a white sweatshirt and pants with white tennis shoes, or purplish-pink sweats with blue shoes, or oversized overalls, and she looks no more than twelve years old.

"If I were an animal," she says, "I would be a fish or a bird. It's the peace and beauty of the ocean, the silent language of it. It seems like a womb, protective. The sky too. I love all colors, but blue mainly, because it's transparent like the water and the sky." Sometimes, because of the poetry of her talk and her sublime beauty, she seems not quite of this world. Then, in a jarring moment, her ethereality disappears: "Today Howard told me I was getting fat," she says after polishing off a plate of antipasto and another of spaghetti. She pats her behind and says, "I get fat here." She laughs. "I told him he was right."

Kinski can be sexually charged, sultry-sweet, alluring. At dinner she wears a light blue short knit dress, dark blue tights, red high heels, and a wide red belt. There is not a hair on her arm. When she lifts her hair off her back, you see her neck is long and curved, like Queen Nefertiti's in all the pictures. Suddenly she leans back and crosses her legs like a man. She appears not to know you can see straight up her dress. During a party at Los Angeles's chic Ma Maison, wearing a black leather miniskirt, black pointed flats, a V-necked blue sweater that keeps falling off one shoulder, she gets very drunk. She shatters a champagne glass against a wall, then puts her arms around a statue of a man in a corner and kisses it passionately.

She is tumultuous but also spontaneously affectionate, lighthearted, and she delights in the smallest things, like chocolate or a fresh breeze. Named after Dostoyevski's Filippovna Nastassia in *The Idiot*, she constantly says things like "full and empty at the same time," "everything and nothing," "painful and a relief at the same time." She seems to walk a kind of Tao in the naturalistic religion she has created for herself. Some of her favorite words are *truthful*, *flow*, *unfold*, *breathe*, *planet*, *confront*, *drug*, and *long for*. She takes herself very seriously as an artist and struggles to express herself. When she does take after take of a scene, her body remains taut, at her command. She concentrates so intensely, she quivers. Her eyes liquefy as she recedes into a character, and her face flushes.

She says, "The period I'm going through now is a transition. You know when you're in the middle of puberty and you don't know what to do with yourself? I feel like that now. It will be a transition into something very good if I work hard enough at it. But it is a frustration and an emptiness and a lack of confidence now. I feel young and I feel old. I feel twenty years below zero and old. I put a lot of demands on myself to know this and that, to be here and there. I've got to really do one thing at a time all the way. I've got to stop wanting to know and do everything at the same time. It's like you have a home stuffed with beautiful things—statues, books, lamps—that give a little bit, a little bit, a little bit, and you have nothing. And then you go into a house where there is a great light and one object and you could sit there all your life studying it, and one discovery about the object would give birth to the next, and it would be totally fulfilling. Right now my life is cluttered and unfulfilled. But to fulfill it is up to me. You get up with your body and you can't run away from it. If I weren't attached to this body I would have left it long ago."

Kinski says love is the most important thing in her life. "I always fall in love with someone while I'm working on a film. It's a joy to get up in the morning. Sometimes when I'm not infatuated, I just make things up in my mind. Making a film is such an intense thing. You're eliminating everything in your life and you're absorbed into the world of the movie. It's exciting. It's like somebody saying you have an illness and you only have this short time to live. Then you live it and that life is over with. Good-bye. You never see any of the people again. But meanwhile you have this short life in which you can do and feel and fantasize about all kinds of things because you know it will soon be over. So I always fall in love. Then you slip out of it, like a skin you take off, and you're naked and you're cold but it's exciting because there is going to be something new. My relationships are as intense and as giving and as short as my parts are. I would pump everything into a person. I would give my left arm that it was for life, but it dies so shortly. And when it dies, it doesn't even leave traces. The relationship vanishes into space. When I finish a part, it's the same feeling. I leave people and people leave me, I leave parts and parts leave me. I say it is 'the flow of life,' but it affects me terribly. Every once in a while I have such a breakdown, question every move."

To Nastassia, filmmaking is an art, and the greatest artists are the directors who can pull her soul out of her body and lay it on her skin to be seen. "I idealize my directors," she says. "It's true. I need to. I need to. I don't know if idealizing is a bad thing or a good thing. But I just want to get up in the morning and work for somebody. I want to make his dreams come true. I really do. I want to get a glimpse of his eyes searching things inside of me. For some I want to go to hell and to heaven. It hasn't happened with everybody. There are certain people I idealize. Others are very good, and I want to please them, too, but in a different sense of the word. In the past directors have always portrayed me as this strange girl who hardly talks but who has a great effect on people. They don't give me a chance to do something more, let more out of what is inside of me. The time is only coming up now when I feel I can open up. I have been almost a creature of these directors' imaginations. I guess that is what they saw in me and why they picked me . But if I was an object at moments in movies, I was also alive. I wasn't dead. I always gave everything I could while I worked. I could give maybe more today, but I gave what I could then."

On the set of *Unfaithfully Yours*, Kinski is extremely self-critical. After the director says "cut" to a scene, she invariably asks him if they can shoot it one more time. "In a way, I am panicked about each new take, but on the other hand, I want a new one like a drug. I do scenes over and over again, and then when I make sure that no one can do them again, I tell Howard, the director, what I did wrong and what I should have done. It is perverse. Then I sit back in painful pleasure and think about how much better it could have been. Howard laughs, but he is frustrated too. It is the same with many things I do. I make sure it's too late, and then I really attack it. I take pleasure in diminishing what I've done and try to top it with something that can never be done."

When she was just thirteen, Nastassia played a mute juggler who lives with an older man in *False Movements* (1975). It happened by chance. Nastassia went to a rock 'n' roll club called the Sahara in Munich every Sunday night with her girlfriends. The wife of the director of *False Movements* saw her there, went up to her, and said, "Who are you? Where do you come from?" Later the woman called Nastassia, who says, "I never had dreamed of doing a movie. My father was an actor, but I never thought of being one. I was pathetic. I was giggling before they said action every time. They told my mother I was sweet, but a lot of trouble too."

In 1977, Kinski played the daughter in the British horror film *To the Devil a Daughter*. "I don't know why I did that," she says. "I read it and I thought, 'That's fun, a nun and a devil.'" She made a television movie with German director Wolfgang Petersen (*Das Boot*). Nastassia was fifteen at the time and became an instant celebrity in Germany. "They thought I was wonderful," she says. Next she appeared with Marcello Mastroianni in the Italian film *Stay as You Are*, the story of a young woman who falls in love with a man she later finds out could be her father. "The story," she says, "was intriguing, but the movie didn't do the job."

Kinski did nude scenes at the director's request. "He described the girl in the movie to me as being young with nothing to hide, and she is in love and doesn't wear anything when she has breakfast and talks with her lover. All this made sense to me, so I said okay. And then *Playboy* took the picture without my saying yes and showed it all over the world. Sometimes they even clipped Mastroianni off. I felt awful. I saw how other people reacted to nudity, and that made me feel bad—not that I did it, but that they were exploiting Nastassia nude, saying here you can have her, any magazine and anybody can look at her. And I don't know any of those people who look at me, they look at me, they throw me in the toilet, in the rubbish. Dirty kind of men, I don't know. That's upsetting. Today I think I shouldn't have done it, but still, in context, it is part of the girl's character. I wasn't complexed about it, I wasn't even thinking if it was right or wrong. I saw my parents go about nude from the time I was a baby. That's how I grew up. I don't want to sound stupid and innocent and say, 'Oh, I didn't think it was bad.' I guess I have to eat my soup. Today, if a director asked me to do nude scenes, I would say that I wanted artistic control and put it in the contract. I never did nude scenes because I thought it was cute. I always respected the wishes of the director. I am not like that anymore. If a director asks me to do it and it doesn't make sense to me and I think more can be shown and felt without nudity, I won't. Nudity in a picture is such a delicate thing, and it is so rarely right. But it can be right if it's done by people with beautiful vision and if it becomes part of the melody of the situation. The body, after all, is a beautiful and secret thing."

When she was fifteen Nastassia met director Roman Polanski at a party in Munich. He was working on the opera *Rigoletto* and invited a few people from the cast to his hotel. Kinski went with two girlfriends, one of them a friend of his. Kinski says, "We all said, 'Oh, I want to meet Roman Polanski.' He was really fun. He was light. He served us dinner and drinks. He wasn't paying a lot of attention to me, and then later we started talking and that's how we met." Polanski asked her to be a photographic model for the 1976 Christmas issue of *Vogue*. Polanski suggested Kinski go to America to study the language and take acting classes in Los Angeles. She says, "I went to the Lee Strasberg School, but I never really got involved. I always sort of watched and observed it from the outside. At that time I wasn't really sure I was going to do acting. By that time Roman and I were great friends. One day he told me about a book and he gave it to me to read. And I read it and I loved it. It was *Tess of the D'Urbervilles*. He said, 'I might do this film, and I thought you might be right for it. But you have to lose your accent, and not only that, but you have to be this girl from head to toe.' So he sent me to Dorset, England, and I lived in the country for a while, and then I went to London to study at the National Theatre to learn the right accent. I still didn't know if I had the part. Roman never really made me feel he was serious about it. We rarely talked about it on the phone, and then it just happened. I went to France and I guess that was it. I never dared to ask.

"As a director, Roman is very humane but very firm. Roman digs into people's hearts, gets really close. He is a true poet. He is very cruel sometimes too. He just wants the inner part of you. He is every character in the movie. He is Tess and Angel and the countryside and everything. You feel he is the boss. I love that. I don't want a director who wants to be like everybody else. The great present Roman gave me was to leave me in peace so much of the time. He knew the most important thing was for me to find it out myself, to grow into that earth person and that different time and rhythm. We actually talked very little during the movie. He made me feel I could do it and made no fuss about it. He had such pleasure and love for the story. *Tess* is about the evilness of a mass of people. It is the story of how laws and society can destroy only the purest people, how the purest and truest are trapped by the spiders. Roman told me he wanted Tess to stay the same, whatever happened. She's much deeper than revenge. She is always the same, knowing she would die again and again for the same thing. He had wanted to do it with his wife [actress Sharon Tate, who was murdered by Charles Manson], which a very confusing thing for me. He wasn't really sad about it. She was Tess, she was always there, anyway, with him, although I would be the one to make it visual for other people. Polanski is innocent and reborn. He talks about everything, a book, a play, a movie he wants to do, with such freshness, like he was just born and discovering it for the first time. But he's lived so many hundreds of years. He is always awake.

"*Tess* was really my first confrontation with myself, my own thoughts and feelings. Spending a whole year in the country, the real country, changed me in some way, brought me closer to myself. Everything was shut off, and I was in the middle of big fields of flowers and mountains. Before, I was hyper all the time, and then I started having conversations with myself that I never had before. At five o'clock in the morning, sitting in the middle of a field, watching the sun come up and hearing the grass and hearing myself, feeling my pulse and my blood, I heard thoughts I never heard before. I got addicted to being with myself, watching without saying I am the flow of life. The book became like a drug to me. I reread it and reread it all the time. And the more I discovered, the more I realized there wasn't that much to discover about the character. There was just this one river so clean and blue within her, and I felt totally myself through the character and nature. It was a rebirth for me. *Tess* is the best thing I've ever done, not in terms of performance, maybe, but the purest and the most beautiful thing."

Kinski had to learn to walk a high wire for her part as an acrobat in *One from the Heart*. She says, "I started real low. It isn't like walking a straight line. It is like life in the toughest sense of the word. Gravity pulls you down everywhere and you really have to find the ultimate center of yourself. And because of my impatience, I got so frustrated and kept falling all the time. Then I found an image of something pulling me up, something positive from outside and within, and it worked and it was like magic to me. I loved the circus people. Actually I thought of leaving everything and going to the circus. Those people put their life on a tiny string all the time. They know what might happen, but they're together and confront it all the time."

After *One from the Heart*, Nastassia's second movie of 1982 was *Cat People*. Although she and the director Paul Schrader had a brief affair, the two ended up disagreeing violently about the film, particularly about one nude scene. She says, "I didn't agree with the way the film was done. Overall I didn't like my performance in *Cat People* at all. I wanted to do the movie in a much rougher way, getting more into the souls and passions of these people. Who cares about blood and flesh smeared all over the place? I blame myself because I listened to the director. I should have rebelled. I followed his path. I sort of melted into what Schrader thought was right. I used to think you had to do what the director tells you to do, but you can't. You have to put your own individuality into it, your own thoughts. I didn't. I let myself be trapped. I don't regret it, except that we didn't go where we had to go.

"When we were filming the scene where I seduce John Heard, I was supposed to go behind a window and pull off my pants. I told Schrader I didn't think I had to do that, I would just mime the gestures. Schrader said to do it. He said it wouldn't show, anyway, because it was so dark. It was very dark, so I thought, Oh well, but when I saw the film, the shot showed my pubic hair and everything. And I said to Schrader, 'You promised me it wouldn't show,' and I begged him to edit it out. It was just two seconds of film. He said no, he wouldn't cut it out, it would take away from the art of the movie. Bullshit. Then he should have taken all the other shit out that wasn't necessary and gone more deeply into the souls of the characters. When he refused to take out the nude shot, I went to the heads of Universal and I begged them to help me. They all sort of smiled at me and said, 'We'll see what we can do.' But they were all on his side. I know I agreed to do nudity in the film. But I'm nude so much in it, and I gave so much of it. Toward the end what is important is their looks and their feelings. What upset me so much was that he lied to me after all we'd been through. He knew exactly what he was doing. He lied to me so I would do it. This movie was a big disillusionment to me. After that incident I felt I had to take more control over my movies. I'm not just a piece of meat they can use. They are the directors and the creators, but there is no creation without actors. If you're in the hands of a great director, you can rely on him. But if you're in the hands of someone who is not great, then you should work on yourself harder and harder and pull it through yourself."

Kinski says her acting is all instinct. "Each time when I tried to prove something, when I said, 'I want to do this, this will really show them what I can do,' each time I failed. I could only go back to the truth. I don't understand acting. Sometimes I only understand it while I'm doing it, and sometimes not even then. You cannot study acting. You can get new tools to use or an opening, but you can't become something by studying, you just can't. You can become better. But some people can't even do that. They are best when they are very young because they are restless. When the restlessness settles, the acting goes. When acting goes for me, I'll just stop and do something else. I hope I always will get better and better, meaning bigger and bigger and more courageous and deeper and lighter and more flexible. But when it's time to go, it's time to go. There is no use trying to ride a wooden horse."

Nastassia's father is the German actor Klaus Kinski, fifty-six, best known for his roles in two Werner Herzog films. In *Aguirre, the Wrath of God*, he plays a madman who must face the South American jungles alone but is secure in the knowledge he is God; in *Nosferatu*, he is a creature who feeds on blood. Kinski is one of the great movie monsters, and he brings with his abilities a reputation as a difficult if not demonic performer. Klaus met Nastassia's mother, Ruth Brigitte, forty-two, when she was seventeen. She was selling gloves in a Berlin store. He saw her through the window, went in and pretended to be interested in gloves, and took her home that day. They sent a telegram to Brigitte's mother and then went off to shoot a movie somewhere. Nastassia was born January 24, 1961, the month after Brigitte turned twenty. The Kinskis' marriage lasted about eight and a half years.

Brigitte has been with Nastassia in Los Angeles for the last several weeks at the Shangri-La, a refurbished, Art Deco–style hotel in Santa Monica across the street from the ocean. I meet Brigitte there, and we sit on a bench by the beach and talk. She is much smaller than Nastassia, shorter and finer-boned. She is dressed in offbeat black: black Bermudas, black stockings, black flat shoes, black sleeveless top, and an accordion-pleated black jacket. Her eyes are blue, she wears no makeup, and her skin has the same milky quality Nastassia's has. Brigitte is writing a book of poetry and her autobiography. She has not yet been published. She says, "I never really came to be an artist because I had my child and my affairs, which were the most important things in my life.

"Klaus and I lived actually in a place from Kafka. Every night and every day I was on stage in our home. He created a play and I had to react. It was sometimes terrible. It was a hell and a heaven. I was convinced one hundred percent he was the devil. It was *Richard III* ten times or *Dr. Jekyll and Mr. Hyde.* He was extremely jealous. No one ever had the right to put the name of me or Nastassia in their mouths. He wanted me to have a child every year. It was impossible. He was so possessive, he was jealous when I gave Nastassia milk from my breast. It was as if he had built a religion around us, the Madonna and child. It was ten times *Romeo and Juliet* with their child. It was beautiful in a way, but hell too. We lived very intensely for eight and a half years. One day was like months. Our relationship was crazy, but we always did by our instinct the right thing for Nastassia. We gave her her freedom. She was extremely fanciful and she played always with herself. She created from one little thing a world. And when she needed me to embrace her or play with her or be sweet, I was always there, but I never forced her to do anything. Our relationship didn't hurt Nastassia. It doesn't bother children if they feel in their own minds that their parents love each other. We loved each other. So she was always fine. She wasn't even scared of her father. After the breakup I never let my child feel my own vibrations when they were negative. I felt I had no right. Somehow I did it.

"I felt it always very strongly that Nastassia would become an artist. Whatever she was doing, whether it was dancing at three years old to classical music she had never heard, or falling into poses, or when she was painting, whatever, I felt it. When she was four, she blended colors together as the old painters did. She never used real red or real blue or real yellow, always the old colors, red-brown, English blue, to involve the colors so they had the harmony of old paintings. She always painted princesses with long necks and extremely tiny waists with two balls coming out of the neck, the breasts. I knew what was coming when she was two years old when her father filmed her. Two years old with such sensitivity and such an attitude of pain in her face, and beauty, a woman already, and a child at two years old. The pain was not as a human being would feel pain but as a rose, as a flower would feel pain. But I always wanted to keep it away from her so it didn't come too early. It was not for us to push her in any direction. Klaus and I never spoke about it. It was an unspoken law. We never said, 'Look at her, she will be good in film.' Klaus never talked about acting with her. She is not a film kid. I wanted her to have a normal life before the destiny took her away.

"She was a bird. Always a bird. She'd flow. She was always busy. She got up very early in the morning and always said, 'I've got so many things to do.' She played, she sang, she painted. What this child gave me in beautiful vibrations and love, it's a beautiful desert. She has kept her imagination. She was always so naive and wise, so far, so far that it was in my mind that she lived already once. I don't know. The extreme of the characters is so strong. I myself grew up very late with my intellect, although my instinct was always very large, and maybe that was good for Nastassia. I never had this attitude to force myself to be somebody in the establishment. It didn't interest me. I lived myself, too, in a fantasy world with my child. I was very young and I had to find the secret to life, to growing up, to find my own identity.

"At fifteen, when she decided to quit school, it was terrible. I went to the highest head of the school system in Munich and I begged him to make Nastassia stay in school. Sometimes she said she was going to school and she didn't. Between the ages of fourteen and eighteen, Nastassia gave me a very hard time. I'm melodramatic and melancholy, so I cried all the time. I couldn't understand it. I felt completely unguilty. I still don't think her rebelliousness against me was natural. She has said she created her own problems, wanted to be an outsider at this time. I never gave her any bourgeois attitudes to rebel against, like don't wear those pants, don't wear makeup, come home at ten o'clock. I didn't love her too much that I wanted to keep her. When you see your child happy with eyes like candles and a smile in the face and the whole body restless, how can you say no? But don't ask me how I suffered because it was dangerous. All of Munich was after her because of her charm, her spirit. All day long, 'Is Nastassia there?' Boys, girls, it doesn't matter. They all wanted something from her. This unspoken secret freedom, karma, she has had always, which stimulates people to be around her. When the boys came with their big motorbikes, I died. I was so worried about accidents, drugs, everything. But she was protected by love. How do you say when you eat something and feel satisfied by it? She wasn't hungry for love. She had no vacuum in her. She was a tomboy, too, played sports. She gave boys and men a hard time, but not to be coquettish, not to play. She fell in love for a short time and then forgot. But not in a nasty way, she was like a cloud, she would just drift away. It still happens.

"They gave Roman Polanski an evil image in this country in his relationships with girls. A man can never force a girl when she doesn't want to make love to him. Polanski is a very sweet, charming, intelligent person. That's why the girls like him. He's probably dangerous too. But girls make up their own minds. He liked Nastassia very much. And he gave her at that time all the strength and attitude she probably should have gotten from her father. Never did I try to direct her relationships with men. When my child is happy, it's supposed to be the right man for her. And every one of us must make her own experiences. I couldn't say who was right for her.

"I have never supervised her since she was a child. I help her decide about her films. I told her from the beginning not to appear nude in films. When she went to Italy to do *Stay as You Are*, we had a fight at the airport because she wanted to be on her own. I didn't know she would do a nude scene, it wasn't written in the script. I didn't sign anything that said she could do nude scenes. I said, 'You won't do it again, will you, Nastassia?' And she said, 'No.' And then she did it again in *Cat People*. I got so mad. I couldn't understand it. She is so strong and intelligent, and on the other hand she lets people manipulate her so easily. I've told her, 'Your face is magic and so erotic that you don't need to show your body. Millions of girls have beautiful bodies, but you have this face, this expressive dark magic.' Oh, she is so stupid. If she didn't have that magic and elegance, she would be finished.

"She is now so restless. She must find her calm. In so many aspects she is trying to find her identity. To change identities in films is a hard job, anyway, for grown-up people, and even harder for such a young person. She is living like a gypsy now. Sometimes she says to me, 'I have the destiny to live my life fast and get the most beautiful things in life because I will die early.' And when she says it, it cuts into me like a knife and I say, 'Stop, don't say that.'"

Nastassia and her mother are so close that neither one can describe the feeling. Nastassia says, "My mother and I have this really strangely close relationship. No other relationship can come close to it. It's frightening. Even when I'm in a relationship with a man, I compare it to my relationship with my mother. She is a friend, but she is still a mother, and everything a mother needs to be, she is. She is really observing and caring and doesn't want anything but giving because it's her joy. Even when I can't bear anybody, not even myself, she's like the sun coming up to me. She dedicated all her life to me. Sometimes I feel that she gave her life to me and now it's my job to maybe take her somewhere. But what is it she doesn't know? She knows things I couldn't begin to know. Yet she is so fresh with ideas which I already take for granted. She sometimes wakes me up and says, 'Don't you see?' and she makes me see and feel things again. Nobody, not my father, not anybody, has done that for me, except movies.

"When I was little, she knew instinctively when I needed peace. She let me be and be and be. Sometimes she thinks she wasn't strict enough. She says I took it for granted. But I didn't. She gave me freedom, the kind in which you let the child be but you always know when you have to be there. Protection was always there. She is just like a lion's mother. She'd fight for me for anything, the slightest thing. She would never have me on a leash, but she would kind of watch out, every instant, every second, of my life, and if anybody turned against me, she would go crazy. She might be wrong or she might be right, but she knew the most important thing was to protect her child, that you only have one another. Everything else is like a jungle.

"My mother never said to me, 'You're too young or too old.' The first time I fell in love was when I was thirteen turning fourteen. He was a year or two older and he waited for one year, watching me when I was playing on the street with my friends or when I went to coffee shops, before he even dared to say hello. It was the most romantic love story. That was my first real experience. My mother didn't object to the fact that I was having a relationship at fourteen. She couldn't. She left us in our own world. She didn't try to break into our world. We were in love and we were two children and she wasn't against it. She understood. A lot of people aren't like that. They want their children always to be their children. I'm very grateful to my mother for that. You know how you can get screwed up by your first love. Your parents make you feel it's dirty. That can unplug something in you, the tiniest, most precious part of you, and that will be it. The same with Roman Polanski. My mother and I never really talked about age. She knew I felt very strongly about Roman, more as a person than anything else. He was this man who all of a sudden paid attention to me and didn't say, 'You're too young to talk about this or to know this.' He talked to you like a person. My mother always said, 'Whatever you do, right or wrong, I'm sure is right if you follow your fate. If you suffer, that's right; if you're happy, that's right. I want you to do what you feel.'

"There was a very difficult time when I was fifteen, when I started to be less of a child, trying to be more of a woman and independent, thinking I had to do it on my own. My mother didn't understand. She said, 'I'm so open with you, you can do anything you want anyway, just show it to me.' I saw all my friends having problems at home, leaving, having nervous breakdowns, so I thought that was the way it ought to be. But our problems were never about school or drugs. It was because we loved each other so deeply, and all of a sudden there was a cut. I was mean to her because I loved her so much. I wanted to get away from that love and experience rough, unprotected life. I went away and left her brokenhearted. Sometimes I stayed in friends' homes. It was just too good. I wanted bad. That period in my life will always be a part of me. Rejecting love and rejecting the good things and trying to destroy them and just before they're gone build them up again. When I went to Italy to do *Stay as You Are*, I went alone and I longed for her so much. After *Tess* I lived in France and had my own house for the first time. But as soon as that separation was settled we came back together again as strong as ever. Today when we're together and we talk it's like total ecstasy. Men become jealous of my relationship with my mother. It is such an incredible thing to know that whatever happens, somebody will be there. Even if you murder. The more crimes you commit, the more they love you. I can't explain it. It's not just because she's my mother and gave birth to me. I guess I'm just one of the lucky ones. It hurts me when I hurt my mother, but when I do, it's only because I am bleeding myself within. And I want to give her that as a present. She's the only one I can give it to because she is the only one I truly love.

"My father loved us so much, but he's the kind of person that chokes you. He doesn't leave you your own pleasures. If you think or feel one way and he feels the other way, he won't accept it. My mother wanted to work. People wanted her to do movies, but he just wanted her to be at home, be a mother, be a wife, be this Venus, this planet he could land on anytime. We were this one thing, the three of us, which was great. This togetherness I hardly see anywhere, but it was also choking, just too much. It wasn't 'they separated or they didn't.' They just had to separate. I was eight. I remember I wasn't surprised at all. I wasn't very hurt because everything was always in the open. I always felt things, saw things. Children can see things, even more than the people who are involved. I knew it had to happen. After the separation my mother, for the first time in her life, lived. She was very young, like a little girl. She was very bright but young, and all of a sudden she was free, free to play around. And she did. And it was a different life for her and for me too.

"When I was about ten or eleven, my mother lived with a painter and sculptor. We didn't have any money. He was the kind of guy who could do anything, but he didn't do anything. He could build a house but would only build it halfway. So my mother sold everything she had, like jewels, and we put everything that was left, carpets and lamps, into a huge van. We cut out the windows and made it livable. It was beautiful, and we traveled with it all through Europe and Greece and Turkey. It was an adventure a kid dreams of. It was great for me. I started painting with my mother's friend. All of a sudden colors meant a lot to me. I painted faces of beautiful women with mirrored eyes, or fairy women, women flying with wings, or queens. I spent hours painting tiny flowers onto the queen's gown. I always painted women, never men. For months we traveled. Then we dumped the van and flew to South America. Caracas, Venezuela. I went to school in Rome, Berlin, Caracas, then Germany again. That's when I learned languages. My ears were tuned. I speak German, English, French, and Italian fluently. When I was fifteen, I decided to leave school. The things I wanted to learn I would learn, but I felt school was a waste of time. There were lots of things I didn't know and still don't know, but there were things I learned when I left that aren't teachable. It was an instinct."

Nastassia does not like to talk about Klaus. They have only met once or twice for lunch or dinner in the last eleven years. She says, "My father is so expressive that things he feels even before they are thoughts are visible on his skin. He heats up. What other people work on, he was born with. He's got eyes like the sky and like hell at the same time. They're so clear and blue and alert and serious, and then they're like hell. That's how he is. He is total light and pureness and then hell. He gives totally or he gives nothing. He is like the sun, then an iceberg, then nonexistent, and then the sun again. Which is fine. It's a lot better than most people are.

"I wasn't really sure what my father did when I was little. I thought every father did what my father did. So I saw him coming home and going through these mood changes, and I said to my mother, 'What does he do outside of our house? He comes home and goes crazy.' Even my dog, when it heard my father's footsteps, would slink down behind me. But I wasn't afraid of him. He would be so sweet to me and bring me a basket of marzipan fruits. That was my favorite. He was very tender. He made my mother and me laugh by imitating the way all animals from a flea to an elephant go to sleep. We'd go crazy. We were all playacting, my parents and I. It was free theater without any curtains, without any visitors. My father showed me experience is there for the moment. It's not to put in a little cupboard and keep it. Life is full of nows. He was the tenderest, most delightful, beautiful, open person, and in a second he would turn into a beast, and then be on his knees begging forgiveness for being the beast and literally start crying because he would hate himself for it. And all of a sudden the beast would take over again. That's what made him so amazing. When he went insane, it brought things out in you that never would have been brought out, and then, after forgiveness, when he turned into the most tender, silent, flower again—it would totally throw you off. It would clean you out, and you wouldn't have things stuck in you. But then when you wanted to clean yourself out from within and give your own personality, he put a cork in you and you couldn't express yourself.

"He would talk to himself a lot. He would say, 'What am I doing? It's not enough, I want to do more.' That was basically what he said. He was frustrated because he was really a great actor and he really didn't have the opportunity, as far as I'm concerned, to show that and work with great people. For twenty-two years he worked on writing the story of

Paganini's life. He always wanted to do it. But his main dream was to have a ship and never land on any land. He used to talk about it and said, 'Someday we'll be on the ocean in our ship and we'll play with the fish and go all over the world and never be dependent on anybody.' He had big white rolls of drawings of ships, and he would sit there in front of those drawings for hours, obsessed.

"But as soon as he had any money, he spent it. It went upside down all the time financially. But that was great because the value of things stayed with us. I would know how to live without money in an instant if I had to. He would give us a castle some year for a month, and then we'd be broke again and sit in some little place and he would borrow money just to make us happy. He wanted my mother to be queen and me to be the princess, like in a fairy tale. We had this enormous house once when I was seven. It was in Rome on the Via Appia Antica. It used to be a church. It had paintings that had been hanging there for years. It had huge land with snakes and a guest house. One lady's husband died and he came back and visited her every night in that house. She had proof. The place was haunted. My father was so jealous that he wouldn't let any male protectors stay there while he was out of town working. Doors and windows opened. Paintings fell. My mother and I huddled in a corner, and the moon glistened through the windows and the shadows were alive. It was like a movie. We used to hear the sound of cucumber chewing and the smell of it in one room. I promise you, it's true. We weren't crazy.

"My father was obsessed with one thing all his life. When he is with his family, his child, nothing else exists. But then when he separates, he separates. Memories may stay with him, but he's in a new life, and because he's so obsessed, he can only give his attention to his new life. But while he's giving it to you, it's all the way. I've never seen anybody like that in my life. When I see him today, he's in a different world and he gives himself there and doesn't give himself to us anymore. Once I understood that, I accepted it. So I don't despise him anymore. He and my mother are the best things that ever happened to me. They unfolded me and gave me everything I long to re-feel. My childhood was the most beautiful period of my life. It was then, and it will always be within me. I see now how precious and amazing my father really was. Nobody that I see now is like that. Nobody in my life is that giving and demanding and open. He is every extreme. Nobody has ever loved me that much, I guess. Only now can I see what really happened. My father pushed down and then said, 'Let it out,' and as soon as it was out, he wanted to push down again. All these things were bad and good, but I couldn't have dealt with only the good.

"I think maybe in my life I've always been looking for someone like my father maybe to re-create something I felt when I was little. But now I'm looking for just the contrary. I couldn't unfold with a man like that. When I was younger, I was attracted to older men. I liked the fact that somebody would take me and teach me things, that they had all this history behind them. They balanced me out because I was always jumping around and searching and wondering. I always had the feeling I could give them more than I could give to people my own age because what I had they needed, and what they had I needed. So it was an exchange that was right. But now the exchange I need is different. I want to experience things and see things with somebody who has never seen them before. Also, younger people are less full of complexes. They are more ready for life as it comes. They just take it as it comes. Sometimes they're crueler but much, much clearer.

"I haven't seen all the movies my father has done. I refused for a while to see him even on the screen until I began to accept him. Now I'll see one of his movies if it is running. I think he is great and could be great. He is great in moments when he wipes out everything and anything. But he needs to work with somebody who is as far out as he is, or somebody who is totally calm, but some force that brings out the things he doesn't want to bring out. He used to blow people away on the stage in Berlin. He was like a man from the moon. It makes me happy when I see myself in him on screen, but because we've gone so deep in our relationship, the happiness is just like a slight perfume or a breeze over something that is burning inside me and him that we can't deal with. I would like to act with him in a movie. Before, I thought I never would. Somebody would have had to kill me before I did that. Now I would act with him. Maybe that would be it for me. It would be like giving antibiotics to someone who is sick. The disease is the cure."

Klaus Kinski doesn't want to be interviewed. On the phone he says, "You're just mad about your child. Whatever your child does is beautiful. There is no high point or particular behavior. I cannot say she was like this or like this or like this or like this. I was just in love with her all the time whether she was a baby, three, four, five, ten, seventeen, or twenty. There is no difference. There are no childhood stories to tell." A few calls later he agrees to meet. He lives in Marin County, north of San Francisco. He waits on the steps of an Italian coffee shop in Sausalito, a town just across the Golden Gate Bridge. He isn't much taller than 5'6" or 5'7". He is wearing blue jeans, clean and faded, with a hooded, white cotton blue-striped top, and black rubber boots up to his knees. He looks weather-beaten. His hair is full and white. His curved lips are Nastassia's. His eyes are huge and blue, jumping wildly every second, as if they were caged and trying to get out. It looks as if his two front teeth are false, and every once in a while a hissing sound escapes from them. There is a cold sore on his lip. It is impossible to think of the sore and the hiss as anything but signs of the entrance to some underworld or lair in him inhabited by God knows what. He talks incessantly, although by his own account words are meaningless and distract from life. "Words and words pulled me, pulled me away from life," he says, and he mimes being pulled and pulled until he chops his arm in a sudden gesture. We eat lunch at a Japanese restaurant where he orders a plate of sushi. He argues with the solicitous owner over the way his tuna has been prepared. He won't allow me to take notes or use a tape recorder. He says he prefers to get to know me before he talks. Instead he rambles about the nature of life, language, journalism (more bad words). And about Nastassia: "She is so young, young, young, younger than she is." And: "She was my daughter before she was born." And: "I don't try to justify myself or defend myself. I've always done what I had to. She should know for herself that I love her, that I've loved her always, always. Those years you can't replace by words, though. After years and years, words get weaker and weaker."

After lunch we go back to the Italian café, and Klaus starts to brawl with the waiter because the cappuccino takes too long. The incident prompts him to discourse on what is wrong with society. He then says he would be more comfortable talking where he lives because it would be silent and he wouldn't feel claustrophobic. We get into his four-wheel-drive truck and start. The backseat is littered with the toys of his son, seven-year-old Nanhoi, the child from his now ended third marriage with a Vietnamese woman half his age. (Nanhoi lives with his mother but visits Klaus regularly.) There is a pair of tiny leather shoes dangling from colored string behind the driver's seat, a little brown cowboy hat, a basketball, football, and soccer ball, and an Oakland A's green-and-yellow satin jacket. On the forty-five-minute drive to his house through the hills of Marin County, Klaus talks more: "The essentials: life, love, life, death." "Nothing changes the day of my death, the day of my birth." "I want to be simple. I want to be simple." "I am impossible to live with." "I don't listen to music when there is wind." "Nastassia is of me, as I am of something else." He also talks about the vibrations in nature and reincarnation.

We finally near his house. We start up a hill. Cows are grazing outside the window. As we enter the woods, the road turns into nothing but a deeply rutted trail. Deer and rabbits run about. We drive by a white Indian tipi about ten feet high that he has had made from surrounding trees for his son. We finally get to the house, on top of the hill. There is no path to his door except what he has beaten with his own passing. The house is one room, all wood. One wall is all windows opening out onto a balcony hanging above the hill and trees. There is a modern bathroom in an alcove off the main room, a modern kitchen built into the opposite wall. But for those, it is like walking into a child's playhouse or a tree fort. There are toys everywhere: a paper tiger kite, big and orange, hangs on one wall next to a multicolored giant paper dragonfly. There's a child's desk made out of wood covered with coloring paper and crayons, a trundle bed with little boy's clothes, blue-jean shorts, and a few shirts carefully folded. Pictures of Nanhoi are framed and hanging everywhere, along with the child's drawings signed, "To Papa. I love you." A miniature pair of wooden clogs is on the floor, next to bigger ones. There are snowshoes on one wall. There is a circular wooden staircase to the loft upstairs: more windows, a king-size bed with no sheets, *Grimm's Fairy Tales*, and a set of Louis Vuitton luggage. In the main room the basic piece of furniture is a large wooden table with two benches piled high with a typewriter, a Nikon camera, boxes of typing paper, and a phone. There is a hearth fireplace, the only heat source.

We talk, or rather Klaus rants for a couple of hours. He is elemental and powerful. My face feels sunburned from the encounter. His virtual monologue touches on Nijinsky, Baudelaire, critics, the French use of the word *genius,* competition, directors ("They're growing now like mushrooms after rain. Is someone going to tell me how to die, how to cry?"), van Gogh, then finally Nastassia: "*Tess* I saw, and I was deeply shocked in my feeling. This sort of shocked me, this deepness, this depth. I didn't even care what movie it was. It was just this . . . words are too weak to speak this out, that's why I wasn't ready all the time to answer people who said, 'Aren't you proud of your daughter?' What does proud mean? Are you proud of somebody you love? It's like if you stopped on the street and went to a woman with a baby and said, 'Hey, you, do you love your child?' What does this mean? They would probably scream for help and say he's a madman. At the Cannes Film Festival the movie was there, and there were advertisements for *Tess*, posters on the hotels. And every time I passed this poster I saw this face coming down, this look. My impression was so strong, I did not know I had to tell her, and I didn't tell her how great she is. But she didn't know. I was shocked. When I saw it, I had this feeling that I have had very few times in my life. I was shocked, crying and holding my face, and I was embarrassed that anybody could see me, but I couldn't help it, just because she appeared on screen. It was going in me. I didn't even think. The word *shock* came into my mind afterward.

"I saw *Stay as You Are* and *Tess* only. I didn't ask her if she saw every movie I did. [Klaus has made more than 180 movies, most or all of which he did for the money. He is proud of this.] I could never think about that. Why do I have to see every movie she did? Why? Sometimes she did movies with people I was bored by. I don't care about this or that director. So if she is so beautiful in a movie, it is because of her, not a director. So why should I see the movie then? As long as I am not blind, I don't need a dog to see. If I am blind, maybe I would like the dog to lead me. I am not blind. I don't have to see her movies. I know my child.

"I have made many things wrong in my life. I should have made many things better in my life, not only to Nastassia but many things. If someone said to me, 'You did everything wrong in your life,' I would say, 'Okay, maybe you're right.' But my way is the only way I can exist. I can feel and express things to understand how true something is. People in my life have tried to change me, and I have blown up even more violently and I said, 'What, do you really want to distort me?' What's left, you have to do it your way. I don't need a Bible to tell me I'm doing wrong a hundred million times in my life. Everything I did wrong in my life I am suffering a long time. It's coming back and back and back and back to me for years. I am not ashamed to tell myself what I am doing wrong, but there must always be a way to understand that's all I can do. What I want to say is I tried, okay, I tried, and I'm not breaking my head that it's not happened. It's like a growing plant. This tiny thing is coming out, you can feel it coming out, it's breaking through, so it may be one day that she will understand many more things than she understands today. Nobody can come to me and say, 'Why haven't you seen this and why and why.' I know what I have to do.

"I respected her as a little child. I never felt I am the one who could give orders because I am bigger. That's ridiculous. In my brain doesn't exist politics, doesn't exist religion. Nastassia was growing up in love, always from her mother, except maybe mine was missing when I was not there. From the beginning she was naturally so much a part of me, a part of me, a part of me, that I didn't have to look at her because I just felt her, like a sleeping animal will cover its child with his fur. He doesn't have to look there, he is just doing, it's like your own arm. That's nature. People make this distance in life only by talking. When she was a child, I had no dreams for her. You know when a star is falling and you wish something? I always did it when I was a boy, but I could never say just one thing. I was always wishing something which was unspeakable by words. It was so much farther than anything. So how could I have this wish for her? I could only have for her all my deepest feelings, like a bird that takes off. One dream would have been too limited."

When Nastassia learns that I have seen her father, she says she is much more his daughter than she admitted earlier. "Wanting to isolate myself becomes like a drug, and I know I can't have it yet. I am becoming closer and closer to nature, and the vision of the origin of it just pumps up into me all the time. But I don't want to become like my father, not dealing with anything and anybody. My father's a coward in a way. So am I. We both are. I'm a coward because I pull back and put myself in neutral when it comes to relationships and people I really love. In my life I go toward something or someone with total energy and strength, and then all of a sudden I stop short like a rabbit and make a right-hand turn. I go on to the next, to a new surprise. I'm afraid to commit to anything, like my father. He does not want to be truly confronted, so he goes out and hangs on to the sunlight. I do the same thing, and that's why

I reject it in him so much, because I see it in myself. So, I'm in neutral. I have to find pleasure and pain because pain—pain is just a word— pain is good. Through pain there is relief and sudden understanding and love. It's all connected.

"Other people tell me I'm like a butterfly, settle here, and I enjoy the moment, and then I fly away. They say it's nice but it's really the pits. It's nice for a moment, it's like a rain shower, but then it stops and I'm just indifferent or cold, and then I fly away again. I always have this image of a planet, and the closer I get, the smaller it gets, and then when I have it in my hand, it is nothing. And as soon as I let it go, it flies away again far and lights up. It doesn't want to be with me yet. I repress so much. I express it with myself mainly. I write. It's not a diary, it's a friend. It's the better part of me that connects with the confusing part. I don't write for weeks, then writing is all I long for. It's like breathing. When I write, the pores open and I feel cleansed. I'm like two people. Not the good way when sometimes you're the beast and sometimes you're the angel. But the beast within the beast is still a great beast. It's not that. I can't pin myself down. I can't make a commitment to anything. The indifferent, cruel, and ruthless part of me tries to pull the rest into it, but I have one gift, the gift of instant joy, like vitamins. That joy is stronger than the pull because the joy is connected to something higher, something beautiful and strong. This is what is the truth: I create something, and in the next second I am capable of destroying the purest thing in the world. I could drop my best friend or my mother at the most important moment, and then I would turn around and awaken desire to help out a complete stranger.

"My father told me never to follow a religion. He said it's all phony and hypocritical. If you want to be religious, he told me, love the days and love the flowers and go through life with open eyes and don't lie. *Morality* was a word my parents never used. *Truth* was the word. Truth and facing things like an animal. I worship the consistency of nature. After all that happens, it keeps renewing and growing and growing and growing, and whoever created that is God. Whoever made that live. Who knows who God is or what God is? But it's the best thing we have, and it's the only thing to hold on to. The question of how the universe began tortures me. Starting with the insects. How many thousands of different little beautiful little perfect little insects are there? And then you go on and on and on and back, and you can't find any beginning. There are facts and you can read books about it, but it is still so unapproachable. And the earth actually flies, like our souls, I guess.

"Whatever I love is connected to my parents, what they've loved and listened to. I grew up with Chopin. My father had records of African music, ugaduga, ugaduga, real jungle African music. Bongo drums. I used to listen to that music, it was like the rhythm of the body. I love Dostoyevski and Gogol and Kafka and Goethe. It's not that I read it and loved it because of my parents. But we happen to have one thing, the three of us. These were the things, the books and objects I had at home, and these were the first things I was confronted with. Everything else I read after that was paler. In a way Dostoyevski and Gogol and Kafka and Goethe all say the same thing. They crave the same thing. It's so crazy. It all ends up in one spot, and it all ends up in what I learned from my parents too. The one thing is relief. It's growing from young to old to young again. You can become young again only when you're really old. And it's longing for pain, to know feeling exists, longing for darkness to know light exists. It is longing for self-destruction to know what it is that is great about love and realizing when it's almost too late that you have to live."

Kinski says she wants to direct but not star in a film she has written called *Day and Night.* "It is like a fairy tale that shows the day and night of human beings. There are two characters: a beautiful woman about thirty-five, who has never really lived, and a boy about eleven or twelve. They are not related. They are not lovers. During the day the woman screams at the boy and hits him, but at night she changes into a loving, nurturing person. To keep the day beast away, they resolve to swim out into the ocean at night, as far as they can, then wait for morning. They do, and when day breaks, the woman tries to drown the child. He holds on to her and they both drown, hugging each other."

April 1983

Kinski has changed the spelling of her first name to Nastassja. She married Egyptian businessman Ibrahim Moussa, thirteen years her senior, in September 1984. They have two children, a son, Aljosha Nakzynski, born in 1984; and a daughter, Sonia Leila, born in 1986. They divide their time between houses in Paris and Rome. Kinski's last Hollywood film was Revolution, *with Al Pacino, in 1985. She regularly acts in European films.*

BOB DYLAN DOWN EXECUTIONER'S ROW

*T*he sun is slipping fast under the edge of the silver ocean when I reach Malibu. Halfway down Blue Water Street there is a high hedge growing along a chain-link fence. I follow it and turn left into a dirt drive. On the right in the middle of an open field are a guardhouse and a dog. Lined up along the fence on the left are ancient, disabled cars: one a green-and-white ambulance with pointed fins, another a battered white trailer with no wheels. A gate hidden in the fence opens, and Bob Dylan's assistant, Carol, asks me to follow her. We walk past a vegetable garden. Dozens of chickens are scratching and pecking in the yard. A Mexican man feeding the chickens smiles at us. Dogs run around and bark. We take a path to a cabin some distance from the main house, which fades into twilight.

The walls, floors, and ceilings of the cabin are made of dark wood. There is a blaze a foot high in the corner fireplace. A stereo is sitting on a cardboard box by the door. There are a couple of couches and a coffee table with a bouquet of pink peonies on it. A room on the right is completely bare. There is a kitchen on the left. A wooden stairway leads to what must be a sleeping loft upstairs. I look out a window and see a brick patio with a Jacuzzi. Feeble light comes from a lantern near the fire. I sit down, and Carol brings in coffee and a plate of chocolate finger wafers. She says, "I'll go get Bob."

Dylan stands in the shadows of the doorway for half a second. It is chilly, but he is wearing light blue cotton shorts, almost like men's boxer shorts, and a Hawaiian-style blue short-sleeved shirt that is open to the waist. He has a pair of blue thongs on his feet. He gets a cup of coffee and sits next to me on the couch. He has a pack of Kool cigarettes in his chest pocket and smokes maybe five or six while we talk. His fingernails are all very long and pointed. It looks as if he files them to keep the points. His hair is curly and brown and reaches almost to his shoulders. He has stubble on his face. There are bags under his eyes, a diamond stud in his left ear. He doesn't smile, but he laughs a few times. He seems slightly harassed or tired and he keeps rubbing his eyes and running his fingers through his hair and pulling it. Once or twice he leans his head on his arm against the couch. While he sits he sometimes pulls his bare legs underneath him.

He seems oblivious to his surroundings. It is cold and dark, and grows darker as the fire dies out. Once Dylan gets up to put on another log. It burns quickly, and finally we are sitting in near total darkness. I can't see my notes except where I have highlighted them in pink, yellow, orange, and green fluorescent marker. Outside the door, dogs bay without stop. We talk about *Biograph*, the unprecedented five-record retrospective of his career just released by Columbia Records; we talk about a few other things. Dylan, forty-four, is intense but vague about all details. There are long, aching pauses in the conversation when he considers his thoughts. He cannot be hurried. He is rambling and repetitive but then speaks a word or phrase that stuns, that conjures truth. As he talks I get the sense of waves slapping the side of a boat, or of many rings circling a planet.

Biograph

"It wasn't my idea to put the record out. This record had been suggested in the past, but I guess it just didn't come together until recently. I think it's been in the works for like three years. I had very little to do with it. I didn't choose the songs. A lot of people probably had a hand in it. The record company has the right to do whatever they please with the songs. I didn't care about what was on the record. I haven't sat down and listened to it. I don't know why. I guess I just never did. Even when I make a record, I listen to it once or twice before it's out, and then once it's out, I don't really listen to it anymore. I'm always doing my current record. Last year's record is sort of in the past. I didn't really take a hand in this because my enthusiasm for making records might not be what it was twenty years ago. I don't know."

"This silence of tongues it was building"

"This five-record set could have been all unreleased songs. If it was worth my while, I could put together a ten-record set of unreleased songs of mine, songs that have never gotten out and songs that have been bootlegged. Some of those unreleased songs I have, some I have in fragments. I have a lot of the stuff in different places, just cassettes we made here and there. I would have to call some people, I guess, and say, 'What have you got that I can't remember?' Yeah, I've got songs I can't remember. Everybody's got songs they can't remember. I'm the final judge of what goes on and off my records. This last record I just did, *Empire Burlesque*, there were nine songs I knew belonged on it, and I needed a tenth. I had about four songs, and one of those was going to be the tenth song. I finally figured out that the tenth song needed to be acoustic, so I just wrote it. I wrote it because none of the other songs fit that spot, that certain place. So now what would happen to those four songs? One of them really didn't get finished, the others just got left. When I go back in the studio next time, I'll look at all that stuff. I'll sort through it. It's on twenty-four-track tape somewhere."

"Robbed my boots and I was on the street again"

"Yeah, a lot of my stuff has been bootlegged. What can you do, you know? If you don't want some stuff to be bootlegged or if you want to save it or if it's something that you're working on, you just won't show it to anybody. It bugs me when the stuff I've never finished is bootlegged. I don't know. There was one kid who showed me a record that he got on me of stuff that I was working on. I don't know why anybody would really go out of their way to want something like that. It interrupts your natural working habits. I mean, if there is something you would like to do with some tune and you see that it's already out there, it can get discouraging. Some of the stuff hasn't gotten out, but most of it does. I'm always real surprised that it does. I think it happens to most everybody. The *Basement Tapes*, they were bootlegged. I didn't pay much attention to the *Basement Tapes*. I thought they were what they were—a bunch of guys hanging out down in the basement making up songs. I never really cared much for bootlegged tapes of concert shows because usually the sound quality is so bad that a lot of what really goes on, the excitement of it all, really gets lost. I don't listen to the bootlegged stuff. I really don't have any feeling about it one way or another. There's nothing you can do about it. Bootlegging is a big business. It's like the dope business—it's supposed to be illegal, but a lot of people make their livelihood off it."

"Got to play your harp until your lips bleed"

"Years ago I didn't spend much time recording. I was putting a lot of pressure on myself to do it right and fast then, because of the confinement of the studio. But nobody else works that way. Now technology has made it kind of difficult to work that way. You have to fill up the space on a record now because the space has a noise of its own, whereas before, when you were working on a four-track or an eight-track, the space was something that had a spontaneity and a life of its own. Now it doesn't. It's just dead space. So therefore you have to fill up the sppace. People's ears have become accustomed to hearing every space filled up, and they're throwing everything in. More is there to make you think less. If you hear a song now with space in it, it doesn't sound right, it doesn't sound quite as together as something that's got multilayers of sound and multi-rhythms. To me, the machinery is making sound the thing, not the song. I'm trying to find a balance. You know the old Sun Records, the way they would sound with just the upright bass and a guitar and a snare drum? That's the sound I love the best, just that simple sound. My sound is basically backbeat and Stratocaster guitar or an old Martin guitar. But you can't record that way anymore. It won't sound the same. It will sound sterilized. You have to work within the sterilization of the industry. Anything raw you put in, it's going to come out sterilized. My thing is playing live, but that's even been affected because a lot of groups, they don't play live. They use a lot of preprogrammed stuff to make things sound like they do on records. It's not really too uncommon to be thinking that in a few years when you go hear a live band, that won't sound right either because people's ears will be so programmed to be hearing what they're hearing on records. I don't use synthesizers. I know I could if I was taught how, and put some time into just working the machines. But playing with a synthesizer is not really as much fun as playing with an instrument. I guess those machines are for people who are more inclined to be visionaries, who imagine something and work it out. As opposed to people who carry it around with them. That's what I do."

"Come around you rovin' gamblers and a story I will tell"

"I go through different periods when I'll write a bunch of things, then go through long spells where I don't really write anything. I just jot down little phrases and things I overhear, people talking to me, stuff like that. I write them on paper, write them out with my hand. Usually when I have some kind of deadline pressure I'll get prolific. When I do work, I work for long periods of time, then I lay back for a minute. I'll work for, like, twenty-four or thirty hours, fourteen hours at a time, and then readjust after that. Then I do it again four or five days later. I write a bunch of different ways. Sometimes I'll be able to hear the melody and everything right in my head, sometimes I'll play on the guitar or piano or something, and some kind of thing will come. Other times I'll just go into the studio and play riffs with other people and then later on listen to the tapes and see what that wants to be. Sometimes the words and music come together. Other times the melody will come first, or the words. You might write a song because you feel a certain way about a certain thing, like the Sun City record—Steve Van Zandt felt a certain way, so he wrote a song. I've done that, and then I've done the other way where the song is not really about any certain thing but it all seems to be focused in on a feeling. As I go on, I find it harder to hold on and develop a certain idea. You have to be almost a monk to hold on to something and explore all the possibilities of it. I haven't really done that as much as maybe I should or I could. When I play live, I always find stuff in my songs that I could have done a little better, could have written a little better. I don't know. It's not for me to understand my songs. I don't need to understand them. I don't make that a part of it. They make sense to me, but it's not like I can explain them. I mean, while I am doing them I have an understanding of them, but that's all, you know."

"And in comes Romeo, he's moaning"

"What voice I have, what little voice I have—I don't really have a good voice. I do most of my stuff with phrasing. I think of myself as just having an edge when it comes to phrasing. I guess my voice sounds pretty close to a coyote or something."

"Idiot Wind"

"What is that, rock? I don't like rock, just plain rock. I don't know what rock is. Is that Twisted Sister? I don't know what that is, rock. I hear people talking about it all the time. I like rock and roll; now that's a different thing. Rock is hard; that don't mean nothing to me. But rolling is smooth and easy. A lot of the roll is gone from the music I hear, sure it is. Look at the buildings you see every day. They're huge, towering skyscrapers. Concrete and steel. Massive coliseums is where they play rock. It's the environment, right? Hard rock. Things got to have roots. There are still roots, but they're only there on record. It's like people studying literature. Who do they read? They read Shakespeare. Literature must have been at a high level when Shakespeare was writing his plays. You can't say that today if you go and see a play. It's going to be very far down the line from Shakespeare. The same way with rock 'n' roll, rhythm and blues, and all that. We're living in a time where you can still feel it. It might be remote, but you can still feel it, whereas fifty or sixty years from now, it's only going to be a dream. How many radio stations play Howlin' Wolf or Jimmy Reed or Muddy Waters? Most young black guys don't even know who those people are."

"Too much of nothing"

"There's no way you can listen to the radio now and think that all those songs are on because of the music. Something else is putting them on the radio. It's not because the songs or the music is so good. It's something else entirely. I don't much listen to radio. Every time I hear it, it's depressing. Most of the stuff isn't meant to be heard by someone who is in anything but an up mood. I'm not in an up mood most of the time, or half the time. My moods vary. The stuff you hear on the radio would make it seem like everything's all right everywhere. You really have to seek your salvation in some other place than the popular radio. It used to be you could hear in the different parts of the country different types of music. I don't remember when this was, maybe in the sixties. Wherever you went, you would hear different music that was popular in different regions. What was popular in Los Angeles was different than what was popular in New York. There would be different music playing in Nashville than in Austin or Seattle or Chicago. Now, wherever you go, it's the same. If it's the Top 10 in New York, it's the Top 10 in Miami. Why do you suppose that is?"

"Something is happening here but you don't know what it is, do you Mister Jones?"

"I have never cared whether critics liked or disliked my albums, but I have cared that they didn't understand where they were coming from or what I was up to. I can truly say that there have been a lot of critics who have listened to my stuff, and they have been just deaf. They haven't really heard what the heart of the matter is. They haven't heard what was there to be heard. All they heard were preconceived ideas of their own, which they brought to whatever record of mine they were listening to. I haven't understood the critics' evaluation of my stuff. It's deeper than 'He's trying to do this' or 'He's trying to do that' or 'He's not succeeding at this' or 'There's none of this.' Critics reviewed the movie *Renaldo and Clara* saying that was an ego trip, whereas, what is an ego trip? Bob Dylan up on the screen is an ego trip? Who made Bob Dylan a myth, anyway? Isn't *Scarface* an ego trip? What's not an ego trip if you make a movie? I don't know. The criticism of the movie was not about the movie. It was about what the movie could have been or should have been or something like that. That carries over to my records. Some intellectual critics who want to see things keep evolving, who want to feel the same kick at forty-five or fifty that they felt when they were fifteen and sixteen, a lot of those intellectual people, they stand in my way."

"'Twas in another lifetime"

"My first five albums? I don't even know what the first five were. I don't know if I could name all twenty-nine of my records, but I could name some of them. I liked a bunch of albums I did in the eighties. I liked *Street Legal* a whole lot. I did that in the seventies. I liked all the albums, sort of, I guess. There's always something on all the records I liked. When you make them, you like them. My favorite songs of all time aren't anything I've written. I like stuff like 'Pastures of Plenty' and 'Mississippi Mama and Me' and 'That's All' and 'I Get a Kick Out of You.' My favorites are old forties songs, I think."

"Ezra Pound and T. S. Eliot fighting in the captain's tower"

"At certain times I read a lot of poetry. My favorite poets are Shelley and Keats. Rimbaud is so identifiable. Lord Byron. I don't know. Lately if I read poems, it's like I can always hear the guitar. Even with Shakespeare's sonnets I can hear a melody because it's all broken up into timed phrases so I hear it. I always keep thinking, 'What kind of song would this be?'"

"Jokerman"

"There's some humor in my songs. I don't know, I think so. Some other people might not get it. I think there are funny things inside a lot of them. Some there aren't. It's kind of mixed up so much that I wouldn't be one to just point and say, 'This is funny.' Some of these things are just foggy, some of these things I just don't have a fix on. I'm not really a good authority on my stuff. I'm a better authority maybe on Woody Guthrie's stuff than I am on my own stuff."

"Tomorrow is a long time"

"For me the sixties seem just like yesterday. Time has a strange way of eluding you, you know. I mean, spiritually there is no time. There's no sixties, no eighties. When we say the sixties or the seventies or the forties, I don't know, we can't touch that. What are the sixties? We can't reach out and touch it any more than we can touch the nineties or the 1800s. I'm not so overwhelmed by sixties, seventies, fifties. It seems, though, that at a certain time there was more to discover all the time. It doesn't seem that way now. Kids grow up real fast. I've got kids. They grew up fast, faster than I grew up. A hundred years ago they grew up even slower. You ate by candlelight then, you know what I mean? All the comforts are real deceiving as to what life's all about. All the crutches. Society, you know. Western civilization."

"The truth was obscure, too profound and too pure, to live it you have to explode"

"I don't think each person has his own individual truth. How could you have your own personal truth? Who would give it to you? If you had it, why would you have to go to school? Why would you have to get a job? If you had your own personal truth, even truth you think you might know, whose truth is it? Is it your truth? Did you make it up? What's inside is just confusion. But what's inside has been put inside, you know. Whatever culture you're in, that puts it inside. So when you're searching inside for something and you say, 'Well, I have my own thing inside,' well, that's been put inside by cultural forces. They just bombard you. It's an all-out attack to stick stuff into your brain."

"You were born with a snake in both of your fists while a hurricane was blowing"

"Well, people tell me about the myth, you know. Some people are in awe. It doesn't penetrate me for some reason. I wish it did because then I might be able to use it to some advantage. I mean, there must be some advantage to it. I haven't been able to figure out what it is as of yet. [He laughs.] I don't really think too much on myself, you know. It's a waste of time for me to think like that. Oh, I don't know where I fit in now. God, life is short enough without having to dwell on how you fit in. The best you can do is just survive through it."

"And muttered underneath his breath, 'Nothing is revealed'"

"Prophet. I might be that. [He laughs.] I still might be. You never know anything for certain, especially something like that. But when you think back to certain events, there's a possibility they may be true. Or you may just think they're true. Who really knows?"

"Oh, Mama, can this really be the end"

"I've never felt that it was over for me in music today. I still feel like I've got more to do. As long as I can do it live on stage, I'll still be doing it, and as long as I'm performing live, making records just goes with that. A while back I started writing a novel called *Ho Chi Minh in Harlem*. He was a short-order cook there in the twenties before he went back to Vietnam—it's a documented fact. It excited me there for a minute. It's possible I'll finish it if I get dedicated to it and decide that this is something that really needs to be done, or I need to do this. I did this song with Sam Shepard last year. It was called "Danville Girl." A long ballad, about fifteen minutes. I heard some people talking about making a movie out of that. I'd like to write some short stories, but I'd have to go to a log cabin in the mountains somewhere and say, 'This is what I'm going to do.' I will do an album of standards. I think I'm going to try to do that with Richard Perry. We were talking about that. I don't know what's going to be on it, but I will do one. I've always wanted to do a children's album too. But how would they release it?"

"He not busy being born is busy dying"

"I don't want to talk about what I've become or became because that sets people off into role playing. You can't lead people by role playing, and you can only muddle things up. So, whatever it is that I am manifests itself through what I do, what I say, not by what title I want to put on myself, or other people may want to put on me. That's why I've stayed away from all that stuff all the time. I mean, I know you can call somebody something like 'born again' and then you can dismiss that. As long as you can deal with it on a level of, like, a cartoon, you can dismiss it."

"Preacherman seeks the same, who'll get there first is uncertain"

"I've always played the guitar and sung and wrote songs. That's all I'll ever do unless there comes a time when I decided not to do it anymore and started to preach or something. But even preaching would be an extension of what I am and what I do and the music I play. People who don't play the music, who don't know what it feels like, they tend to overintellectualize what I do. They overestimate the lyrics in my songs. My stuff has always been lyrics and guitar, strumming, always. I mean, I would not make a good street poet. You put me on the stage without a guitar and I probably would hide. I feel uncomfortable in front of people without my guitar. What people have never understood is that the words were important because no one else was doing it and I broke through and I did it, but there wouldn't be the songs or the words without the guitar. To me, the guitar has always been just as important, if not more important, than the words. You see my lyrics printed in books, and to me they look silly. They don't really have the same effect because they're meant to be sung or recited in an odd kind of way. People put on a record and take out the lyrics and say, 'What's he saying?' and they kind of listen to what is being said, as if it's being spoken to them. They're waiting to hear some voice to put everything in perspective for them. Everything's not going to be put in perspective for them.

"People who have lived through the fifties and the sixties and the seventies and who now are living in the eighties, they're downright insane if they were to take all those periods seriously. There's none of them you can hang on to. People who are living in the eighties are living a different life-style than they were living in the forties and the fifties and the sixties. But there are some people who don't get changed by the times. They can be living in any kind of time period, and I'm one of those people because everything gets filtered through me, and it gets filtered into the music I play. I was the same twenty, thirty years ago that I am now. My values haven't changed. Sure I've gone through lots of different things and I've learned a lot and my life isn't what it was. My life is different all the time, but my values haven't changed. There comes a time and a place for me to tell people what I've experienced or what I've learned. If I clarify it for me, and that's what I do in the songs in some kind of way, that's all I can do. I don't judge myself and I don't really judge others. I don't watch or look at what's happening, I just take it or leave it.

"When you get high and then your bubble busts and you get down low again, lower than you were when you started, you have to have values. You have to know what the great big picture is, how it operates, and it has to be busted down in simple terms because sooner or later everybody gets to that point, and that's what makes people confused. There's too much everything, too much traffic, too much food in the super-market, too many clothes, too many this, too much that. And there's going to be more and more of it. But I've never been caught up in that, it doesn't do anything for me. I have to make things, I have to do things. The only thing I get a kick out of is playing or performing or some kind of artistic thing. That's just the way I always have been. I don't get a kick out of nothing else. But that's okay because throughout history it's been one big mass spectator sport. I don't know. Am I making any sense? When you write a song, you always work with common things, clichés, that everybody can identify with. If you're working with something like that, then most people can understand. You always have to be in that area where everyone knows what you're talking about. But from that point you can use it how you see fit and go as deep or as shallow as you either choose to or have the talent to. The deeper you go, the fewer people who are going to go with you. There's nothing you can do about that, because in the end it's not up to you to know who you're supposed to reach. It might be one person. You know, it's true, that old saying, 'Leave all and follow me.' And it's a point not too many people can ever allow themselves to get to because they're too busy hanging out. Unless somebody has experienced that, even for a minute, you're stuck in the flesh. So everything revolves around that, what feels good, what tastes good, what looks good, what smells good. I mean, it's all like the last meal down on executioner's row. Striped candy or something."

"Blowin' in the wind"

"In life, well, I mean, I feel like I fall short in just about everything. In music I can do just about what I need to do. I feel pretty calm most of the time, but then if I review my situation at all, it always seems like I'm up there walking the plank. I'm probably a driven person. I always feel like somebody's cracking the whip. Somebody or something. It's just mostly because so many things happen in my life and they're all going at the same time, but I don't know how else to live my life. I never felt like I was searching for anything. I always felt that I've stumbled into things or drifted into them. But I've never felt like I was out on some kind of prospector hunt looking for the answers or the truth. You won't find that in any of my songs. I never went to the holy mountain to find the lost soul that is supposed to be a part of me or whatever I am. I don't believe in that stuff, and I don't feel like a person has to search for anything. I feel like it's all right in front."

It is utterly dark now. Carol knocks on the door to retrieve Bob. But first he picks up a flashlight and, as he walks me to my car, says, "I wish I could say something exciting or preposterous." I ask him about the property, and he says something vague like, "There are a bunch of houses here." He tells me, "You can call me a couple of months from now or next year or if you ever need to reach me for anything. If you ever need a quote or anything. If something's happening." Then he says good-bye. Before I can turn on my headlights, the gate in the hedge is closed.

November 1985

Under the pseudonym "Lucky Wilbury," Dylan harmonized with George Harrison, Roy Orbison, Jeff Lynne, and Tom Petty on the record Traveling Wilburys. *Dylan can be heard singing on* Folkways: A Vision Shared, *an album of Woody Guthrie and Leadbelly standards, performed by musicians as diverse as Bruce Springsteen, Brian Wilson, Little Richard, Willie Nelson, and U2. Dylan and the Smithsonian Institution came up with the idea of a commemorative record to generate royalties for sub-sidizing Folkways Records, a historic label with deep folk roots. Since* Biograph, *Dylan has released* Real Live, Knocked Out Cold, *and* Down in the Groove.

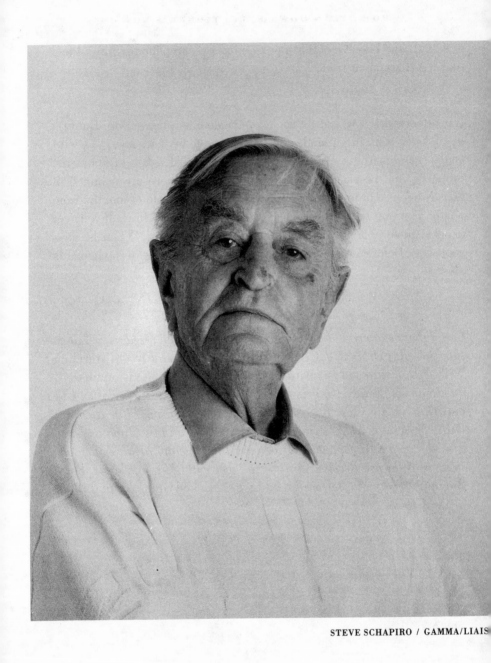

DAVID LEAN ON THE FAR HORIZON

*O*ne day during the hectic shooting of *A Passage to India*, David Lean stopped and stood for a moment on a hilltop, admiring the sweep of the spectacular Indian countryside. A member of the crew scurried up behind him to ask a question and waited to be acknowledged. "Isn't it beautiful?" Lean wondered aloud. The man confessed he had been away from home for too long, was sick of Indian scenery, and wanted to get back to England. "Then," Lean said, "get your ticket and go. If that's what you want, you should work in a factory."

Voyager to distant lands and the movies' great poet of the far horizon, David Lean, the master British filmmaker who directed *Brief Encounter* (1945), *Great Expectations* (1946), *Oliver Twist* (1948), *The Bridge on the River Kwai* (1957), *Lawrence of Arabia* (1962), *Doctor Zhivago* (1965), and *Ryan's Daughter* (1970), has made his first film in fourteen years, an adaptation of E. M. Forster's classic novel *A Passage to India*. "I think people who make movies," Lean says, "are in a very privileged position. It's the only new art form—since what? It's wonderful. It takes us all over the world, and we see fascinating places and meet fascinating people and have one hell of a time. We are very lucky doing what we do. Once I asked Alexander Korda why he didn't direct more films. He said that for him it was like going down the mine. What he meant was, when you go on a studio stage, the big doors are shut behind you. There's no mine about jungles and deserts. It's a great privilege, making films. I've seen places and sights that no tourist would ever see. I always think, wherever we are, of all the people who work in white boxes every day of their lives. I'm jolly lucky. If there hadn't been film, I don't know what I would have done. I think I would have been a pretty good failure. I love movies. And I never thought I would have the luck to go into them. They were in the dream department. I think they still are."

Sir David—the director was knighted this year—is seventy-six, but nothing about him, except his hands, betrays his age. His hands are ancient, huge, gnarled with veins, and dark brown. They bring to mind Forster's description of the Marabar Caves: "Fists and fingers thrust above the advancing soil." There is a birthmark under his left eye that has faded into a smudge on his sun-dried face. His hair is silver and cut meticulously around his ears. His eyes, blue-gray, do not waver as they take your measure. "He has eyes like the sea on a cold day," an actress said a long time ago, adding, "but not the Mediterranean." He is handsome, startlingly so, with the look of one who could be the last of some warrior race. Lean groans that he has gained thirty pounds while editing *A Passage to India,* but nevertheless he looks fit and trim. He habitually wears black pants with creases like folded paper, black socks, and plain black shoes, a navy cardigan sweater with maroon trim on the pockets and down the front, a starched light blue or white shirt buttoned all the way to the collar, no tie.

The entire time we talk in his suite at the Bel-Air Hotel in Los Angeles, he is slightly distracted, as if thousands of feet of film from *A*

Passage to India were unrolling in his head. One can't resist the feeling that there is a lot of Forster's Mrs. Moore in him. Underneath an almost majestic presence, he is cranky, and one can well imagine him saying, as Mrs. Moore does, "And I held up from my business over such trifles!" He is very reluctant to speak of his personal life or past. Several times he says, "I don't want to talk about those personal things." He begins to reminisce about his lifelong travels only when a large atlas of the world is spread out on the table in front of him. He touches it and his eyes warm. He traces a path with his finger from city to city, continent to continent, and names all the places he has ever seen.

"I have been through the Panama Canal twice, I've been to New Zealand, all around French Polynesia, the Cook Islands, Tahiti, the Tuamotu Archipelago. I've sat on top of Mount Cook in a helicopter. I've been to Uruguay, Argentina, South Africa, Morocco, Egypt several times (marvelous place), Jordan, Ceylon, all over India, Bali, Indonesia, the Fiji Islands, Singapore, Hong Kong, Spain, Finland, Italy, France, Yugoslavia, all over Europe. I've lived in Los Angeles and New York, been to Jamaica on holiday. My wife and I have a house in Rome. I love it. We remodeled it and made a lovely garden. We put a lot of love into it. We haven't been there for several years now. Lately, with the kidnapping in Rome—it's very frightening—I might be a good one to have my wife captured. I wouldn't trust it, so we haven't been back. But I haven't got the heart to give it up. We lived for three years in Tahiti in a hotel, I've forgotten the name of it. We had a sitting room, a bedroom, and the sitting room next door, which we turned into a kitchen, and a dining room with a terrace. We had two Boston whalers docked in French Polynesia, one of them in Bora Bora and one in Rangiroa, which is my favorite place in the world. It is an island an hour's flight from Tahiti on the atolls. There is a little lagoon fifty miles long and twenty-five miles across. Wonderful place. I lived in the Grand Hotel in Venice for years. Altogether I suppose I've lived in Kenya for about a year. We fly around game parks there, don't hunt, take photographs only.

"I like to travel by boat, I love big ocean liners, any kind of boat, really. I rather like watching the sea go by. Driving is a different thing. I always try to drive my own car when I'm making a film, because all day one is absolutely surrounded by people, and when I get in that car, I'm on my own. I have time to think, and I just get a kick out of driving. I like a good car. I used to take my Rolls-Royce everywhere. I still have a twenty-year-old Rolls-Royce now. It's in England. It's equipped with left-side steering. I never drove it in England, just on the Continent. I wouldn't have a phone in a car if somebody gave it to me as a present. That would be the last thing I'd want. What a horrible idea, isn't it, that you can't even escape in a car.

"I've lived in hotels all over the world. I still don't have many clothes. I sort of traveled in a car and put my clothes in a case and left the case in the car and wandered around. I've always traveled quite light. I think that there are various things that I've left all over the world and forgotten about. I don't even know what they are. It happens. Only six months ago I realized that I'd lost an overcoat and I could not think where it was. I went out and bought a new one. I know it's in some hotel somewhere. That sort of thing. Various radios I've lost, I suppose. I always carried radios with me whenever I went out in the wilds. I always tuned into the BBC Overseas Services to hear the news.

"I travel so much because it gives me such an enormous kick. I owe it to my father, really. One of the great things he did was he took my brother and me abroad a lot when we were on holiday from school in the summertime. We went on ships. We went down to the south of France. I'll never forget the first time I saw the Mediterranean. I gradually realized that there was another world out there when I had always thought that London was the last word. I'm always absolutely fascinated going to strange places, seeing strange trees. The other day, walking up to this hotel, I saw ferns that gave me a little kick of excitement. Of course I've seen them growing naturally in New Zealand. But just seeing strange, exotic plants gives me a kick. It's different from the London suburbs, and so were the movies.

"I was traveling and working on films most of the time, really, and I didn't have a home. I lived in hotels and wherever the films took me. *The Bridge on the River Kwai* was the first time I really went out and smelled blood. We worked in the jungles of Ceylon. We built a bridge with elephants. The elephants used to tug the timber down the hillside when it was cut and push it into the river. I just enjoyed doing it, and the movie came off. The lucky thing was I made some money out of it. They all thought it wasn't going to be a success. Then the money came and I got some of it. I loved being out in the jungle. It was wonderful.

"I think probably the greatest film experience I had was *Lawrence of Arabia*. I lived in a trailer with the wheels taken off on top of a Mercedes truck. The trucks were tough trucks. I was right out there in the desert. We lived in one place—I think it may have been in Saudi Arabia—but nobody quite knew. We had a small airplane and we used to go out on reconnaissance flights to look for locations and we'd land on mud flats, dried mud flats. Those first scenes when Lawrence went out into the desert, when he first sees it, we wanted something very big and broad. We had to bring water in by tanker from two hundred miles away— incredible. It was as distant as that. We lived very well. Couldn't do it now, I'm sure. Everybody would think it was mad. It was wonderful. God knows I wouldn't like to live there forever, but I lived there for a year. Marvelous experience. I remember saying out there, I'm not surprised that most of the great religious leaders came from the deserts. Because you feel terribly small, and also, in a strange way, quite big. This vastness, a sort of pitilessness combined with enormous beauty."

Lean's sixteen films in forty-two years have earned forty-five Oscar nominations, including six for his direction (he won two, for *Kwai* and *Lawrence*), but *Ryan's Daughter,* Lean's last film, created so ugly a critical outburst after its release in 1970 that he fled the movie business. "I didn't want to make a film then, really," Lean says. "Partly for lack of subject, but I had such terrible notices that I really lost heart. I can't remember the last time I got a good notice. *Ryan's Daughter* got the most appalling notices. I don't think it's as bad a film as the critics said it was. I'm still quite proud of the storm sequence in it. It is frightfully hard shooting a picture in Ireland because the weather is changing every ten minutes, literally. I did make a big mistake on the movie, though. I photographed it in two different styles: a very ordinary sort of photography; then when Rosy got an obsession about this young chap, I went into wildly romantic photography with cumulus clouds and I made everything very lush. Unfortunately I failed to say so. I should have had the priest say, 'Now look, Rosy, pull yourself together, you're seeing this through rose-colored glasses.' And it would have worked. It's one of the fatal errors you can make. Everybody pounced on me for making an absurdly romantic picture. I didn't mean it that way. I meant that when you are in that state, to put it cornily, you are seeing things through rose-colored glasses. Nobody got it. And nobody got the fact that it was based on *Madame Bovary.*

"The notices for *Doctor Zhivago* were dreadful. That's when I caught the first real packet from the critics. But the notices for *Lawrence of Arabia* had started to be dreadful. I remember after *Lawrence* there was, mercifully, a newspaper strike in New York, but unfortunately *New York Times* critic Bosley Crowther got on the radio and, I'll never forget, started his review with: 'The film is as devoid of humanity as the desert sands it portrays.' And I remember a critic at one of the big Sunday papers in London headed her article with 'Two-and-a-half Pillars of Wisdom.' *Newsweek* reviewed *Doctor Zhivago* saying it had 'cheapjack sets' and 'pallid photography.' Both those things are completely untrue. After the premiere of *Doctor Zhivago* at a dinner in a big hotel in New York, the room was like a morgue, with everybody reading these terrible notices. Then I went to the London premiere, hoping the notices there would be better than the American ones. They weren't. They were worse, even worse. Then—I'll never forget this—I put my car on a transport plane to fly across the Channel to France. I put my passport down on the counter, and the Automobile Association man looked at the name and he said, 'Mr. Lean, I'm so sorry, what happened?' I said, 'What do you mean?' And he said, 'I've always liked your films, what happened?' And I realized of course that he had read some newspaper critics, and I said, 'I really don't know. Go and see it. You might like it.' I left England. That was it. Thanks to the head of MGM, who put more money in advertising for *Doctor Zhivago* and kept it in one or two theaters, receipts started to climb after word of mouth started. In the end, of course, it made more money than all my other films. [It has brought in more than $200 million worldwide at the box office.]

"Then, after *Ryan's Daughter*, this New York Critics Circle asked me around to the Algonquin Hotel. It was a Sunday night. The restaurant was closed to the public, and we sat at a long table, maybe a dozen critics, in this vast, empty, darkened dining room. It was rather like the setting in *Citizen Kane*. The critics started firing questions at me. One of them led off with, 'Can you please explain to us how the man who directed *Brief Encounter* can produce this sort of rubbish?' And then Pauline Kael said to me, 'Are you trying to tell us that Robert Mitchum is a lousy lay?' And it went on from there. It lasted about two hours, and I thought, 'Why in the hell am I making films? What's the point?'

"I didn't have the feeling, not at all, that I'd lost my touch. You don't feel that, really. But the critics are the intellectuals. I'm always frightened of intellectuals. I don't know, I think one tends to take the critics too seriously. I suppose we're all terribly sensitive about critics. Because you can't, as it were, meet the general public, and if your mother or aunt tells you the movie is great, you say, 'Yes, very sweet of you, but you would.' The only people who really don't give a damn who are out there giving their opinions are the critics. They are the only people, as it were, you can believe. You read it there in black and white and think it must be true. I don't know about this country, but in England they're not mad about success. If a film goes, really goes, with a big public, the critics are very wary of it. I think they say, 'Well, that's just a circus.' Well, we are sort of a circus, the movies. I think we provide everything, don't we? From Slim Pamphlets to Barnum and Bailey, and I think that's good. But the critics hurt me enough to make me not want to do any more films. I had plenty of money, and I thought, 'Well, I won't do anything for a bit. I might do something one day.' And I just went off.

"For three years during that time—1978 to 1980, I guess—I was living in Tahiti working on *The Bounty*. I got hooked on it, thought it was a wonderful story, the true story of the *Bounty*. Captain Bligh is a much maligned man. I think he was a terrific chap, though he had no sense of humor and wasn't a typical movie hero. Christian was a young man who just got swept away by the South Seas. Dino De Laurentiis was going to produce. We were going to make two films, which I still think would have been a good idea: the first part ends with the fantastic voyage of Captain Bligh in the open boat across the Pacific to Australia; the second part was the search by a terrible man called Captain Edwards for Christian and his men. Robert Bolt and I were writing the scripts in Tahiti. We actually had built a full-scale replica of the *Bounty* in Tahiti from the original designs. It looked lovely.

"Then Dino came out, and I don't know what the full reason was, but he said he hadn't got the money to make it. He said the whole thing would cost $50 million, and he backed out because he said that was too expensive. It broke my heart because I think they were the best scripts I've ever had. Dino De Laurentiis gave me some weeks, I've forgotten how long, to sell it to somebody else. I gave up every penny that was due to me, taking a chance on getting it going again. I couldn't get it going with anybody else. They were all scared. And when one person becomes scared, you're cooked. There were all these stories going around about me at the time because of *Ryan's Daughter*, saying I would wait three weeks for a cloud and then it became I would wait three weeks for a wave. In the end, poor Robert Bolt was struck by open-heart surgery and then a stroke. I turned the two scripts into one, and still I couldn't sell it. I regret *The Bounty* terribly because I think it could have been a very, very good film. It's a terrible thing to work on something for all that time very, very closely and then have it taken from you and read in the paper that you walked away from it. I think *The Bounty* is the biggest regret of my whole career. I wish I'd never met Dino De Laurentiis or any of that lot who made the film *The Bounty* that came out earlier this year. I haven't seen that.

"I don't understand, really, why I didn't make a film for fourteen years, and I don't know really what I did during that time. It wasn't a harrowing experience, though I missed making movies. I probably went to Africa. I'm always going to Africa. I had a very good time. I love taking pictures. I take hundreds of still photographs. I have a sixteen-millimeter camera that I adore, so I've got thousands of feet of film I haven't yet edited. It gives me great fun taking pictures. I had a good time, I went all over. I saw a lot of places." Although Lean shrugs off questions about depression during this long period in his life when he wasn't making movies, his friend and colleague Maurice Jarre, who has composed the music for every Lean film since *Lawrence of Arabia*, says, "I saw David during the time when he was not working and something inside of him had died. Then, when he was making *A Passage to India*, he became younger and more dynamic and he had back a very sparkling light in his eye."

Lean says, "I started thinking of doing *Out of Africa*, based on the book by Isak Dinesen. I was sort of toying with it and wondering how to do it, and then this phone call came about *A Passage to India*. It was just over three years ago when Lord John Brabourne, who works with another producer, Richard Goodwin, called me. I had only met him once. He rang me up in a hotel in London and said, 'Look, I'd very much like to come and have a talk with you.' And I said, 'What's it about?' And he said, 'Well, it's just a subject. Could I come, then, to talk with you?' And I said, 'What happened in the caves?' And he nearly dropped the phone. I'd heard a rumor that he'd bought *A Passage to India*. He came to see me and said, 'I'd very much like for you to do it.' And I said, 'I'll do it.' And he said, 'Don't you want to read it again?'

"I got a Penguin copy and read the book a lot. I underlined in ballpoint pen everything I thought would be good in the film. And I had a notebook, and every time I got an idea of how to put the book into film terms, I wrote it down. What I do is I sit down and I write down what I'm imagining I'm seeing on the screen. I'll write, 'Scene 42: Long shot of so-and-so.' Then if I think it will be very effective to go to a socking big close-up, I'll write that down, 'Scene 43: Big close-up—Adela.' I really sort of see it oblong and try to write it down on paper. I wrote the script for *Passage* in a room at the Maurya Sheraton Hotel in New Delhi. I couldn't stay in New Delhi for more than six months or I'd be caught with Indian income tax, which is hefty. So I wrote and moved out just before six months. I went to the Dolder Grand Hotel in Zurich and spent about three months there, finishing it. I wrote the whole script in my own handwriting and then typed it out. Then my wife typed it properly. She went to an American missionary school in India in the Himalayas and learned typing as part of her course, which no English school would ever do, of course—far too practical. I always write my scripts out in longhand and I type them. I only type with two fingers, which is a huge advantage because it slows you up and you get to know every word and examine everything more carefully than if you just rattle it off.

"About twenty-five years ago I saw the play *A Passage to India* in London, and at the time I wanted to buy the rights and make it into a film. Forster was alive and living in Cambridge. Forster didn't trust the movies. I don't blame him. He said, 'No. I don't want to let the movies have it because I think they'll either come down on the side of the English or on the side of the Indians and I'd like a balance to be struck.' The truth is he didn't strike a balance in his own novel. He was very, very pro-Indian and anti-British, and my guess is he didn't want to perpetuate that. I think he was terrified that the movie would come down on one side or the other. I think the movie is pretty well split. Mrs. Moore, Adela, and certainly Fielding, are English and completely fair-minded. I thought Forster had gone too far in saying all the Indians are angels and all the English are villains.

"Forster left the rights to the book to Cambridge, and King's College had an okay on who was chosen to be the director. After the script was finished, John Brabourne and Richard Goodwin took me to King's College—lovely-looking place. We had lunch in the dining room, and the dons were all friendly, old-looking gentlemen. Old gentlemen? Younger than me, I think, who turned out to be some of the greatest experts on English literature you could find anywhere in the world. I'm glad I didn't quite realize that at the time. We sat down and I had about two spoonfuls of soup and one of them turned to me and asked why I had done a certain thing with the script—I don't remember now exactly what—and I said, 'I wish you'd left that for the sweet.' At the end the dons said, 'Well, good luck, good luck.' As a matter of fact, they liked the script very much.

"No movie is faithful to a book. It cannot be. One of the most important things about the novel is that it has wonderful characters: Fielding, Aziz, Mrs. Moore. I've done my best, as far as I am capable, to make them true to the novel. I have shortened the narrative, picked up certain threads, and made them more important than Forster made them. I hope people find the movie true, as it were, to the book. One of the troubles with making a film from one of these great big novels is that obviously, if you made a picture of the novel to please everybody, you would end up with a film twelve to fourteen hours long. Also, it's a different medium, so I think to put a novel on the screen you've got to do it in a cinematic way. It's another language, it's a language of pictures. You've got to do it in such a way that it looks like the book but isn't.

"I think the characters are straight Forster. The biggest cheat is Ronny. In the book he is 'the red-nosed boy.' I thought, 'I don't believe it in a movie. For a girl to come out to India and make up her mind whether she is going to marry the red-nosed boy—impossible. She'd know yes or no in England.' So I cast against type. In the book Miss Quested is a bit of a stick, and I found it a little difficult to believe that that prim young woman could suddenly be attacked by Doctor Aziz in the caves. She was very much of a stick. After I saw the play and read the book, I was fascinated by what actually did happen in the caves. Did he or didn't he? I always said to myself, if I make the film, I'm going to make that one of the talking points. If a group of four people saw the film and then went out to dinner, I hoped they would start arguing and have different points of view. I wanted to prepare the audience for what happened in the caves, so that they could say, 'Yes, it could have happened.' I tried to say that she found new depths in herself. I gave Mrs. Moore lines like, 'India forces one to come face to face with oneself.'

"I added the scene of Adela bicycling through the fields and finding the ancient Indian erotic statues in the ruins of a temple. I used that scene to show her as-yet-untapped sexuality. I always imagined to myself—although nobody ever said so, Forster certainly didn't—that she was brought up in some vicarage somewhere and both parents died. She was a very repressed girl. I wanted to say she was opening out. One of my favorite places in India is a place called Khajraho. A couple of Englishmen were hunting tigers there and found themselves in the forest with a lot of undergrowth. They saw stone figures amidst the vines and soon discovered that they were erotic figures. In fact, there were more than sixteen temples covered with this erotic statuary. I've always been fascinated by that, and it gave me the idea of showing Adela in a new light. Also, I enjoyed doing that scene—I think it's a piece of cinema. It is the same sort of thing Forster introduces with Aziz, that he reads sexy magazines, that, as McBryde says, 'He is a widower living alone.' I wanted to set them both up.

"After I finished the script, this was in 1982, I gave it to John Brabourne and Richard Goodwin and they went to America to find financing. Every studio turned it down. It doesn't make any difference that my films have made millions of dollars. I hadn't made a film in fourteen years. The studios thought, 'Maybe he's lost the touch. Maybe he's forgotten how to do it. Is he strong enough?' They all kept on saying, 'What's the bottom line?' In the end I had to initial every page of my own script—130 pages—to promise that I wouldn't invent a herd of elephants or something which would cost more. It's humiliating; the money people have you over a barrel. They're just frightened people. It's one of the things about movies today. Instead of the old boys like Goldwyn, Mayer, Selznick, Cohn, who, though some were absolutely illiterate, loved movies, the new people at the top don't care about movies. I hardly meet a person now who loves films. They love money. They're all obsessed by money. They're just in it for the money, and I prophesy if they keep on like this, they will lose it all. We've got to get back people who love movies. Anyway, I thought, 'To hell with this. They'll find the money somehow or other.'"

John Brabourne and Richard Goodwin had originally written a

budget for about $14 million, only to find that it was too much for their original backer, EMI, to put up. So they went to Hollywood. Goodwin says, "We went to every major studio except MGM and Columbia, and to several of the smaller companies. The first people we went to said to us, 'We are not going to make this movie, nor will you find anyone in Hollywood who will make it.' I guess at the outset everybody thought we had a director who could easily fall into the class of 'uncontrollable.' Quite wrongly so, of course. We tried another studio, and they told us they would make the film if there was an explicit rape scene in the cave. These people meant it, they genuinely believed there should be a rape scene. And they were people who had made some wonderful films in the past. We were just so shocked and appalled, we didn't say anything. It was complete idiocy. Another studio, actually this was an English company, said that instead of Mrs. Moore meeting Aziz in the mosque, Miss Quested should. They said, 'It would be a pity to lose this wonderful romantic scene on an old dame, really.' One powerful studio chief said, 'I thought Forster had only written Captain Hornblower stories.' Somebody else said, 'Oh yes, that's a shipboard romance, isn't it?' Everybody said, 'Well, what's the bottom line? Why are you doing it? Who is it going to appeal to?' We kept saying, bleating, perhaps, 'Well, we think it will be a good film, and we think the public will respond to that.'" Goodwin and Brabourne eventually worked out a complicated deal with five partners, including Lean. "It was a legal nightmare," says Goodwin. "The stack of documents was more than fifteen inches thick. The legal fees to get the deal together added up to about $250,000. There was nobody who was able to say, 'Shut up, lawyers, just do it.'"

Meanwhile Lean was scouting locations for the movie. He says, "I bought a Mercedes station wagon, and my wife and I and Eddie Fowlie, the location manager, and his wife, all four of us, went off to India. We drove all over. We finally found a place in Bangalore next to a maharajah's palace. The grounds were tremendous, I don't know how many acres, in the middle of the city. And the place was within five miles of the big hotels. An Indian film was shooting there, and it suddenly dawned on me over twenty-four hours that here was a captive studio in the middle of the town. We shot most of the film in the maharajah's palace where we built the sets. Nearly everything in the movie is a set. Every shot in the streets, every bazaar scene. You can't work on the streets in India. The Indians are absolutely film-mad. It's their great entertainment. As soon as you bring out a camera on an Indian street, crowds, thousands of people, appear. People said to me, 'Why are you building sets? This is terribly extravagant.' But of course it is much cheaper to build a set. It's better than a real street because you can control it. It is the difference between a painting and a photograph. You can make the painting much better.

"I like Indians very much, and I think the scene where Aziz gives Fielding his collar stud is wonderful. It is so simple and very touching, and it is also typically Indian, absolutely typical, that over-the-top kindliness. Indians are very emotional. I took awful chances every now and again. In the trial scene where Aziz is in the dock saying, 'Mrs. Moore, Mrs. Moore, where are you, Mrs. Moore?' I mean, who in the hell would say that? It's terribly touching. It's the same with the extras for crowd scenes. Indian crowds are wonderful to work with. You explain to them as clearly as you can what the scene is about. They say, 'Oh yes, very good, very good, very interesting, now come along then, off we go.' And at the end of each scene after one, two, three takes, I'd say 'Print take three,' which I knew was going to be it. I would say 'Cut' and then start to clap, and they would all clap like mad, and that was the acknowledged end of the scene, you know.

"One of the great things about the book is the interplay of human beings. There are two wonderful scenes showing the two cultures: one in the mosque when Aziz meets Mrs. Moore, and the one in Aziz's house when Aziz shows Fielding the photograph of his wife. Wonderful attempt to communicate and give to another human being. I think it's terribly touching, and that's always relevant, isn't it? I don't think we human beings vary very much, do we, year to year?

"When I shoot a film, I am always trying to make a positive out of a negative I am holding in my head. It's always a compromise; very few times do you actually hit it. Forster wrote the cave sequence about a place in northern India. Richard Goodwin went to see it, and the government told him there could be no filming there because of bandits. Goodwin took pictures and made a tape of the echo. I was rather disappointed. The echo was all right, but the caves Forster wrote about were at the bottom of rocks only thirty feet high. I'd always seen on the screen in my mind caves and caves at the bottom of a cliff face. Eddie Fowlie went out on a fast reconnaissance trip near Bangalore. He found some rocks and cliffs. We went to look. The trouble is, if you have a cliff, you generally have boulders at the bottom of it, and we couldn't find a place without the boulders, and they were too heavy to move. Then Eddie found a place for Mrs. Moore's cave, that first cave they go to. And I said, 'I don't think that's any good, is it?' And he said, 'Just think a minute.' And I thought about it a moment and I looked at it and there was a great big bowl in the rock, covered with scrub about ten feet high, and he said, 'Imagine that all cleared out.' And he was dead right. I'm very grateful to him. We cleared the whole thing and we made it just bare. There were wonderful water marks running down the rocks. When the monsoon comes, water pours down and over the years has made those marks. We of course had to make holes in the rocks for the cave entrances, and it is such tough rock we had to send out for special drills from England.

"That was the beginning. Then I wanted to find the line of caves where the group climbs up. It was jolly hot, and I was quite tired and I said, 'Well, come on, then.' And we started climbing up and up these rock slopes where in fact the elephant climbs in the movie, and then this high cliff started to disclose itself and a wall and old ruins and that was it. We drilled a series of holes, and I was so thrilled because it was pretty well as I imagined it. Very old rocks, you know, worn, not sharp, with an old, old animal, an ancient, ancient, animal going, plodding on, almost back into the past.

"Shooting *A Passage to India* I didn't feel I was getting old. I didn't feel more tired than I used to. It's a curious thing, you know. I feel I've got much more experience, but I feel really as I did when I was twenty-five. I am very healthy. I am very healthy. I have never been ill in my life. You get very trim doing these big location pictures. When I'm out on my feet all day long, climbing rocks, doing God knows what, I stay fit. I didn't feel while I was filming this movie that it would be my last. Of course, I have had thoughts that this might be my last one. One of the terrible things about movies is the difficulty of finding a subject. It's frightfully difficult. If I make another movie I'd like it to be good. I don't want to make a movie for the sake of making a movie. Although I just do love being behind the camera taking pictures. There just aren't that many good ideas and stories floating about. I have no ideas for my next project. In my daydreams I think about all sorts of things. I'd love to have a go at a musical, like *Singin' in the Rain*. I think I'd be quite good at it. There is a Hindu proverb, I nearly put it into *Passage,* that says, in very simple terms, 'We're like a leaf on a river and we've got a very small paddle or we can use our hands. We can go this way or that way, but only minutely. But we're on that damn river, and we're going to be taken down it to some destination.'"

Lean was born March 25, 1908, in Croydon, a sedate suburban community on the southern edge of London. Lean's brother, Edward Tangye Lean, three years younger than David, died in 1974 at the age of sixty-three. For twenty-five years he had worked for the BBC, much of that time as the head of Overseas Services. Lean's father, Francis, lived into his nineties. He had been a senior member in the accounting firm of Viney, Price, and Goodyear in London. His mother died around 1950.

"I didn't come from a wealthy family," Lean says. "On my father's side it was a family of headmasters. On my mother's side were inventors. Her maiden name was Tangye. They were Cornish on both sides. They came from Cornwall, down in the tip of England. There were a lot of tin mines there. My brother always used to say, 'David, we've certainly come up from the mines.' He may have been right. My mother's family was an interesting lot, and rather artistic. My mother's sister could draw quite well. She didn't teach me. I wanted to and tried and failed dismally. I would love to be able to draw. My grandfather invented gas engines. I remember when I was a boy going to the various train stations seeing 'Tangye Gas Engines,' great posters up.

"My grandfather also invented a very famous hydraulic jack. Apparently there was a boat, I've forgotten the name of it, the *Great Eastern* it might have been, a steam engine, that was built. The launching ceremony came, and the boat wouldn't budge. They tried everything to get the damn thing to go. It was a national joke. Then these two brothers, my grandfather and his brother, went along and asked if they could have a go at doing it. Everybody said it was ridiculous. They had invented jacks that were about three or four feet high. I don't know how they did it, but they put a series of these jacks under the boat, and down it went. I think that made their name. Then I know my grandfather invented a safety lamp for coal mines which I think is still used today, or at least the idea is. I don't really remember him, but I remember going to the house where my grandparents lived in Warwickshire, a great, big rambling house. I remember off the drawing room there was a big conservatory where there were black and white grapes growing. There was a glass roof. There were chairs and you had lunch. It was lovely.

"Almost immediately after I was born," Lean says, "my mother and father moved from Croydon to a place in the country, and they had a nice house there. Then the time came for me to go to school—I must have been seven or eight or something. My mother and father were Quakers, fairly strict. Because we were Quakers, the local school, which was Church of England, wouldn't have me. So we had to move back to Croydon. We lived in a rather large house there, and we had what in those days was known as a charwoman who came in to scrub the floors and do the rough work. She was called Mrs. Egerton. Her husband was a cabdriver, a horse-drawn cabdriver. In those days Quakers thought the stage was rather a doubtful place of immorality, and films certainly were. I wasn't allowed to go to movies. Mrs. Egerton was mad about movies. She was mad about Charlie Chaplin. We had a kitchen in the basement with a big table, and I used to sit in the corner and she used to act Charlie Chaplin for me—running around the table and skidding around the corners. I remember saying to her once, 'But I don't understand. When they talk, what happens?' And she said, 'Well, it comes up in writing.' And I said, 'That can't work.' And she said, 'It does. It looks as if they're talking.'

"Then, when I was thirteen, I left school at Croyden and went off to a Quaker boarding school called Leighton Park in Reading. It was a very nice school, very sort of broad-minded. We used to have various nationalities there, which in those days was rather extraordinary. I think there were Indians and a Chinese boy. There were special holidays when the boys were allowed to go see a movie, but I used to sneak to the cinemas on Wednesdays and Saturdays. So if you went in in the dark, when the movie finished and the lights went up, you were terrified that you'd find one of the masters sitting there three or four seats from you." The first film Lean saw was a 1921 version of *The Hound of the Baskervilles*. "That beam of light traveling through the smoke had an immediate magic for me," he remembers.

"My first camera was the biggest compliment I've ever been paid. It was given to me by an uncle when I was about twelve years old. It was a Kodak Box Brownie. In those days it wasn't common at all for boys to take photographs. Now everybody does. But this chap gave me a small camera, and it was the biggest compliment I've ever had. I was looked on as a dud, you see, and it was a wonderful thing. I started taking pictures and developing the film myself. I was fascinated with that. I spent most of my free time when I was at school in the darkroom enlarging pictures. I've always been fascinated by pictures, by photographs. It was the only thing I was ever any good at, I suppose.

At school I was an absolute dud. Hopeless. I wasn't any good at it. My father, he used to be able to count up four columns of figures like that, go right up it and add. As a result, of course, son not competing with father, I still use my fingers to add anything. I was hopeless, and I never thought I could do anything. My brother was very clever. He had two books published before he was twenty-one. I don't know that they were terribly good, but he had them published. I remember one of them, which he wrote when he was there, *Storm Over Oxford*. My father sent my brother to Oxford because he was very clever. I didn't go to university because my father didn't think that would be worthwhile. He said, 'I don't know what to do with you. You'd better come into the accounting office.' It did hurt my feelings, but that's as it was. I went into the accounting office and wore black-striped trousers, a bowler hat, and carried an umbrella. I remember my father going for me one day— he saw me wearing a pullover sweater and he said, 'You must not wear that, it's not professional enough.' I lasted about a year.

"My mother was a sweet woman, rather pretty. I remember my mother a few years before she died saying, 'David, tell me, what exactly do you do?' In fact, it's not as foolish as it sounds. She had gone to see a film, it may have been *Great Expectations*, and she saw 'directed by.' Now what in the hell does a director do? I'd find it difficult to explain if you'd just arrived from Mars. I wasn't very close to my brother or my father. My father was tall, and I think he was handsome. He wasn't a stern character. He left my mother. I must have been in my early teens. We moved into a very tiny little house in Croydon. I didn't like it. It was sort of a bad part of my life, really. My father, poor man, was plagued by guilt. In those days it was a dreadful moral stigma. You felt you were the most wicked person in the world. It is a difficult thing in the best of times, but in those days, and being a Quaker, you can imagine. He didn't get married again. He went off with somebody else. She was a nice woman. I got to know her later. I don't really want to talk about these personal things. But you know, I think he was a sad man. I think people who did that sort of thing in those days—and it still happens today, of course—were riddled by guilt. They feel that they're wicked people. That's the thing about Anna Karenina, isn't it? One of the points surely was that she really agreed with the people who condemned her.

I'm not a Quaker now, though I have kept a lot of my Quaker upbringing. Moral overtones, really. Never tell a lie. Never cheat. And be highly suspicious of great show. I find it very difficult when I go into a place like St. Peter's in Rome and I see people swinging a lot of incense and gold about. I feel it is too ostentatious. Quite wrongly. I don't know why one shouldn't be too ostentatious. But that's from way back in Quaker meeting houses, you know. I think it's a very good religion, very good. I like the simplicity of it. I think it's quite good to go to a meeting, which I don't, and sit for an hour in silence every week, and just think a bit with other people. I don't know what I am now. I don't think, as Mrs. Moore says, that it's a godless universe. But I wouldn't know what God is. I cannot believe it's all accidental. We're still trying to find out, like plumbers trying to mend Swiss watches, what makes us tick, aren't we? I don't know. I just don't know. Nobody knows."

After the dismal year at his father's accounting firm, Lean entered the film industry when he was nineteen as a "teaboy" at Gaumont Studios. His job was to bring morning and afternoon tea to the workers on the movie sets and to load film for the camera department. He earned ten shillings a week. He quickly graduated to "number-board boy," holding up boards with the take numbers for the directors during every scene, and then to "third assistant director." Lean says, "In those days I was film-mad. I was twenty and too junior to see the rushes every day, but I made friends with a projectionist. I still remember his name. Matthews. I suppose he's dead now. I used to go into the box when they were showing the rushes, and he let me look through the projectionist's hole into the theater.

"I remember one day Matthews said, 'I'm running some cut stuff.' I went in and looked through the porthole and I saw stuff that had been cut. When you cut from a close-up of you, as it were, to a close-up of me, you can make it look as though we are looking at each other. I knew the scenes had been shot hours apart, and I was fascinated. Somebody looks up—cut—a bird flies in the sky. I thought, 'What a magician's trick.' It is a new language, of course, and I became absolutely fascinated. I used to ask the directors if I could go into the cutting room and help them. I used to wind up the film for them and look after the trims, because in those days the directors always cut their own films. There were no Movieolas. They would look at the film through a magnifying glass. I can see it now: The director would get a piece of film, measure it from the end of his nose to the end of his hand, three foot, six foot, nine foot, and then—cut. That was in the days of silent films. I became really fascinated by this."

When talkies came in, Lean learned how to synchronize sound with pictures. By 1930, when features were preceded by the news and a two-reel comedy in the movie theaters, he became the chief editor of the Gaumont Sound News. Later Lean edited newreels at British Movietone. He says, "Editing the news was done terribly quickly, about a thousand feet a week. There were two editions per week, one on Sunday night and one on Thursday night. It was a wonderful training ground. You cut with scissors straight from the negative, so you got used to cutting negatives, which of course nowadays would seem absolute madness. At the Movietone News I edited newsreels for four years and then got into features. Of course, I overcut like mad. When you're in newsreels, you're lucky if the cameraman gets a goal in the football match or a car dashing down the street. Then, when you suddenly come to cut a film, you have everything: long shots, medium shots, close-ups, and the result is you overcut terribly. It jumps around. I was just so pleased to have all these shots, I overcut. I remember working on a film and the producer, Alexander Korda, fired me off of it for overcutting. It was a very good lesson.

"After a while I became a sort of film doctor. If they had a film that was much too long, or a film they were in trouble with, I used to come in and recut it, that sort of thing. In fact, if I get too old to direct a movie, I wouldn't mind going back to that. I love the feel of film. I love the smell of it. The smell has changed slightly. We used to make the joints with acetate, and the cutting rooms would have this perfume around them. Now that's gone. Go and sniff nail-polish remover nowadays if you want to call to mind the old rooms. Editing is terribly exciting. You're putting the whole thing together. I always try not to have a foot of film cut until the end of shooting. Most pictures now are cut starting the first day of shooting. I don't like that because I try to keep the excitement of telling a story in pictures. I start at the first shot of reel one, and then I get the second shot and I'm sort of building it up as I go. If it was all cut, I wouldn't get the same freshness and excitement. I think you sort of get a flow doing it that way. It's a fascinating job."

During the mid-thirties, Lean became the top editor in England. He cut films like *Escape Me Never* (1935), *Pygmalion* (1938), *Major Barbara* (1940), *One of Our Aircraft Is Missing* (1941), and *The Invaders* (1942). Lean would spend his days editing and his nights in theaters taking in film after film. He says, "I'll never forget. In those days I was brought up on American films. I just loved them. I loved the sweep and the action. My great idol was Rex Ingram, who was a great director in America. He was the top director at Metro, especially after he had done *The Four Horsemen of the Apocalypse* with Rudolph Valentino, and *The Prisoner of Zenda*. Ingram was a wonderful director. Through watching Ingram's films I realized that there was somebody behind the camera controlling what was shown when. I remember seeing a film called *Mare Nostrum*, a silent film. Ingram directed it. There was a scene where the villain smashes a chair against a glass door and the camera catches it from a low angle. Nothing in those days was shot at a low angle. I thought, 'My God, that's good.' Generally people were in a longer shot. And here was somebody saying, 'Look at it from here,' and making it more dramatic by the choice of angles. I realized that there was some sort of guiding light at the back. Then I became terribly interested in directors, of course."

Lean codirected his first feature, *In Which We Serve*, with Noël Coward in 1942. He recalls, "I always had a fear that the doorman wouldn't let me on the sound stage. It was guarded, you know, and I thought I looked rather young to be the director. But they always let me in. I remember Celia Johnson in *This Happy Breed*. Wonderful actress. Wonderful gift. I wish she were alive. Lovely, lovely. I remember one day I was very cross because there was a scene in which she had to cry. But she and John Mills had a joke. I don't know what the hell it was. I said, 'Look, quiet, we are about to take.' And I realized that they were laughing so much the tears were pouring down their faces. I was very cross. I said, 'Now, look, we've got to wait. Bring on eye drops, bring on some face makeup.' It took about five minutes before she looked all right. And I said, rather impatiently, 'All right, let's go, action.' In thirty seconds I was crying, she was so wonderful. Oh, she was terrific. Then in *Blithe Spirit*, well, I was out of my depth on that one. High comedy is one of the most difficult things to do because you have no yardstick. Nothing is really true. A man with two wives, one a ghost and one living. We can see the ghost but the wife can't. Very, very difficult. I don't think I did it very well. It was rather frightening. I was a very frightened rabbit in those days.

"I was starting to do *Great Expectations* down at a place called Rochester, which was a very rough neighborhood. I wanted to see the first print of *Brief Encounter*, which I had just finished, so we went to the manager of a nearby theater and said, 'Look, would you run a new film and call it the premiere and give us a chance to see this first print?' He put it on, and during the first love scene somebody way down at the front—I'll never forget the voice—started to laugh in a high-pitched 'hee, hee, hee,' a terrible laugh. One or two people said 'Shh,' but then other people started to laugh with her. And as each love scene came along, she laughed more and more, and so did more and more people. When I got back, I was so ashamed of it. I lay in bed that night in the hotel where we were shooting *Great Expectations* and I thought, 'How can I get to burn the negative?' You're terribly ashamed when the whole audience is rocking with laughter. You think you've done the most fearful thing. It was really a terrible shock. The movie went very badly in all sorts of places. I remember them coming to me and saying that they had to take it off in Turin, Italy, after three days. Then gradually it became a sort of cult movie, and a few people wrote it up and said it was good, and now it's sort of Bible country.

"*Great Expectations*, well, I suppose it was the first time—I went out on a Sunday night and saw queues around the block and I think the first part, particularly, I think it came off. I enjoyed that. Wonderful working down in the marshes. I think *Oliver Twist* is a better film than *Great Expectations*. It was cut to bits in America because they thought it was anti-Semitic. I didn't mean it as such. I just thought I was doing a story with a rather comic Jewish fellow. But it wasn't taken as such. They cut whole lots of stuff. They cut most of the humor out of Alec Guinness's performance. I remember them saying, 'We'll allow you to keep in what is necessary for the plot.' It was too bad, because I think they messed it up.

"Well, you know, in *Hobson's Choice*, working with Charlie Laughton, a pleasure. The terrible thing is he immediately puts the director in the position of an audience. You roar with laughter and you should say, 'Now tone it down a bit.' But you just let him go. I think I let him go a bit over the top. But he's wonderful, wonderful, Charlie. I liked him enormously. We used to go have drinks in the pub around the corner beside the Thames. A dear chap. And *Summer Madness*, well, that's Kate Hepburn. Terrific. I've been friends with her ever since. I think I could call her one of my best friends. She's wonderful. She's got this extraordinary command of technique apart from her gifts as an actress. I remember saying to her once, 'Look, Kate.' It was a scene in which she was standing in the middle of a room and I said, 'Look, I can give you no possible reason for it, but I've somehow got to get you over to that window so that you can look out of it and see — I've forgotten what now.' She said, 'Oh, that's okay, that's what I'm paid for,' and she walked over to that window as if it were the only thing she could possibly do. Wonderful gift.

"*Lawrence of Arabia* was the first time I worked with Peter O'Toole, of course. I saw a small picture, *The Day They Robbed the Bank of England*. Peter was playing a silly-ass fisherman. There was something about him. I'd never heard of him, but there was something about him. I thought, 'I'll go for that.' And I did. Of course, he came out wonderfully. I don't think I identified with Lawrence. Sympathized perhaps is a better word. Lawrence was a wonderful man in his way. Wonderful man, strange character. He thought the best was Hindu. But the unfortunate thing was he didn't believe it, couldn't believe it. I think it's quite true.

"I found Omar Sharif for *Doctor Zhivago* on a postcard that Sam Spiegel, who produced *Kwai* and *Lawrence*, had got. Someone had cast a European for the part and he was absolutely hopeless. Sam produced these photographs of Egyptian actors and I said, 'Let's try him.' And it was Omar. It was very thrilling to try Peter O'Toole and Omar Sharif, two unknowns. Then we were looking for a girl to play Lara. I saw lots of films with young girls. I looked at *Billy Liar* and suddenly on the screen came this girl walking down the street swinging a handbag, and I said, 'That's her, let's go.' It was Julie Christie. She was terrific. I wish to goodness I'd worked with her again.

"I think every film is difficult in its own way, mostly because, you see, no actor is absolutely bang-on correct for the part. By the time I'm finished with the script I know the characters almost personally, know what they eat for breakfast in the morning. So when the actors are rehearsing I say, 'He hasn't got enough sense of humor.' Or, 'I wish he were a bit more lumbering.' Or, 'I wish one had a feeling that he's holding something back.'

"I don't believe much in improvisation. On the set, at the last minute, you're in the middle of the trees and you've got to be very careful." Maurice Jarre visited the set of *Doctor Zhivago* one day and recalls, "I saw the rehearsals of the scene where Rod Steiger says to Julie Christie, 'You are a slut' and then slaps her face with his glove. David was like — you know when you see someone feeding a bird with a little food — he was doing the same thing with the two actors. He was feeding words to them, one by one, and then lines, one by one. He was rehearsing for a full day that one little scene until it was perfect."

Lean admits, "I've often had to use a stopwatch in rehearsals to speed actors up. A curious thing about the screen, it slows things up. Some actors do tend to love long pauses so they can be on the screen a little longer, but I think it can be terribly boring. I'm terrified of boring people. I've very often asked the continuity girl to use a stopwatch. An actor will rehearse his lines and I'll say to the continuity girl, 'How long was that?' And she'll say, 'Twenty seconds.' I'll say to the actors, 'Let's have another rehearsal. Try to speed it up a bit.' Then I'll say, 'How long was that?' And the continuity girl will say, 'Fifteen seconds.' Then I'll turn to the actors and say, 'Do you know you lost five seconds?' They can't believe it because they haven't lost anything. Actors will very often complain about the speed, and I've always said, 'Look, I promise you, if you think you're speaking too fast when you see the rushes, I'll retake it.' I've never had to retake. I always see five seconds going through at twenty-four pictures a second, and that's a lot of film. I just like a tight film, a film that keeps the attention of the audience.

"I like some actors, some I find ghastly bores. Perhaps if we were actors, we would be the same, perhaps we are the same, anyhow. They only mostly look at themselves, and mostly they think only of their own parts. Show some rushes to an actor and say, 'Don't you think so-and-so was good when he did that?' And they say, 'Oh, I wasn't watching him.'

Terribly tough being an actor. You're up there in front of that glass eye. A good part of my job is trying to put actors at ease so they'll perform in front of the camera as well as they performed that morning in the bath when they were rehearsing the part themselves. To a certain extent actors are like puppets. Being a puppet is part of the job, isn't it? They are playing somebody else. At the end of a day of working with actors on a scene, I am terribly tired and I feel like a sponge that has been squeezed dry. At the end of it I want to get in a car or go and sit and do something completely different so I can come fresh and excited to the set the following morning.

"Judy Davis and I had tiffs on the set. Alec Guinness and I usually do. Alec and I have worked together for years. He virtually started his screen career with *Oliver Twist*. When you deal with anybody who has a mind of his own, and certainly Alec and Judy Davis do, of course you disagree on occasion. I like working with these people. It's awfully interesting. I'd rather have them than have an absolute dope. In *Bridge on the River Kwai*, I think Alec wanted to play Colonel Nicholson as more of a funny character. I think he was frightened of becoming a bore. I wanted him to play it absolutely straight, and he did and it worked. On the face of it, the character, Colonel Nicholson, is a bore. All sorts of people were offered that part, and they all turned it down. Stars like motivating things. In *Kwai*, everything happened to Colonel Nicholson. He got an obsession with the bridge, it was the first creative thing he had done in his life.

"All the time I'm making a film I keep thinking of the audience. I'm not pandering to them. I feel rather sort of like a conjurer saying, 'Ladies and gentlemen, see this man entering the room, he is being watched very closely by that girl sitting in the corner.' It's telling a story. I'm telling a story to an audience and I'm thinking of that audience when I'm telling it, hoping they understand the way I'm telling it, hoping I haven't left something out. I don't like mystifying people. Although in a sense the whole of *Passage* is a kind of mystery. I guess I like mysteries but I don't like muddles. My old friend William Wyler used to say, 'If you're going to give the audience a shock, just before it, almost reduce them to boredom so that 'bang, they sit up.' He's quite right, of course. I've done it quite a lot in my films, I think. It's rather like a roll of drums. A simple example: In *Passage* you don't know if Aziz has gone into the cave where Miss Quested is. Then you cut to Mrs. Moore waking up with a jolt, and then she says, 'What's happened?' And you hear a voice say, 'Oh, nothing, elephant taking a bath, Memsahib.' And she says, 'No, something else,' and she stands up and looks around and I hold it for quite a little bit and then—cut—to a rock going 'bong bong bong bong bong' down the hill—cut—a hat doing the same thing down the hill—cut—the girl going down the hill. It's like the roll of drums when someone is doing a tightrope act. It is sort of an orchestration of pictures.

"I do become obsessed by a movie, in a sort of maddening way, I must say. I go and have dinner, and whoever I'm sitting with says, 'Are you all right?' And I say, 'Yes, I'm all right.' And in fact I've got a close-up of somebody superimposed over the soup. It's that sort of thing. You cannot get the pictures of the day out of your head because you have concentrated so much. I'm still doing it. Right now, with the prints, I'm thinking, 'That shot of Mrs. Moore was a bit yellow,' and off it goes again. It is sort of maddening. Pictures are chasing around a bit. I have pretty good eyes. I don't quite know what it is. I think over the years—I just loved seeing things—and over the years if you're a movie director or you like taking still pictures, you start to see oblong. You put a frame around things. I'm an awful bore. I often tell people, 'Oh, do look at that.' And they say, 'Oh, isn't that beautiful. I hadn't noticed it.' Well, it was there. It's a bit of a bore sometimes. I've just begun to dare to think I perhaps am a bit of an artist. I always felt a little bit presumptuous to think that because artists, I think, are wonderful."

In the past, Lean, who has a son by his first wife, has sacrificed his married life to his moviemaking. "He was not the sort of man that husbands are made from," said Lean's third wife, the British actress Ann Todd, at the time of their divorce in 1957. "Too tense. Too mercurial." Leila Devi, Lean's fourth wife and a native of India, met the director in 1954 and eventually divorced him in 1978. "David and his work are more important to him than I am," she has said. "He really only lives when he works. Life has only one meaning for David—his filmmaking. He is obsessed. He will do the impossible for a film. He will go to the moon. The film is his father and mother and brother and son. His concentration is total. I never talk to him until he talks to me. Even if he is just shaving or tying his tie. If I speak to him, it startles him. His greatest love apart from making motion pictures is taking still ones. He has the most marvelous eyes. He can see a spot on the horizon that no one else can see."

Lean is stunned when I asked him about the nonspeaking role his fifth wife, Sandra Hotz, has as Mr. Fielding's wife in *Passage*. "Who told you that?" Lean is anxious to know. "I've been trying to keep it a secret. I met my wife in India. I don't really want to go into that." The two met in the late 1960s when he checked into a hotel in India owned by her parents and she showed him to his room. They lived together for quite some time and were married four or five years ago. Sandra speaks Hindi and carried out extensive liaison work with the Indians during the shooting of *A Passage to India*. Lean does say, "My wife is not an actress and doesn't want to be. Somebody else suggested that she play the part of Stella Moore. It is awfully hard to cast certain people, and it was essential, really, that Mrs. Moore's daughter not be an actressy-looking person, and they're hard to find. Somebody said, 'Well, why don't you put her in it?' And I said, 'Good God.' So she did it."

Lean then invites his wife to join us in the sitting room of their suite at the Bel-Air. She is elegant: tall, slim, tan, gracious. She is wearing classic gray wool pants and a cowl-necked gray print blouse. Her perfect nails are painted red. She speaks with a proper English accent. She appears to be in her mid-thirties. "My wife and I have bought sixty yards of waterfront property on the edge of the Thames," Lean says. "It's down in the docks. We've remodeled an old Victorian warehouse and pulled down a modern one to plant a garden. I love gardening. But we haven't moved in." We drink tea, and Sandra happily brings out photographs of the as yet incomplete house and garden that they have helped design. The house's interior has simple lines. It will be re-finished with light woods and have spectacular views of the river. Is it a place to settle down or another whistle-stop in the life of a tireless voyager? Lean admits, when pressed, "Yes, I feel that I am a romantic. I don't know if in my life, but—I don't know, I suppose, romantic, yes. I don't know. I have been a bit of a wanderer, yes. It's a wonderful thing, you know, going to strange places."

December 1984

David Lean and his wife are divorced. A reassembled version of the original uncut Lawrence of Arabia, *recently edited by Lean, was re-issued by Columbia in February 1989. The director has been working on the screen adaptation of Joseph Conrad's "Nostromo," which started filming in Spain in early 1989.*

DAVID HUME KENNERLY

THE DARK SIDE OF GEORGE LUCAS

*That face you make. Look I so
bad to young eyes?
. . . I do, yes, I do! Sick I've become.
Yes. Old and weak.
. . . Soon will I rest. Yes, forever
sleep. Earned it, I have . . .*

— Yoda

*G*eorge Lucas slouches on a couch in the airy
office of his home in the rolling, oak- and bay-
covered hills north of San Francisco. The thirty-
nine-year-old creator of *Star Wars* looks limp and
worn and almost never smiles. He has lost twenty
pounds in the last six months. He is wearing faded
brown, slightly bell-bottomed jeans, an oversized

shirt, and a brown vest. His glasses are brown. His brown hair and beard are flecked with gray. "I am burned out. I am burned out, period," Lucas says. "I was burned out a couple of years ago, and I've been going on forward momentum ever since. *Star Wars* has dominated my life, sort of grabbed it and taken it over against my will. I've got to get my life back again before it's too late. The sacrifices I've had to make at this point are greater than what I've wanted to make, ultimately."

Whatever personal sacrifices Lucas has made, he and his pal, Steven Spielberg, will go down in film history as Hollywood's two most popular filmmakers. *Star Wars* (1977) and *The Empire Strikes Back* (1980) rank No. 2 and No. 3 on the list of all-time biggest money-makers. *Raiders of the Lost Ark* (1981), a Lucas idea and story, executive-produced by Lucas and directed by Spielberg, is number five. Lucas's *American Graffiti* (1973), loosely based on his own experiences as a small-town adolescent racing souped-up cars, is one of the most profitable movies ever made. It cost Universal $780,000 to produce and has grossed more than $145 million worldwide. And Lucas's upcoming *Star Wars* film, *Return of the Jedi,* the third in the trilogy, looks to be no less a blockbuster than its brethren.

But George Lucas is tired. Soon he will rest. Earned it, he has. He says, "My life, once I got into film school in 1965, was like pushing a 147-car train up a very steep slope. It was push, push, push. I pushed it all the way up there, and then *Star Wars* came and I reached the top. I jumped on board and started going down the other side, and I've had the brakes on ever since, pulling and pulling on all these levers, with the wheels screeching and screaming, trying to stop. There's no way the brakes are ever going to stop it, and it's all been work, work, work. I'm about to jump train. I've got this slim chance right now to decide whether I'm ever going to climb back on again and see if I can find some level terrain for the train to travel on.

"I am afraid that if I did another *Star Wars* movie now, I'd be straying from my path. To me that would be like being seduced by the dark side, but more than anything else, I think I'd be unhappy. *Star Wars* is a book. I look at the movies as three chapters in a book. I have made the last chapter and put the book on the shelf. I wanted to finish it so I could say, 'The End.' Up to this point it has been incomplete. Whether or not I'm going to write another book, I have to decide. This book practically killed me. I didn't know after I did the first chapter if I could finish the book or not. I was ready to quit then. I wanted to quit then. But I kidded myself into thinking that if I stopped directing, it would be like quitting. I thought I could just oversee it. But it didn't work that way. *Star Wars* is so uniquely my vision and so incredibly complicated to do that I ended up having to get involved. It's bigger than what one or two or three people can do. It needs a giant team of people. I relinquished endless control. It didn't bother me to give up the control — I couldn't have kept it.

"As it was, I could barely oversee these films. It is hard to describe the amount of detail, the amount of work involved. It's a three-year deadline with two years of really concentrated, serious work, ten to twelve hours a day, six days a week. There are two periods of four or five months in those years when the work is sixteen to eighteen hours a day. You get not much more than five hours of sleep a night. And that's hard. On Sunday you're wiped out and you're still thinking about the movie. People usually don't understand the implications of what I'm saying, living this way, day after day, but it's awesome. You can do it for a couple of months, but year after year it gets to be grim. I've been doing it for God knows how long. It's more and more pressure and I'm more and more unhappy, and tired and exhausted and dragging home endless problems at the end of the day. I'm not having much fun. It's all work. It's very anxiety-ridden, very hard, very frustrating and relentless. The extent to which one's personal life is usurped cannot be overestimated. It has made me less of a happy person than I think I could be. It has disrupted my family life. I have a wife and a two-year-old daughter, and they are the most important things in my life. My family is it for me. Amanda is two years old now, and she's magic. She's this little girl and she ain't going to wait for me. She's going, she's growing. The last thing in the world I want is to turn around and have her be eighteen and say, 'Hi, Dad, where have you been all my life?'

"I thought it would get better after *Star Wars*, but it hasn't. It's just gotten worse. The anxieties and the frustrations get worse as you get more removed. I'm afraid I'll end up at the end of my life saying, 'Well, that's all I've done.' Sure, there is a creative high in fixing a sequence, but there's a much bigger high in holding your daughter. Raising a child is a much more significant accomplishment to me than having made the movies. I just wish I could figure out how to do them both at the same time. I love *Star Wars*. I think it's great, but I just don't want to sacrifice my entire life for it. I don't want to be an all-consumed workaholic. I want to enjoy the better things in life like a normal person—just, say, go out and stand on a hill and enjoy life. I really am lazy. A lazy person would rather not be doing what I'm doing. I am lazy unless forced to get going, and I've really been forced to get going.

"I don't think I'll ever let other people take over the *Star Wars* movies if I don't do them. I'd rather not have them done than have them be done badly. I'm not going to turn it into *Planet of the Apes*. This story is finished, and whether I go on and do another story, who knows? If they are done at all, I'll do them or find someone like Steven Spielberg who is willing to do the next three. But it would have to be someone like Steven, whom I have complete confidence in. I don't know if I'd ever find somebody else like that. The important thing is, this finishes it for me. I can walk away from the whole thing now and get my personal life in order. I'm going to put my company, Lucasfilm, on hold for the next two years. I'm going to take a two-year sabbatical and try to make my life full and rewarding. I want to relax, go to the movies, learn more about computers, study social psychology and architecture. I want to do a little writing. To read a book has been a luxury beyond anything I've been able to know. There is more to life than movies and work, no matter what the accomplishment. *Star Wars* is an accomplishment. It's a thing and it exists. I created a small work that stands on its own, that is what it is. It's given people a certain amount of joy in a certain time of history. In a thousand years, ten thousand years, it will be nothing more than a pretty minor footnote in the pop culture of the 1970s and 1980s. I have to decide what my next accomplishment is going to be."

Even now, on the eve of the movie's release, Lucas doesn't know if *Return of the Jedi* is any good. A chronic pessimist (a recurring line in *Star Wars* is, "I have a bad feeling about this"), Lucas says, "We didn't know until two weeks ago when an audience saw it whether the film worked or not. I feel the same way I did about *Star Wars*—it is either the worst film or the best film. There is just no way to know. I'm still not sure. When you're working on it, you just have no way of knowing. I'm so wrapped up in it and I've worked so hard, I've lost sight of the thing. I mean, here I've got a ten-year-old story—that's pretty old—and it was written as a dumb kind of thing, and suddenly it's become this giant phenomenon and you say, 'Well, gee, is this going to live up to . . . Shouldn't there be more? Maybe I should redo the whole thing. Maybe I . . . Gee, maybe this isn't what everybody thought it was supposed to be.' I feel more confident about this film than I did about *The Empire Strikes Back*. *Empire* was the big risk. It was a departure. It didn't have an ending. This has an ending. This is more of an 'up' movie; *Empire* was a 'down' movie. But I am really worried about this too. Well, they've seen two already; maybe they're going to be tired of it. And, well, gee, is it going to pay off? So you finally get to the end of the shaggy-dog story, and then everybody says, 'Is that it?' I thought a lot about whether I should try to do something else, but then I said, what the heck, this is the way the film was written, this is what the film is. I said, 'Well, that's all there was.'"

Return of the Jedi is the climax of the trilogy, and both *Star Wars* and *The Empire Strikes Back* build up to it. *Jedi* also has three times the budget and nearly twice the number of special effects that *Star Wars* had. Initially, Twentieth 20th Century–Fox allotted *Star Wars*, which Lucas both wrote and directed, $3.5 million. The figure was upped to $10 million, and the movie came in at between $10 and $11 million. *Empire* cost $25 million. Irvin Kershner directed it. *Jedi*, directed by Richard Marquand, will have a final price tag of about $32 million. Lucas was the executive producer of both *Empire* and *Jedi*. *Star Wars* had 545 special effects, compared to *Empire*'s 763 and *Jedi*'s 942.

The movies got bigger and bigger largely because the wizards at Lucasfilm's special-effects company, Industrial Light and Magic (ILM), kept making breakthroughs in technology just to translate Lucas's vision onto film. Lucas, with his driving perfectionism, was finally able to do in *Jedi* what he had wanted to do in *Star Wars*. "*Jedi* was the hardest of the three films, technically and logistically," Lucas says. "At every level it was harder. Special effects, for example. In *Star Wars*, the battles in space were faked, done by sleight of hand editorially. There were only one or two ships in each shot, and there was no continuity between shots—a ship couldn't fly from one shot into another. There were very few ships, and the ships moved slowly, and the moves were simple. In *Jedi*, each shot has thirty or forty ships, they're all moving continually between shots, and their moves are very complicated. You can say, 'Why bother to change if the special effects worked in the first film?' That was what I wanted the first film to be, and I had to see if we could actually accomplish it. Plus the audience has become more sophisticated and the space battles in this film are the way the audience will remember them in *Star Wars*."

Tom Smith, ILM's general manager, says, "I can't think of anything that we know how to do that we didn't do for this movie. George actually made two movies, one a gigantic special-effects movie, the other a character movie." Twice a day for a year Lucas has held forty-five-minute conferences in the projection room at ILM to look at special-effects film. He either said "great" or, with a pointer on the screen, explained what was wrong with a shot and how it could be made better. "George has Superman eyes," says Smith. "It is a very unusual physiological thing. He can see through things to the very essence of a picture and know what is right and wrong with it." For the past four months 150 technicians at ILM have worked twenty-four hours a day, seven days a week, in shifts, to finish the movie's special effects. Smith says, "After Christmas we gave up our private lives."

Lucas also kept his "Superman" eyes on the development of the monsters for *Jedi*. He says he barely managed to get twenty simple monsters in *Star Wars*, then decided to put all technical energies into making just one sophisticated monster for *Empire*. *Jedi*, however, has more than one hundred sophisticated monsters, thanks to the marriage of computers to puppetry, achieved in part in *Star Wars* but perfected in *Jedi*. The creatures aren't hatched whole in Lucas's mind. He will visualize a monster and characterize it to his creature designers, Phil Tippett and Stuart Freeborn, or his art director, Joe Johnston. Jabba the Hutt, for example, Lucas described as "a large, repulsive, sluglike creature, half slob, half Sultan—the ultimate slob Godfather. They'd work for months coming up with designs and designs and designs and I'd reject them or accept them," Lucas says. "Phil Tippett would give me twenty-five little sculptures of various creatures and I'd pick two or three. I'd say, 'Change the nose on this one, put the ears from that one onto this one, and I'll take it.' I wasn't the main creative force behind the creatures," Lucas adds. He told Johnston and Freeborn that Yoda should be "blue-green, have sort of a big head, giant ears, and a funny little pug nose." It took about ten months for the team to approximate Lucas's vision of Yoda.

Lucas had always wanted a primitive, free-spirited society to end up battling the high-tech evil Empire. Before *Star Wars* was made, the Wookies were going to be the primitive race. But in *Star Wars*, Lucas had already shown Chewbacca, a Wookie and Han Solo's copilot, to be highly civilized. Wookies are tall, 7'5", so Lucas decided simply to cut them in half, and make them primitive, short-haired, short people. He scrambled the letters of the word *Wookies* and came up with Ewoks. "That's where the idea of the Ewoks came from," Lucas says. "In the end, part of the decision in designing the Ewoks was not to worry about the fact that they were cute. It's just in the nature of things that anything short and fuzzy ends up looking like a teddy bear, so I just said, well, look, we'll just make them cute, what the heck. I have a feeling we are going to get trashed for making them cute. I don't care if everybody thinks they look like teddy bears. Critics will say the movie is just an excuse to sell teddy bears, but I don't care."

However well done the special effects are, or however real the monsters look, Lucas is rarely satisfied. He says, "After *Star Wars* I used to say that only twenty-five percent of what I intended was up on the screen. In the next movies a lot of those goals were made a reality. But I have learned that no matter how hard you try, no one has control. It isn't how well you can make a film, it's how well you can make the film under the circumstances. That's the challenge. You always have limited resources and extenuating circumstances, acts of God. That's the joy and the heartache of it too. Sometimes the lack of control makes the films better, sometimes worse. But you have to accept that the movie isn't going to be as good as you wanted it to be. The bigger the movie is, the less control you have and the more you have to go with the flow, go with whatever happens."

Just one example of *Jedi* go-with-the-flow production problems: Forty dwarfs were hired in London to be Ewoks, and each one was fitted for an Ewok suit. Individual plaster casts were taken of the actors' hands and feet so that perfect-fitting latex gloves and boots could be made, to which hair and nails would be added later. The boots turned out to be too heavy for the stage platforms of the Ewok village built in the trees twenty feet off the ground, so new plaster casts had to be taken and lighter boots made. Forty new dwarfs were found in the United States for the Ewok scenes shot in the forests of Crescent City, California. Again, each was fitted for costumes and plaster casts were made. Then a choreographer had to be hired solely to teach the diverse dwarfs how to walk and run and move like Ewoks. During filming, after each Ewok shot, the actors had to take off their masks or their plastic eyes would fog up and they wouldn't be able to see where they were going.

"Making movies is the art of compromise," Lucas says. "I hate com-

179

promise. It really used to depress me. You have a vision and you see a movie on the screen that doesn't come near the vision. After I stopped directing, it didn't bother me quite so much anymore. Once I felt personally, creatively, off the hook, I wasn't as committed to the vision and how well it got accomplished." Lucas can't say if *Empire* and *Jedi* would have been better or worse if he had directed them. "They would have been different. I know they would have been because I was there on the set watching the director and I knew I would be making this or that decision differently." Lucas says it is difficult to compare Kershner and Marquand. "They're just different," he says. "It's even hard to say what I would have done in certain situations. It's like taking three people and putting them in front of an easel with three different colors and asking them to make three different strokes. Which is better? Who better? You end up with three different interpretations of three strokes with three colors."

Lucas says he always works with the directors and never pulls rank. "I've never directed over anybody's shoulder. It's impossible. It's too subtle an art. It's always been collaborative. If there is a question, I talk to the director back in a corner. Occasionally there is tension, but I've tried to be very conscious of it. I've worked with the crews since *Star Wars*, so it's very easy for them to ask me a question, but I defer to the director. Within reason, I've always tried to let the director make his movie his way. Sometimes I'll pull him aside and discuss why I think something else would be a better idea. I don't think I've ever said, 'This is the way it's going to be. This is final.'"

"Only once did I get conflicting directions," recalls Carrie Fisher, who plays Princess Leia. "When I came into Jabba's throne room disguised as a man, Richard told me to stand like an English sentry. Then George walked in and said, 'Carrie, you're standing like an English sentry. You want to be more swashbuckling.'"

"What I do," Lucas says, "is go around offering suggestions. Walt Disney said he went around pollinating little groups of people. I go around saying, 'How about this?' or 'I got an idea, what if . . .' I act as a glue. There are a lot of gaps unique to *Star Wars*. Questions only I can answer. I act as the ultimate source. 'How would this robot walk?' 'Should this creature have a radio antenna?' I'm the only one who has the whole vision, and I know it intimately. A director comes to one of these films and has a pretty good grasp of what's going on, but he hasn't lived with it for ten years and he can't give an instant [Lucas snaps his fingers] answer to any question that could possibly come up. The directors relied on me as a backlog encyclopedia.

"There is an enormous amount of grossness to filmmaking. But into the grossness you put a lot of little details, subtleties. How are the mosaics patterned, the door handles shaped, the niches carved? A film starts out with a giant brush and ends up with a team of artists painting in the details. In the *Star Wars* saga I have a lot of control over the giant brush-strokes, the sets, the plots, the casting. I try to add in as many details as I can, but a team of thirty or forty people adds the rest. You can pan across one seam in a set, and suddenly the audience is jolted out of it because of a carpenter who didn't do the right thing. The scene is destroyed by a detail. This is especially true in fantasy films like *Star Wars. Star Wars* isn't like *The Wizard of Oz*, with giant purple sets and phony little trees. With *Star Wars*, if you let yourself go slightly, the world is sort of real. It's very hard to create an immaculate reality out of nothing, to make what's totally incredible credible. I've always tried to create a reality you can believe in without going that far to suspend your disbelief."

"A long time ago in a galaxy far far away . . ." is the beginning of every *Star Wars* story. Lucas says, "*Star Wars* movies are basically entertainment. You go, you eat your popcorn, you have two hours of entertainment, you feel good, and you go home." But he adds that "there is a lot in them that never gets talked about. The *Star Wars* movies are just fairy tales, but fairy tales aren't just silly old made-up stories. There is a lot going on in them that makes them work. At the same time, though, they're not done with a capital *A* for 'Art' or *S* for 'Significance.'"

Lucas read myths and fairy tales the entire time he was writing the scripts for *Star Wars*. "I consciously went into it wanting to make a fairy tale, and I studied a lot of fairy tales." He read Joseph Campbell; Bruno Bettelheim; *Grimm's Fairy Tales*; Greek, Islamic, and Indian mythology. He also read Carlos Castaneda's *Tales of Power*. He read C. S. Lewis and J. R. R. Tolkien, as well as popular science fiction like Frank Herbert's *Dune* trilogy and E. E. "Doc" Smith's *Lensman* saga. Lucas read C. G. Jung, Edgar Rice Burroughs, and Frazer's *The Golden Bough*. He read a lot but doesn't admit to any one particular influence. He says, "Yes, I've done a fair amount of reading, but a lot of *Star Wars* just came intuitively. The reading gave me feelings for motifs and themes, but ultimately most of *Star Wars* is just personal.

"If I ever consciously used anything that I read, it was to make the story more consistent with traditional fairy tales. For example, if there was a part in which Luke had two trials, I would try to make it three, because three is more consistent with hero myths. But if adding a third trial jeopardized the story, I wouldn't do it. I can't give any specific examples. I just don't remember, and the scripts changed a lot. It is hard to go back without studying it. It becomes academic, and when I was doing it, it wasn't academic. Also, you're talking about ten years and a lot of work. The basic themes are 'quest of the knight,' 'father and son,' 'good versus evil,' 'renewal of faith,' 'test of becoming a man or a knight,' 'primitive versus technological,' 'man versus machine.' A life spirit is stronger than what a machine can create. That's all it really comes down to. A large technological force that tries to destroy the human spirit is ultimately very vulnerable because it's a machine and all you have to do is unplug it. But it's always dangerous to analyze these things. It's always better to let people watch and decide for themselves what something is about. I don't like to get too intellectual about it. I'd much rather have people think of *Star Wars* as entertaining little movies. The thing stands on its own, it is what it is.

"There is more of me in *Star Wars* than I care to admit, for better or worse. A lot of it is very unconscious, very personal. You can't get away from that. It comes out of you. It's not something that is done by the numbers, it's very personal. Luke more or less is my alter ego. He can't not be. You can't write a main character and not have him be part of you and not be able to identify with him. I identify with a lot of the characters, and you have to in order to write it. Han Solo and Luke are like twin brothers, the spiritual brother and the warrior brother with the devil-may-care attitude. A lot of people have said Han Solo is a composite of an old friend I used to race cars with and screenwriter John Milius. Who knows where these characters come from? I didn't base Han Solo on any person.

"The idea of the Force evolved. It has evolved all during my life. I've always had a deep interest in the cosmos—the great mysteries of life. I have always pondered it and been fascinated by it. I've always asked the questions and looked for the answers. I don't know if I am any further along now than when I was five years old. I continue to look. If I know anything, it is that we just don't know what's going on. To deny things that don't fit into our sense of reality, like levitating a chair, to say this doesn't exist, and to close one's reality into a rigid mind-set is not the most productive way to try to figure out what the world is all about. The Force is a way of saying that all things are possible. Because you don't understand it, because it doesn't fit into your belief system, you shouldn't reject it." In *Empire*, when Yoda levitates a spaceship, Luke says, "I don't believe it." "That," answers Yoda, "is why you fail." Lucas says, "In order to make something work, you have to have an absolute belief in it. But at the same time one cannot just believe things out of hand. As Luke goes on, he gets more skeptical. If you can keep an open mind and be receptive and skeptical, you might be able to get a smattering of truth somewhere. As I said, the only thing I know is that we don't know. The film has one foot in psychology and one foot in philosophy. These are large and complicated issues. Behind each smidgen of surface is a whole treatise on the power of belief systems, the relationship between a person's belief system and what he is able to accomplish. But *Star Wars* is not meant to be an essay in philosophy. It's just a sketch in a primary concept that also serves a plot force. The movie never stops to have a philosophical discussion.

"Do I try to live the way of the Force? What is the way of the Force? I try to have some kind of relationship with God, and I hope in the future I'll be able to spend more time articulating that. My feelings in that area are very personal. There aren't any really obvious manifestations of how I deal with my spiritual life. I don't meditate. I don't go to church. I don't do est. I've developed my own relationship, which I haven't had too much time for. I'm not drawn to any particular religion. I think they are all equally interesting. The Force is also more or less intuitive. I wanted to move beyond folk gods and make an elemental God, something that people could relate to without getting hung up on a specific religion. I was trying to move beyond religion into a relationship with God. I wanted to deal with it in a very simple and straightforward way. I didn't want the Force to be specific, I wanted it to be general. You know, people love to say, 'Oh, George believes in the Force.' I believe in God. The Force is a label you put on something; it doesn't mean anything. I believe in God, and I also believe there is an elemental God that is reflected in all the religions. It's like the blind man and the elephant: All the religions are trying to describe the same thing, it's just that they are describing different aspects of it.

"These ideas are in philosophical and mystical areas so obscure that you can't really discuss them in anything as glib as a movie or focus them in anything as cumbersome as a fifty-volume work. All I was trying to say in a very simple and straightforward way, knowing that the film was going to be seen by a young audience, is that there is a God and there is a good side and a bad side. You have a choice to make: the good side or the bad side. The world works better if you're on the good side. I wasn't trying to preach, but I did want to try to, say, influence kids in the direction of 'find your God and try to be good.' I sort of took a moral approach to the movie." Lucas's wife, Marcia, says she thinks her husband is "very spiritual," not necessarily religious. "George says he doesn't believe in the Force because he thinks people will consider him a freak if he does. But deep down part of his unconscious believes in it, I think."

Lucas's writing room is what Marcia calls a "tree-house environment," which used to serve as their mansion's carriage house. Marcia decorated the suite of rooms—a writing nook and desk built into a windowed wall a few steps up from a large living room, a bathroom, and a tiny kitchen—with redwood paneling and forest-green fabrics. As you enter, there is a green couch in front of a fireplace and a stack of wood. There are bookshelves around the room and a TV and stereo system on one wall. The carpet is beige. Lucas's desk is stained redwood, and on it are a Mickey Mouse phone, a Wookie pencil holder, a telescope, and several books: Joseph Campbell's *Hero With A Thousand Faces*, *Bartlett's Familiar Quotations*, *Webster's Dictionary*, *Harper's Bible Dictionary*, *The Foundations of Screenwriting* by Syd Field, and *Roget's Thesaurus*, opened to a page that has the word *imagination* at the top. There is a little Sony television to the right of the desk, and five three-ring notebooks containing Lucas's notes and sketches for the entire *Star Wars* epic, past, present, and future. There is also a picture of Marcia and the baby. When he is writing, Lucas spends about eight hours a day in his "tree house," with a short break for lunch. "If I spend eight hours 'writing,'" he says, "I probably spend three hours writing and the rest of the time thinking."

It took Lucas two and a half to three years to write *Star Wars*. While struggling, he snipped bits of his hair off with scissors. He used number-two standard pencils and wrote only in longhand on blue- and green-lined paper. "When I sit down to write, it takes me a long time and it takes a lot of work. I don't just sit down and have all these things pop out of my head. They get dragged out kicking and screaming with a lot of pain. It's a wonder it all comes together in the end. Filmmakers have unlimited options, yet after a while a script becomes its own animal, partly because of its own personality, partly because of fate. You only have limited control over it. You're not making it in a vacuum."

Star Wars is not a fantasy Lucas had when he was a boy. He started writing it in 1973, and the ideas "evolved." He says, "There are four or five scripts for Star Wars, and you can see as you flip through them where certain ideas germinated and how the story developed. There was never a script completed that had the entire story as it exists now. But by the time I finished the first Star Wars, the basic ideas and plots for Empire and Jedi were also done. As the stories unfolded, I would take certain ideas and save them; I'd put them aside in notebooks. As I was writing Star Wars, I kept taking out all the good parts, and I just kept telling myself I would make other movies someday. It was a mind trip I laid on myself to get me through the script. I just kept taking out stuff, and finally with Star Wars I felt I had one little incident that introduced the characters. So for the last six years I've been trying to get rid of all the ideas I generated and felt so bad about throwing out in the first place. The truth of it is, I'm not sitting here with one chapter of a book, which is what I had after Star Wars, and saying, 'The book is incomplete.'"

If Lucas does ever decide to take the story further, he will start by going back to a time before Star Wars began. Then he would make a sequel to the Star Wars trilogy. Lucas can describe the stories, the plots, and who does what to whom in the three movies of what he calls the "prequel" to Star Wars. But he has only a vague notion of what will happen in the three films of the sequel. Lucas's notebooks are full of ideas but no diagrams or mythological maps. The "prequel" is about the breakdown of the fictional galactic republic and the emergence of the Empire as the governing body. Everyone, including Obi-Wan Kenobi, Anakin Skywalker, and the Emperor ("the bad Yoda"), starts out as a normal person, just forty years younger. Yoda is also present. The story explains how all the characters got to be where they were in Star Wars. Luke Skywalker is born in Episode III. Lucas says, "The 'prequel' has more plot and less action than Star Wars, and it's more like a soap opera—really Machiavellian, with lots of political intrigue. I had to create a whole backplot in order to get to Star Wars. How did Anakin Skywalker get to be Darth Vader? Who is Luke's mother? I knew at the final draft of Star Wars that Leia and Luke were sister and brother, but the story started out with two brothers and a father. Everything evolved."

In the sequel Luke would be a sixty-year-old Jedi knight. Han Solo and Leia would be together, although Lucas says, "They might be married, or not. We have never actually discussed marriage in this galaxy. I don't even know if it exists yet. Who knows what relationship they will have? I mean, they're together, let's put it that way." The sequel focuses mainly on Luke, and Lucas says Mark Hamill will have first crack at the part if he is old enough. "If the first trilogy is social and political and talks about how society evolves," Lucas says, "*Star Wars* is more about personal growth and self-realization, and the third deals with moral and philosophical problems. In *Star Wars*, there is a very clear line drawn between good and evil. Eventually you have to face the fact that good and evil aren't that clear-cut and the real issue is trying to understand the difference. The sequel is about Jedi knighthood, justice, confrontation, and passing on what you have learned."

The onscreen world of *Star Wars* is a sliver of Lucas's imaginary universe. Lucas constructed back stories not only for his main characters but for his creatures as well. He is particularly fond of Chewbacca and has concocted a cultural and anthropological history of the Wookie race: They come from a damp jungle planet and dwell in wood-and-bamboo doughnut-shaped houses, wrapped around the trunks of giant trees, a hundred feet above the ground. They are mammals, eat meat and vegetables, and live to be 350 years old. The six-breasted females deliver their offspring in litters. The society is a primitive patriarchy with a complicated lineage structure and initiation rites. Their religion rejects materialism. They have their own version of the Force—a natural empathy with plant life and the ecology of their plant. After an imperial invasion the Wookies are rounded up by slave traders and sold throughout the empire. Han Solo rescues a group of prisoners that includes Chewbacca, and the two become inseparable.

Lawrence Kasdan, who collaborated with Lucas in writing *Empire* and *Jedi*, says, "George is very much in tune with his entire history from the time he was very young, and in a way that is useful to him in his work. He is able to draw on those feelings. That kind of openness to your past, and the influences on you, is a very special gift. George has been able to hook into some basic, universal images. He is able to show that someone very small, like a child or Luke, can face someone very big, like a Darth Vader or an Empire or a Death Star. The central image of the whole trilogy I think comes in *Star Wars* when Luke, against all odds, gets through this tiny little crack and fires one little rocket into exactly the right spot to bring down this enormous opponent. That is the most powerful feeling: 'Oh, it's not hopeless, I can be like David and kill the giant Goliath with a slingshot.' In *Empire*, when Han Solo is maneuvering the Millennium Falcon through the meteoroid field—that's a fantasy every kid has had of avoiding arrows or rocks or an avalanche. In *Jedi*, as the flames chase the Falcon out of the Death Star, that is an image everybody has had: 'Oh, if only I could just beat by a few steps the monster or the mugger or the dog that's on my tail.' And whatever feelings you have about Darth Vader, your father, or authority, how reassuring it is to think that there is something good there too. Luke's insistence on his hope that redemption is possible is very inspiring."

If *Star Wars* ever seems like a comic book or a TV serial, it is no coincidence. Lucas grew up on them. He was born May 14, 1944, the third child of Methodist parents, George, Sr., and Dorothy. He has two sisters, eight and ten years older, and a sister Wendy, three years younger. Lucas's mother was sickly, his father a conservative small businessman who owned a prosperous stationery and office furniture store in Modesto, a small city in the flatlands of central California about sixty miles south of Sacramento. The Lucases lived there in a stucco house on Ramona Avenue until George was fifteen and the family moved to a thirteen-acre walnut ranch on the outskirts of town.

George, Sr. raised his children on a litany of his own values: "Work hard, be frugal, don't waste your money"; "Don't stop until your job is done"; "Be true to yourself"; "Early to bed, early to rise." But he didn't think his only son heard a word: "He never listened to me. He was his mother's pet. If he wanted a camera, or this or that, he got it. He was hard to understand. He was always dreaming up things." George, "a scrawny little devil," according to his father, was taunted by local bullies who threw his shoes into sprinklers. Wendy would come to his rescue. Wendy also was there when George, a dreadful student, needed help with homework. Sometimes she would get up at five o'clock in the morning to correct misspellings in his English papers.

Wendy and George used to pool their allowances to buy comic

books—*Batman and Robin, Scrooge McDuck, Superman*—and then hurry to read them in a shed behind the house on Ramona. When Lucas was in college, he gave about two carloads of comic books to his elder sister's children, but has since repossessed them all. In the scene near the beginning of *Jedi* when the bounty hunter brings Chewbacca to the throne room of Jabba the Hutt, Jabba speaks in Huttese, but the subtitles under a closeup of the monster read, "This bounty hunter is my kind of scum, fearless and inventive." A million villains could have said that, any villain in an Action comic.

When Lucas was about ten, George, Sr., bought the family a TV set, and George would spend hours watching serials and cartoons, his black cat Dinky draped over his shoulders. "When I was a kid, I used to love the old *Flash Gordon* serials on television," Lucas recalls. "They were a primary influence on me. The way I see things, the way I interpret things, is influenced by television. Visual conception, fast pace, quick cuts. I can't help it. I'm a product of the television age."

In his teens, Lucas started listening to rock 'n' roll, Elvis Presley, Chuck Berry. At fifteen he got his first car, a Fiat, and loved the thrill of speeding down Modesto's flat roads. He spent time rebuilding cars and working with pit crews at races. "Just about every day after school," Lucas says, "I'd go to the Foreign Car Service and work on the Fiat to beef it up. For nearly four years of my life, I spent almost every weekday between three in the afternoon and one in the morning cruising up and down the streets, stopping only at the Foreign Car Service and for dinner. I used to grease back my hair with Vaseline, put taps on my pointed black shoes, and wear one grimy pair of jeans. I was friends with a gang that wore blue felt car coats. We hung out."

Lucas's days and nights of endless cruising resulted in the hugely popular *American Graffiti*, but his dreams of a racing career were smashed when he was nearly killed in a car accident just before high school graduation. Lucas was hit broadside and thrown free just before his Fiat wrapped itself around a walnut tree. He recuperated for four months. "It shook me up quite a bit," he says. "That is a transitional age to begin with, and since I have a tendency to favor determinism . . . I don't want to get too specific, but by deterministic I mean a belief in destiny and that one is put in a place for a reason. I do think an individual has choices, and if you're on a path you can go up the path quickly if you want. You aren't a victim of some cosmic force, but there are unknown elements at work. Whatever religion or philosophy you choose, they all focus on the same thing: that there is some sort of logical movement of forces that you have a relationship to. Trying to figure out where the forces are coming from and how things are determined has always been one of the great mysteries." After the accident Lucas took up filming auto races with an eight-millimeter camera. He attended Modesto Junior College for two years, majoring in the social sciences with an emphasis in anthropology and sociology.

Lucas was then accepted by the University of Southern California's film school. He made a bargain with his father: George, Sr., would pay the tuition and also give Lucas a "salary" of two hundred dollars a month. Out of that, Lucas paid for food and rent and everything else. "If I flunked out," Lucas says, "I was on my own." At film school Lucas struggled. He had to take liberal arts classes in order to graduate, and he found them difficult. "I didn't think I was all that intelligent. I did pass the entrance exams and get into USC, but I had been tested when I was in high school or junior high, and my IQ was in the nineties. I just never considered myself intelligent in the academic sense. I was never that good in school. I'm not what you call a speed reader. I'm not the greatest speller. I'm horrible at math. My basic SAT skills are fairly low."

In film school, Lucas made lifelong friendships with fellow students like writer-director John Milius. Milius, who wrote *Apocalypse Now*, recalls those days: "In film school George would be very quiet for a long time and then talk for a very long time. He was a ringleader. So was I. Our idea was to see how much we could get away with. We had very little money for projects and George's fascination was to see how much this small amount of money could get. He was the first person to make a film in color. He knew somebody who owned a race-car track, and one time he managed to get some extra film and he shot a race car going around the track at a hundred and fifty miles an hour. It looked like the Grand Prix, and everybody else was shooting some little movie on campus. He knew somebody who owned an airplane, a P-51, and he said to me, 'Think up a story so we can have a P-51 in our movie. People won't believe the shots we'll get.' He did a student film called *The Emperor*, and it was really extraordinary. It was about a real-life disc jockey who called himself Emperor Hudson. George said, 'I've never seen the titles in the middle. Let's put them there.' He had advertisements in it like a radio show. He played with the concepts. He was free. He said we could do anything.

"Our leader was Francis Ford Coppola, who had graduated from film school before us. In those days we really felt we were going to change everything, that we were going to make the greatest art—and we did to a degree. We didn't have much money, but we didn't need much. The root, the highest ideal for all of us, was to do what we wanted. Not what the studio said to do. Our driving force was to get freedom. We called Coppola 'Francis the Fuehrer.' He was really the reckless one. I'd like to see George be a little more reckless but it's hard to be reckless when you become an institution. When we got out of film school, Francis was our leader. He really gave us our chance. The whole concept of the ideal film community where artists could work free from the tyranny of the studios was Francis's. His philosophy was imbued in everyone. George is carrying out that now with his Skywalker Ranch."

In 1967 Lucas won a scholarship from Warner Brothers to observe the filming of *Finian's Rainbow*, directed by Coppola. The next year Lucas worked again with Coppola as his assistant during the shooting of *The Rain People*. Coppola backed Lucas's 1971 film *THX 1138* (a feature-length version of one of his student films), an uncommercial, bleak look at a futuristic world. Coppola says, "George and I became almost like brothers. We were always dreaming about how it was going to be. I think *Star Wars* is a wonderful achievement, but I don't think those movies are George's best films. George is an extraordinary filmmaker, but *Star Wars* is another matter. It is an extremely popular and entertaining vision, but it is just that. It doesn't show his brilliance or the height of his ability by any means. Obviously, over the years, George and I have talked about this lots of times. Once the George Lucas who made personal films starts making personal films again, it will be something to behold." Coppola went to Universal to help Lucas get financing for *American Graffiti*. Based on its success, Twentieth Century–Fox decided to take a chance on Lucas's strange story of Jedi knights and princesses trapped in holograms.

George and Marcia Lucas have been married since 1969. They live in the tiny town of San Anselmo, not quite thirty minutes north of the Golden Gate Bridge, on the top of a hill in a white Victorian mansion built in 1896. Two sun porches encircle the house—one upstairs, the other off the entrance. On the acre and a half of property there are several smaller buildings: Lucas's office, staffed with two full-time assistants; the converted carriage house; quarters for two gardeners; and an apartment where the governess of Lucas's two-year-old adopted daughter Amanda lives. The carefully cared for grounds have vegetable and *bonsai* gardens, flowers, and little groves of orange and nectarine trees. There is a splendid kidney-shaped swimming pool on the oblong front lawn.

The rooms of the main house are bright, full of green plants, and cluttered with pine and oak antique tables and cabinets. Here and there, Oriental rugs warm the wood floors. The Lucases collect the work of twentieth-century American painters and illustrators. They have Maxfield Parrish's *The Ecstasy* and a number of Norman Rockwell paintings, including *Tom Sawyer Getting a Teaspoon of Medicine from His Aunt*. There is one original Tiffany lamp and several imitations. Marcia thinks it's "silly" to put all that money into real ones. On one of the oak bookshelves in the library sits the gold Oscar that Marcia, a well-known film editor, won for co-editing *Star Wars*. There is also a glassed-in case with a model of one of the *Empire*'s deadly Walkers in it. No one plays the black upright piano in the living room, but it is something Marcia has always wanted. There is an antique tricycle on the floor, and Marcia says, "What do you buy for George Lucas? I buy him old toys."

There is a television room with a large-screen Sony TV. Up on the wall are six gold and platinum sound track albums for the *Star Wars* movies and *American Graffiti*. The kitchen is high-ceilinged and roomy; it has an antique icebox for a refrigerator, and bowls of oranges and giant strawberries are set out. A bay-windowed breakfast nook overlooks the pool. A fixture in the house is Marcia's thirteen-year-old Alaskan malamute, Indiana, the inspiration for the name of *Raiders'* main character and also for Chewbacca's personality.

Marcia Lucas, thirty-seven, is spunky and unspoiled. She wears a huge diamond on her left hand but often has her brown hair in a ponytail on the top of her head, and she dresses in blue jeans, sweat pants, sweatshirts, and tennis shoes. She uses the adjective *real* a lot. Marcia's film editing credits include *Taxi Driver, New York, New York,* and *Alice Doesn't Live Here Anymore.* Her husband says she is "great with emotions and characters, the dying and crying scenes." She cut Yoda's and Vader's deaths in *Jedi.* But she also cuts the space battles. George listens to her very carefully. After she saw a rough cut of *Raiders* she said the ending didn't work because there wasn't any emotional resolution between the Ford and Allen characters. The ending was reshot. "I love film editing and I'm real gifted at it," Marcia says. "I have an innate ability to take good material and make it better, to take bad material and make it fair. I'm compulsive about it. I think I'm even an editor in real life."

The Lucases have wanted children for a long time and finally adopted Amanda two years ago. Marcia would like one or two more children; George, three or four more. She says of her husband, "He is a very private person. It's not at all easy for him to open up with strange people. He's got a very childish, silly, fun side, but he doesn't even like me to talk about that because he is so intensely private. George is a real mensch. He is really centered, a together person. He knows what he wants to do, and he's doing what he wants to do. He is very much in control. He has always been a very normal person. His genius is for entertaining people."

Marcia says she has always encouraged Lucas to find diversions outside film. "He's so mentally stimulated all the time, so creative and so inquisitive," Marcia says, "but he is not a physical person. He doesn't participate in any sports or even have a hobby. He is so intensely in love with his work that his work is his hobby. I've been after him for years to get some other interests to help him relax. He's been skiing twice now, and he's a little more interested in exercise. From time to time we have parties if a friend is getting married, or two or three times a year we have six or eight close friends over for dinner and then go see a movie in the projection room. All our friends are pretty much in the film business. George's chums are guys he went to film school with, guys he's known for twenty years.

"George has always loved news. Before we had Amanda, he would take his dinner plate and go into the bedroom and eat dinner while he watched the CBS Evening News. I'd bring my plate and go with him. He would mimic commercials. Now I make everybody leave at six o'clock so that when George comes home, it's just the two of us and Amanda. Now that we have Amanda, we actually have dinner at the table. I cook, do the dishes, and we give Amanda a bath together. George sometimes feeds her her bottle in the TV room. We just decided to try to keep our lives as normal as possible. We both have very traditional values. When you get a big jolt of money, it's very easy to be in awe of it and lose touch with reality. I don't want to raise children in a fantasy. Amanda is going to have to make her own bed, pick up her own clothes."

The Lucases have amassed a personal fortune of more than $20 million. The money is in stocks and bonds, real estate, and art. Lucas made about $18 million from *Star Wars*. He then put up all his money as collateral to start *The Empire Strikes Back*. "I didn't have any money at all personally until *Empire* was released," he says. After *Empire*, Lucas gave the University of Southern California Film School a $5 million gift. He kept from *Empire* the $20 million or so he had put up for it. Lucas will also keep for himself five percentage points of *Jedi*'s profits. He says, "Being rich is not as much fun as people think. It has made my life more complicated. My wife and I are basically simple people. We have simple wants and needs. Money has a tendency to embellish your life much more than you desire. When you have money, there is a lot of maintenance and it's a lot of work. Once you have more than a million dollars, it becomes a pain. Quite frankly, I think the ideal financial situation would be to have just under one million dollars. I'm not the sort of person who can waste money. I can't just spend it on yachts and good times. To me it's not the money; it's what you do with it that counts. I'm interested in doing something productive with it. I plow money back into my company."

Lucas's company, Lucasfilm, is in a cluster of five buildings in San Rafael, a few miles north of San Francisco. The firm's basic businesses are special effects, a postproduction sound and film editing service, product licensing, marketing, technological research, video editing, interactive video discs, and high-level sound (Lucasfilm created the sophisticated THX sound system now used in many theaters). The company also has invested $10 million in oil and gas and another $10 million in real-estate ventures. The atmosphere is informal. Company executives walk around in corduroy work shirts and chinos; computer scientists with Ph.D.s all wear blue jeans, and most sport beards like their leader. On a given day, broccoli, chocolate-chip cookies, and spaghetti are being made in the employee kitchens. After *Empire*, Lucas put three profit points from the film into a fund to be distributed among the company's three-hundred-odd employees, including secretaries and janitors, based on their length of service. For *Jedi* there is a new distribution structure: three profit points will be apportioned with regard to a person's responsibility level at the company as well as his seniority. Lucas can't recall specifically but believes he gave each of the lead actors in *Jedi* 1.5 profit points. The president of Lucasfilm, Robert Greber, a former Merrill Lynch investment banker, says, "Lucasfilm is a very strange and wonderful company in that the sole stockholder, George Lucas, doesn't have profit as his highest priority. His priorities are not to lose money so he can be active in the things he wants to do. George would also like to make working conditions at Lucasfilm as much like nirvana as possible."

Lucas says he started Lucasfilm only as a way of turning the money he was making from his movies into Skywalker Ranch, the utopian film-making community he has fantasized about since his film-school days. Skywalker Ranch, Lucasfilm's major investment (about $50 million) is a 2,600-acre complex in west Marin County. "I knew I had to have a company if I ever was going to build Skywalker Ranch," Lucas says. "Skywalker Ranch was the original purpose of it all." Lucas's goal is to create an ideal, communal working environment and research center for filmmakers, either those working on movies with Lucas, or others who want to rent. When it is finished, Skywalker Ranch, tucked into the folds of the Marin hills, will have state-of-the-art preproduction and postproduction facilities for moviemakers and an extensive research library. There will be a group of apartments, all furnished in the Ranch's turn-of-the-century Victorian style, where guest filmmakers will live with their families; administrative offices will be quartered in the Main House, Gate House, Carriage House, and Brook House; a recreation area will have two tennis courts, a handball court, a swimming pool, a gym, a spa, a softball diamond, and stables. Cattle will graze on the green land which will be planted with trees, vineyards, and fruit orchards. There also will be a four-and-a-half-acre man-made lake stocked with 3,500 trout.

A glass studio at the Ranch employs seven specialists who are making stained-glass windows for the buildings. The windows will picture native flowers, birds, and animals. In a small brass workshop, two workers cut and assemble the ranch's brass chandeliers, lamps, and stair railings. Fifteen millers are recycling eighty-year-old redwood bridge timbers from the Pacific Coast Highway into ceiling beams and furniture. One hundred and fifty tons of cobblestone from rehabilitated streets in San Francisco are being turned into sidewalks. The floors will be inlaid with oak by hand. The library will have a stained-glass dome, fourteen feet wide with a five-foot rise, colored in shades matching the redwood timbers around it. "I wanted a campus environment," Lucas says, "a very relaxed atmosphere with trees. I wanted to build the Ranch to have a nice place to work, a place big enough so that all my friends and I wouldn't be squeezed together."

Looking ahead, Lucas says, "I might never make any more movies. If I do, they most likely will be abstract, experimental films without plot or characters. I am more interested in films like *THX 1138*—nonstory films that are more visual, more pure. I've sort of mastered the art of popcorn movies, but it's limited. Part of my problem with *Star Wars* is that I'm working from ten-year-old ideas. I've got to come up for air now and take a look around to see if my perceptions have changed. I'm not even ready to ask any questions until I can settle down and relax. After *American Graffiti*, *Star Wars* could have gone in the toilet and it wouldn't have made any difference to me, in terms of what I wanted to do. I was set financially for the rest of my life. It was an interesting life choice I made. When I was eighteen and had that automobile accident, that was the end of the first part of my life. I made a transition into film. I always had a feeling that in twenty years I would be making another transition. So, here I am, twenty years later. The last train, I got knocked off of, and hit a tree. This train I'm jumping off of. I have no idea what I want to do for the next twenty years. I have no idea what my destiny is."

May 1983

George and Marcia Lucas are divorced. They share custody of their daughter, Amanda. Return of the Jedi *made $100 million in its first three weeks of release; it is now the third-highest-grossing film of all time, after* E.T. *and* Star Wars. *Lucas was the co-executive producer of* Indiana Jones and the Temple of Doom *(1984);* Mishima: A Life in Four Chapters *(1985); the executive producer of* Howard the Duck *(1986);* Labyrinth *(1986); and* Willow *(1988). Lucas produced* Tucker *(1988) for Francis Ford Coppola. Skywalker Ranch is flourishing. Lucas has no immediate plans to make any more* Star Wars *films. The mythologist Joseph Campbell, before he died in 1987, called Lucas a modern mythmaker.*

GREG GORMAN / GAMMA/LIAIS

VERY
VERY
BETTE
MIDLER

*M*any things have been said about Bette Midler: that she is Bette the Boss, a Bette noire, a hateful bitch, bitchily comic, a prima bitcherina, a new mama, the last of the red-hot mamas, the last of the tacky ladies, the belle of the baths, a bawd and a homebody; that she is randy and raucous, gleeful and glorious, trashy with flash and sleazy with ease, a vibrant, heart-stopping beauty with a wit that stings like a paper cut; that she is deft and diabolical, fragile and flamboyant, melodious, manic, and madcap; that she is a blooming rose, a wilted rose, a star re-

197

born, a rose abloom again, a cherubic chanteuse, a classic chanteuse, the diva of comic irony, a mainstream diva, a diminutive diva, the kahuness of camp, a camp curiosity; that she's got a sassy walk, salty talk, pluck, luck, wit, grit; that she's a little engine that could, a tugboat, the hardest-working woman in showbiz who's been served to audiences on a silver platter, as a frankfurter, in a high heel, on a clam shell, as a mermaid, in a diaper; that she is six feet of body scrunched into a five-foot frame; that she is serious and shy, buxom and blond, with a funny nose and dancing eyes; that she is the best piece of divinity in the world.

The Bette Midler I meet Saturday night is wearing black leggings, an oversized black shirt, and square tortoise shell glasses. She has on no makeup and her brown hair is pulled back in a ponytail. She is very short, about 5'1", and has tiny, perfectly shaped hands and feet. The Divine Miss M is not giving this interview. At forty-one, Midler is very much the homemaker these days, the loving wife and mother. She says about her husband, Martin von Haselberg, thirty-eight, a commodities trader and performance artist whom everyone, even Midler, calls by his stage name, Harry Kipper, "He is wonderful, stabilizing; he sees to the heart of things. He makes me feel comfortable and trusting and safe. He respects me and supports what I do. And he leads me, too, when I lose my way. Now all my friends want to marry Harry Kipper because they want to have a fabulous life like mine." Midler stops often throughout our conversation to nurse or visit her three-month-old daughter, Sophie Frederica Alohilani von Haselberg. "I adore her," says Midler. "I adore her. It is the most wonderful thing. Her face swims before me when she's not there and I think about her before I go to sleep at night and I dream about her and I wake up and I can't wait to see her. I named her Sophie because it is a beautiful old European name. My husband is European and has a very European-sounding name, and I wanted her name to go with that. Frederica is for my father, who was named Fred. Alohilani is Hawaiian for 'bright sky,' which is what I always wish for her. Bright skies. I realized when I announced her name that everyone would think I named her for Sophie Tucker. I'm going to be damned for this, but I have to be honest—I did not name her after Sophie Tucker."

Midler's husband is gentle-mannered, but when he is not smiling, he has a stern, Germanic, aristocratic face, a Holbein portrait come to life. His hair is cut just this side of punk, and he loves to wear the thirties, forties, and fifties suits he collects. Cooking is one of his favorite things to do, and most of the time, Midler says, he does it. He makes cappuccino for us in their glistening, flower-filled kitchen, and then wanders away. As we begin to talk in a sitting room downstairs from the nursery, Midler shows me a picture of her mother as a child. The little girl in the old photograph is wearing a white starched pinafore, her dark hair carefully combed behind her ears, which are enormous. I remark on the girl's solemn beauty and then impulsively point out the ears. Midler immediately runs squealing from the room, waving the picture, shouting, 'Harry, Harry, here's where she got the ears.' And indeed, Sophie Frederica, though adorable, clearly got the ears. They are like little wings on her bald head. She has her father's face. Midler says, "I had no idea what it would be like to have a baby. It was a complete shock to me—that I would have such deep feelings, and that she would be so much fun. Harry and I are not young, you know. We were two people who—he in his sphere and I in mine—had sown quite a few wild oats between us. I never pooh-poohed family life, but it was not something that I put a high priority on. Now I do."

Besides having a perfect child and doting husband, Midler is, at long last, a movie star and a huge box-office draw. Her new and third Disney film, *Outrageous Fortune*, in which she costars with Shelley Long as two women two-timed by the same man, took in $6.4 million its opening weekend, a record for the studio. *Down and Out in Beverly Hills* grossed $64 million and ranked tenth among the most popular films of 1986. Next came *Ruthless People*, which made $72 million at the box office. Midler just signed a long-term contract to star in three additional Disney pictures. She says, "I have been a very, very, very lucky girl. I never expected to be a box-office star, but I'm happy about it and very grateful. I've worked really hard and been up and down, and this is a kind of vindication for me. The whole package is a surprise: to be a box-office success and to be a box-office success hand in hand with Disney. A real shocker. Never. Walt Disney never would have hired me."

Midler has not always been a very, very, very lucky girl. When she talks about her childhood, she gets teary: "My parents had moved to Hawaii from New Jersey in the late 1930s. They liked it a lot, and when the war came, they were stuck. My mother was pregnant with my sister.

My father was a civilian working as a housepainter for the Navy. At the end of the war they had two daughters and one on the way, me. I was born on December 1, 1945, in Honolulu. My mother named me after Bette Davis. She was nuts about Bette Davis. My mother's name was Ruth, and she sewed beautifully. She made all of our clothes up until the time my sister was fourteen years old. She would make three copies of the same dress for my sisters and me, and when I outgrew my dress, I would get my second sister's dress, then I would get my oldest sister's dress. I was always wearing the same dress. I didn't really care. My mother—oh, my mother was stunning. I loved my mother. She was very hardworking. She didn't drive, so if she had any errands, she always had to walk. She was terribly hardworking. I keep remembering her standing over a washing machine. Just endlessly washing and hanging up clothes, washing and ironing. It seemed like that was all she did, you know. When my baby was born, I was so tired, and I kept thinking, 'How did she do it? How did she do it? How could she have four children and still be standing?' I finally got the message, but it was too late.

"My mother always told us that we could do whatever there was to do in the world. She told us we were as good as anybody, and she told us we could do anything. Whatever we thought, whatever we could conceive of, we could do. She always talked about us getting out into the world, about going to college, making something of ourselves. She gave us a lot of confidence. Even though we were the only white people in a Samoan and Japanese community, she said we were as good as anybody. My mother thought I was just wonderful. She thought I was just great, that I could do no wrong. Once I discovered theater, everything else in my life receded into the background. I was just obsessed with the idea of becoming this person. Even though I was selfish, she just thought I was wonderful. She was all for my having a goal and for my getting started on this journey toward theater and going full speed ahead. She encouraged me completely. When I was the lead in the junior-class play, she came to the show and brought me a bouquet of roses and presented them to me over the footlights. My mother saw *The Rose* before she died. Because my father didn't approve, she snuck out of the house one day and went and saw it. She thought it was wonderful. My mother died of liver cancer in 1980. But she had had breast cancer twice, from the time I was in the fifth grade. It was very, very hard, very hard on her. After she died, we finally opened up a crate that had been sitting in the middle of the living room. Her whole trousseau was in it. She had sewn everything herself."

Midler is overwhelmed by these memories, and she gets up from the couch and lies down on the floor, heaving and sobbing and blowing her nose. She cries and cries, and then laughs at herself for crying so much. When she sits up and returns to her spot on the couch, she keeps a box of yellow Kleenex next to her.

"My father thought I was a little odd. He never chose to see me perform. He saw me on TV on the Johnny Carson show a couple of times. He thought I wore my dresses too low and I was too loose. He thought I looked like a loose, immoral woman. He didn't know it was my act. To him it was one and the same. In those days, actually, he wasn't that far wrong. It was the late sixties, you know. My father was a bit of a tyrant. He wanted respect, and I guess when we got into our teens, we weren't really paying much attention to his needs. He would take all our makeup and flush it down the toilet. My sister Susan used to have to call the cops on him because he'd lock her out of the house when she came home too late.

"I have a younger brother, Daniel. He had a fever after he was born and was left with brain damage. My father taught my brother to read and to write. My father—my God, that was pretty rough. My father hammered at him until he just finally learned. I remember my father used to come home at four in the afternoon, and no one wanted to be in the house. At four my father would start, and it would go on until dinnertime. Daniel would cry and my father would scream. My father would just stand over him and yell and yell and yell until he got it. We would say, 'Leave him alone, leave him alone.' But eventually Daniel did get it. He learned to read, and it's made a big difference in his life. It gave him freedom. I think my father was right.

"He was also very tight-fisted. He felt he had to put something aside for my brother. He wanted to make sure my brother wasn't a burden on the state or on us. My parents saved only through real sacrifice. They never went to the movies. They never had a night out. They didn't do anything. They wanted to make this life for my brother. When we were older, my father started collecting lawn mowers and refrigerators. He must have had twenty-five or thirty lawn mowers all over the yard, covered by tarps, in the bushes. He had refrigerators, all kinds of refrigerators. He died last year. He died in May of last year. He had heart trouble. It was too bad, it was just too bad.

"I adore my sisters. My oldest sister was named Judy. She was a very brilliant girl. She was the one who was the most unhappy. She got anorexia in the late fifties and we had no idea what it was. We had no idea. It was so frightening to see her wasting away like that. After a few years she got over it and then became really chubby. She died in 1968 in a car crash in New York. She was walking on a sidewalk along Forty-fourth Street and a car came out of a garage on the opposite side of the street and hit her. It was a freak accident. I was in a show at the time. Everyone else was in Honolulu, and I had to go to the morgue and identify the body and make all the funeral arrangements. It was a very bad time in all of our lives. I don't think my mother ever really recovered from it. My other sister, Susan, is also very brilliant in her field. She started out working with retarded people and now is in hospital administration in New York and is very devoted to health care. She has made a lot of changes in the New York system. My brother lives with her.

"We were poor. We were really poor. We didn't get a telephone until the late fifties. We lived in what is called *halawa* housing. It was government-subsidized housing. It had been a military barracks during the war. We lived in the middle of the sugarcane fields. I'll never forget when we first moved in there, we were right on the edge of the cane fields, and they started burning the cane. I never figured out if some-body set fire to it or if it was just the harvest. My mother thought we were going to go up in smoke. We had just moved into this house, and it was a paper house. It was just pressed cane. All the people from this housing complex gathered outside because they were afraid the place would burn up. After the fire all the soot blew into the house. Every two years or so the fields were burned, so every two years we got these black windstorms. It felt like you could never get clean.

"It was a pretty rough neighborhood. There were a lot of people on welfare. Most of the people were Hawaiian, Chinese, Samoan, Japanese. We were the only white family. We were always picked on because we were the only white kids in school. White people were called *haoles*, and they were really not welcome there. We always had enough to eat. My parents always shopped at this cut-rate store. It was really mortifying, because it was like dented-can city. And seconds. Always seconds, seconds, seconds. My parents discovered the Salvation Army in the late fifties, and my mother stopped sewing. It was cheaper to buy other people's clothes there. But my mother had a great eye, and she picked stuff that was really pretty, just a little worn out.

"My mother was a musicals freak. She loved musicals. When we were old enough to go to the movies by ourselves, we were only allowed to see musicals. We were never allowed to see horror pictures, drama, science fiction, or cowboy pictures. I guess my parents thought musicals were more wholesome. They were less likely to give us bad dreams, nightmares — less likely to give us bad ideas. I must say the ideas those pictures gave me, they weren't bad ideas. They made a big impression on me and really stuck with me. Really, to this day I have never seen a picture more entertaining than an Esther Williams picture. I just loved being in the movie theater, I loved that smell of cheap perfume, and the hot popcorn machine that they used to stick over in the corner. I love that smell.

"We always had hula lessons. My mother was very keen on hula lessons. There was a little shack, and all the girls were there, and the Hawaiian ladies with their mumus and leis. They'd put the records on and we'd dance. It was just fabulous. I loved it. I remember wanting to take singing lessons, but we couldn't afford it. When I was about ten, my mother took me to a singing teacher and she liked my voice but it was just too much money. The first time I knew I had a good voice was when I was in the first grade. I sang 'Silent Night' in front of my class and I won a prize. After that you just couldn't stop me from singing. In our *halawa* housing I always sang in the shower. I sang at the top of my lungs in the shower. At the top of my lungs. It was a tin shower, and it had a really good reverb. People used to gather outside the window and, you know, yell up their requests or yell up that I was terrific or lousy. I always sang 'Lullaby of Broadway' at the top of my lungs. We didn't have a lot of mirrors when I was growing up. We had one mirror, not a full-length mirror, a cracked mirror. You really had to strain to get some true picture of yourself. You know, in my mind's eye I'm beautiful and tall and thin and glamorous. It wasn't really until photographs of me started rolling in that I realized my mental image of myself and my true image were not the same. I was very, very shocked. Very, very shocked. When really unattractive pictures of me were printed, I would say, 'That's not me. Who is that?' I wouldn't even recognize myself. But I had to adjust. And I adjusted.

"I was a very emotional child. I felt very much everything around me, you know, the way the dust motes floated in the sun. I felt everything in a very, very strong way. There is something about Hawaii, something about the air, the light, the sound of the wind that is so romantic, it's so heavy. There is something in the atmosphere that makes you see every moment so clearly. I was always moved by the natural stuff around me. I felt quite isolated, and I knew I was different. My God, you'd think I had been in Nazi Germany or something. I was just this kid. But I was all right up until about the seventh grade. That is when I started going to school with all these Oriental kids who were much better off than we were. They were so mean. They really ripped into me and my sisters. There was a gang of girls and I was their target. Whenever I came near them, they would move away. And there was always this whispering, whispering—you know, what the hell are they whispering about? It was all calculated to suppress you, make you feel less like a human being, less than what you really were. It really broke my heart. It had nothing to do with being Jewish. They had no idea what Jewish was. But they knew white, all right. They were basically racist. I just kept to myself and made two good Japanese friends. I have always gravitated toward people who won't hurt me, you know.

"On Saturdays my parents would go to all the thrift stores and they would drop us off at the library at nine in the morning and they didn't come back until four in the afternoon. We read everything, all the classics. I loved it. For a couple of summers in junior high I worked at the library dusting books and putting them back on shelves. I made a friend there, an amazing woman. She was the kind of person who made you hang up your paper towels to dry. At the end of the summer she would take my friend and me to the community theater. The first thing I ever saw was *Carousel*. I was twelve years old. The actors had costumes made of satin and sequins and fur boas and little feathers at their neckline. They wore high heels with taps on them. They were dancing and singing. I couldn't get over how beautiful it was. It seems I just knew I was drawn to it like a moth to a flame, I fell so in love with it.

"When I got to high school, things really picked up. I was a very good student and made really good grades. In the summers I got a job as a pineapple packer at the pineapple cannery. I was president of the class senior year. There was a drama teacher named Betty Blake who was fabulous. She was so glamorous, you couldn't even stand her she was so glamorous. She wore high-heel shoes with no backs, you know. She had streaked hair, she smoked Pall Malls and drove this old Hudson. I got into her drama class and started doing these little playlets. I joined the community theater in my senior year and started getting good notices. I met two other girls and formed a singing trio. My dad actually heard us sing and thought we sang beautifully. That was the most he ever said about anything I had done. He said I should have stuck with those girls.

"I went to the University of Hawaii. I got into their theater program, but I was very impatient. I wanted to get going, I wanted to get going. I quit school after three semesters to make enough money to go. Then George Roy Hill came to town to do the movie *Hawaii*. They needed extras. I auditioned and was hired as a missionary. I made $350 a week, which was an enormous amount of money in those days. I earned enough to move to New York in 1965, and it was really as if I had come home. I had never been there, but I felt as though I knew it. My parents were always talking about New York. There we were in Hawaii, the most beautiful place in the world, and my parents were talking about New York as if it were paradise and Hawaii was just some way station. I really believed that New York was the place to be even when I was five years old. I took a room in the Broadway Central Hotel and right away met Tom Eyen and started working for him. Eyen had a troupe of really down-to-earth, Bohemian-type actors, and I became one of his leading ladies. I was very happy. I was nineteen years old. I just loved the idea of getting up in front of a crowd and strutting my Hawaiian stuff.

"I got the lead in Eyen's off-off-Broadway production of *Miss Nefertiti Regrets*. All my relatives from New Jersey came to see me. I wore a bathing suit the whole time. I think that's the reason I got the job: I had a two-piece bathing suit. I played a bimbo-type character. I was always playing these bimbo parts because I had a big chest and a little waist and wonderful legs. I still have great legs. And I could sing, and I wasn't afraid to be ditzy on stage. I was also the lead in another of Tom Eyen's shows, *Cinderella Revisited*. I used to say it was a show for nine-year-old gay boys because it was so ridiculous, so camp. I didn't even know what camp was in those days. I haven't figured camp out yet. Some people think it's great and some people don't. All I know is that it is truly trivial and obsessed with style and fashion and stuff that's all very ephemeral and trendy and doesn't mean anything, except it makes life a lot more fun. Tom Eyen introduced me to camp, and I was always vastly amused by it.

"I got an apartment with a girlfriend on Bedford, six flights up, in the Village. It was great. I still think about it and remember every stick of furniture in the place. I loved downtown right away, and the West Side. I did odd jobs here and there to make money. I sold gloves at a department store called Stern's. I was a typist at Columbia University for a while until the great subway strike in 1966. I couldn't get up there. I was a go-go girl in Manhattan and in New Jersey at some Italian bar. I loved being a go-go girl, just standing in the cage and shaking your tail feather. I wore great big go-go boots, white ones with black heels, an orange leotard, and a red bubble wig. They paid $25 a night. That was a lot of money in those days.

"Then in 1967, I got a part in the chorus of *Fiddler on the Roof.* I had been auditioning for a long time, and I think the reason I was chosen was that I had the gall, the consummate chutzpah, to sing 'Pirate Jenny,' a Kurt Weill song. All the other girls were singing ingenue-type songs, songs from *The Fantasticks* or pop songs. I was singing this Lotte Lenya ballad about death and revenge and killing everybody who ever stepped on me. It's a fabulous song. [Bette sings the song.] I have loved that song since college. I loved Lotte Lenya. I thought I was Lotte Lenya. I loved Anna Magnani. I loved the strong woman, the strong earth-mother character. I never cared for the ingenues, and I never got those jobs, anyway. So I sang 'Pirate Jenny' for my audition and there was like dead silence. Thirty seconds later they said, 'We'll call you.' And they did. They wanted me to be in the chorus and to understudy the role of the eldest daughter.

"I was so happy. I was so grateful to everyone. I was just thrilled to death to be in the theater. The theater smells were all around me, and the brilliant voices. The show itself was so beautiful. The way it was lit—you could die for that lighting. The woman who played the eldest daughter was very kind to me. She saw that I was enthralled with the theater, and she knew my three-month contract was nearly up. So one night she phoned in sick so that I could play the part. Isn't that great? She did that for me. She didn't tell me she was going to do it. She just did it. I got to play the part. It was just great. I think I was okay. I didn't drop the mop. That was a big deal. Then a few months later that part opened up again and there were going to be auditions. It was going to be a real audition. You had to do a scene in front of Jerome Robbins. I learned the scene, but on the day of the audition the casting director called me and told me not to go to the audition because I was completely wrong for the part. I said I came to New York so that I could meet Jerome Robbins, and even though I was wrong for the part, I was going to audition. I don't know where I got the nerve. I really don't. I went to the audition and was totally overwrought, but the scene was the most overwrought scene in the play. It was the one in which the father promises the girl to the butcher, but the girl is in love with the tailor and begs her father not to make her marry the butcher. I was so overwrought, I did the scene as if I would die if I had to marry the butcher and Robbins loved it. I got the job even though I was too small and not flat-chested.

"I stayed with *Fiddler on the Roof* for a couple of years, but I kept on auditioning for other things. I was ruthless when it came to auditions. I went everywhere. I tried to get an agent but couldn't get one. I felt that nothing was moving, nothing was happening. I wasn't stretching. I kept looking. I had a girlfriend in the show who wanted to be a singer. She was going to these nightclubs downtown which let you sing three songs. I went with her one night and I got up and sang. I sang a blues song, 'God Bless the Child.' Something happened to me while I was singing that song. It had never happened before. It was a kind of catharsis. I lost myself in that song in a way that I had never lost myself before. It was such an exhilarating experience that I wanted to have it again and again. I found I really enjoyed standing up on a stage with a piano player and singing.

"I found that there were many clubs in New York where you could sing three songs a night and you could really learn how to do whatever it was you wanted to do. I started making the rounds of these clubs. I would audition during the day, do *Fiddler on the Roof* at night, and then after *Fiddler* I got all done up in this drag and went to sing at the clubs. I got the idea to dress up from an East Village artist at the Theater of the Ridiculous named Black-Eyed Susan who wore a kind of thirties outfit:

gray skirt, black pumps, and a white lace blouse with a jabot. After I saw her, the very next day I went out to an antique clothing shop and bought a velvet dress. It had a long velvet coat with a big rabbit-fur collar, and when I put it on, I just felt that I was doing exactly what I had been meant to do. I started singing songs from the thirties and the forties, some standards but a lot of obscure blues songs, some Bessie Smith. That's how it started to build.

"I was also going to see a lot of films during the day. I was introduced to Marlene Dietrich. I listened to Bessie Smith and Aretha Franklin records. A friend started playing all kinds of music for me, a lot of opera, Ruth Etting, Libby Holman. I was going to the Museum of Modern Art and I was going downtown to the Theater at St. Marks and watching Ginger Rogers and Fred Astaire. All this stuff was completely new to me because I had been in Hawaii and never seen any of it. It was an explosion. Plus I was smoking the tiniest amount of grass, and being in my usual hyperemotional state, all this stuff just burned itself into my brain. I sort of became what I imagined the characters to be, not the actors and the actresses, but what I imagined the characters to be. Joan Crawford in *Rain* as Sadie Thompson. I still haven't recovered from that one. Mae West. I had never seen Mae West. I couldn't get over Mae West.

"All my days and nights were spent looking at pictures and movies and reading up on these people and looking for sheet music. I was the queen of obscure sheet music. I was the only person in the Colony Record Store who was actually allowed to go through the files. I would sit down on a little stool and go through every single file cabinet for hours on end, looking for 'the song.' I didn't read music, so I could only go by the title. If it was a great title, I'd buy it. If it amused me or I thought it was a sad song, I'd buy it. This friend of mine also had a huge collection of old pop music. He had Al Jolson, Mae West, Ruby Keeler, and all those terrible Forty-second Street musicals. I would sit in that apartment night after night listening to this stuff, and the dream machine went on and I would just float. I was creating this idea, this persona. It's not that it was a brilliant idea, but it was something. I liked it. I was having a good time. The tortured torch singer in the middle of the fog with the fur piece around her neck, sharing her sorrows with the world. All those wisecracking, gum-chewing, hardboiled blondes in pictures.

Women in gauzy gowns in smoky bars with dark lipstick on the end of their cigarettes.

"I performed at the Improvisation, a comedy club, and the owner, Budd Friedman, became my manager for a while. Because the Improv was a comedy club, you had to be a little bit funny, so I found myself adding chatter between the songs. Then Budd got a call from Steve Ostrow, the owner of the Continental Baths, a health club that he wanted to combine with a nightclub. Steve said he was looking for an act. I was the second act he booked. That first night Steve asked how I would like to be introduced. I said, 'Tell them I'm divine.' When I was in the sixth grade, I was calling everybody 'darling' because I thought it was the thing to do. I guess it was one too many musicals. I always identified with the Mary Boland character, the duchess in the movie *The Women*. I imagined myself as some kind of dowager type calling everyone 'darling.' So it wasn't unusual for me to say, 'Tell them I'm divine,' because I had seen enough movies by then to think I really had made the transition. Another friend of mine was already calling me 'Miss M.' And the name stuck.

"What had happened was that I was singing the blues and ballads in these clubs wearing my long velvet dresses with my hair pulled back and my eyelashes waxed. I was convinced that I was a real torch singer. I believed that I could sing the blues, that I had the right to sing the blues. I was a sufferer and I sang the ballads for a long time and I wasn't a star or anything but I was getting a name as a blues singer. Then when I got to the Improv, I found myself doing parodies of Mae West, for example. I found myself telling whatever joke I had heard on the street. The audience ate it up. There I was, singing my ballads and crying the mascara off my eyes and in the next breath telling some lame joke I had heard. I found out I could make people laugh. When I was at the Baths, I started to really focus on that because I was a girl with five songs and twenty minutes of chatter and needed fifty minutes, so I just had to wing it. Eventually the big, brassy broad beat the crap out of the little torch singer and took over.

"I've made endless jokes about my chest. Oh, I don't know. It's low, burlesque humor. I've always been attracted to that kind of humor. I used to go hear musicians playing in clubs, and there was always a comic telling bad bazoom jokes. I just think they're funny. From the time I was about eleven or twelve, I grew this chest and I was always kind of embarrassed by it. But after a while, after I got to the point where I could show some cleavage, it suddenly was very alluring. It was no longer a joke. There's something about not taking that kind of sexiness seriously that I find really healthy. It's good for you to make fun of that kind of thing because it takes some of the danger out of it. I've just always done it, and always enjoyed it too. I remember I had a huge success at the London Palladium in 1978. The whole balcony held up this sign that read, WE LOVE YOU, BETTE. Placards. Everybody had a placard. I laughed and laughed. Then they turned the cards around and the cards said, SHOW US YOUR TITS. It had been that kind of night. It was the silliest night, everybody was having a great time, and I was very free. You know how when you're free, you sometimes feel you can do no wrong? I felt that way. I walked off the stage and then I came back. It just seemed like the only thing to do, the crowd was so lovable and sweet. So I showed my tits. The whole house went nuts.

"At the Baths it was warm but it wasn't steamy. I was in the middle of this room with a fast-food counter on one side, a pool, and an enclosed steam room. The guys would check their clothes at the door and get towels. When I first performed there, the guys sat on the floor. Later Steve Ostrow put in seats and opened it up to everybody. Then all these people from the Upper East Side decided going to the Baths was the thing to do. It wasn't just to see me but the whole atmosphere. There was a sordidness attached to it. To me it was completely respectable. I didn't have any idea. I was never in any of the back rooms. I only saw one penis. It peeked out of a towel. My stage turned into a disco dance floor after my show was over. The Baths was gay, gay, gay, gay, gay. It was deeply gay. It was gay in a heartfelt way. They thought my show was *fab-ulous*. They screamed, they shouted, they threw flowers. They just loved me. They were just so happy that anyone was standing in front of them singing.

"In between shows at the Continental Baths I performed at a club called The Downstairs. I worked there for a long time, doing the same kind of act. In 1971, Ahmet Ertegun, the chairman of Atlantic Records, saw me at The Downstairs with an extraordinary crowd. It was a hairdressers' convention, and they had booked the room. They were all drinking champagne and throwing confetti and streamers, and at the end of the show they picked me up on their shoulders and carried me out into the street. Ahmet Ertegun saw this and he said, 'My God, I've got to sign this girl.' So he signed me. I started to make a record with Barry Manilow, whom I had met at the Baths, and another producer. We had a good band, but the record was hard to make because the producers didn't really see eye to eye. I spent most of my time in tears because I was too unschooled a musician to tell them what I really wanted. Ahmet didn't like a lot of the tracks, and in the end he said, 'It seems to me that what you do best is work live, so let's throw a party.' We threw a huge party in the recording studio and I got up with the band and we sang all our songs and it was a big hit. That album was *The Divine Miss M*. It went gold and I won a Grammy for Best New Artist in 1973. I felt at the time that the success I was having made sense because I had worked so hard. I didn't feel jaded or bored or blasé, it just seemed that it was the reward. I felt I deserved it because I had worked really, really hard.

"The second record, *Bette Midler*, came out and sold well, but I made the mistake of reading the reviews and I never really was the same again. Some of the reviews said I wasn't a good singer and they were really cruel. I felt horrible. I had made some mistakes, but I didn't think they were worthy of such scathing comment. I decided that I was really a soprano. I'm not a soprano, I'm an alto. I decided I should write my own music, so I wrote a whole record in 1974. The label heard it and they got really upset and didn't want me to put it out. They went back into old tracks I had cut for my first two albums and slapped them onto a third record. That was the beginning of the end of my interest in a recording career. The worst part of it was they convinced me at the time that I had to chase the charts. I really couldn't chase the charts because I was too idiosyncratic, too eccentric for the charts. I wasn't mainstream, and they tried to push me into the mainstream and I couldn't do it.

"I tried, and that was the heartbreak of it, that I was trying. I couldn't really stand up to those assholes. I wanted to please, and when I couldn't please, I lost interest. But rather than stand up for myself, I made a couple of records that were really not very good. You get into the studio with those twenty-four/forty-eight tracks, and by the time they're done with you, it's not even a human being who is singing anymore. It's a machine. My voice is a very warm voice, and what I have to say, what I have to sell or what I am about, is human emotion, either raw or somewhat refined or humorous, but always human. After a while my records sounded like a machine was singing on them. I cut a record here and I cut a record there and I guess it was apparent that I wasn't all that interested because people stopped buying them.

"In 1971, Aaron Russo became my manager. He shepherded me through 1972, which was a huge year for me, just huge. We did New Year's Eve at the Philharmonic Hall, and at midnight I was lifted out of the orchestra pit singing 'Auld Lang Syne,' wearing a diaper with a huge silver safety pin. Aaron booked me into theaters, and we went out on the road, and lo and behold, I was a big success. Barry Manilow was with me. It was my first tour. We had a great band and we had a backup group called the Harlettes. At the end of 1974, we did *Clams on the Half Shell*. That was a brand-new show. That was the first time little me was onstage with all this stuff. It was enormous, it was beyond me. I didn't get it. I really didn't get it. Things were coming down from the ceiling, things were coming out from the wings. New York City, tap-dancing girls, King Kong, a jukebox, mannequins, and black singers came and went. All this machinery was going around and around, and I was the sole reason for it. It just blew me away. I didn't understand it until the very last week, and then I thought, 'Oh my God, this is such a great show. It's closing, what a shame.'

"We went all around the country with that show and ended up in Los Angeles, and Aaron said, 'Now or never. You have to be in the movies. That's the only place you can go from here.' So I said, 'That's fine. Let's go be in the movies.' Aaron got a development deal at Columbia during 1976 and 1977, and for two years nothing happened. He had a huge office at the studio and I would go and visit him there and wait for stuff to come in and nothing ever came in. Finally Aaron said there was only one thing to do, and that was go back to a project I had been offered in 1971 or 1972, right after Janis Joplin died. It was called *Pearl*, and I had said I wouldn't do it. I had been crazy about her and I didn't want to offend anybody or get anybody angry at me. Finally in 1978, when nothing else was happening, I said I would do it if a lot of things were changed. I said, 'For God's sake, change the title. There were lots of people who had the same story. Why can't the script be about all of them?'

"William Goldman was brought in to rewrite it. It became *The Rose*.

In the end I didn't believe it was Janis's story. When I played that character, I believed I was doing an homage to all those men and women who bit the dust from sheer compulsion. Everyone wonders how I was able to do that. I explained to you, I have a lot to draw on, a lot of anger and a lot of sorrow from my own life. You saw me writhing around on the floor. I had the best time ever making *The Rose*. I looked forward to every single day. I couldn't wait to just strap that angst bag on and just chew up that scenery. I had a ball. I was finally just being as big as life, bigger than life, screaming and carrying on and creating a racket. I loved that character. The movie had a big impact on my life. I thought it was my best work. And I felt that as a rock 'n' roll picture it was very accurate. It was almost like a documentary, that's what I thought. The record went platinum, which was a thrill. It was the first one I ever had, and it won a Grammy.

"After shooting *The Rose* Aaron Russo decided we should go out on the road again. We had never been to Europe, and he decided this was the time to go to Europe. Everyone was pretty tired. I was tired, he was tired. My temper was very, very short at the time. I just wasn't happy. I was resenting him, and he was resenting me, too, because he saw I was pulling away from him and wanting to become more my own person. We had been romantically involved for a very short time when he became my manager, but then I realized we were two very strong personalities and very stubborn, and it didn't work out. Then he resented me for having other boyfriends. We fought terribly on that tour. I was really drinking a lot. I was in bad shape. Aaron and I had a fistfight and I said, 'This is the end. This is just the end.' We split up in 1979. *The Rose* came out, and we really didn't share it. I was sorry about that.

"I went on, and I didn't do all that well on my own. I never hired another manager. I never wanted that again. I couldn't take it. I was hoping that after *The Rose* I would have a career for myself in films, but I didn't. Nothing happened, exactly nothing. I didn't get one script, not one script. I would sit home and say, 'I don't get it. I thought I would have gotten one.' Then Alan Ladd, who had been at Fox when I made *The Rose*, started his own company and he wanted a concert film from me to be the first film he released. I didn't have any money. I never made any money in those years, never. So I went out on the road in a show called *Divine Madness*. I had a lot of trouble because that was the first time I was responsible for hiring and firing people, and I made a lot of mistakes. The players in the band were really good, but they were undisciplined and got into this alcohol and coke binge. They would show up late and were throwing up on stage. It was that low. One day the lone dancer I hired didn't show up, and I had to do the dance number by myself. It was horrible.

"Aaron came to that show. It was the first time we had seen each other in a year, and I guess he must have smelled that I was vulnerable, unstable. The night he came I was ill, I was throwing up. I had my head in the toilet bowl throwing up, and he knocked on the door and I got up and came out into the room wiping my mouth off and he said, 'That show is the worst thing I have ever seen in my life.' I had bleached my hair and he said, 'You look like an albino. The lighting is horrible. Who made those clothes?' It was endless. I just broke down. I went out to eat with him, and I listened to everything he had to say, which boiled down to, 'Don't ruin everything I've built up. Come back with me.' It made a lot of sense, but I was so angry that he had waited until I was so shaky and had pounced on me that way, that I decided not to have anything to do with him. It was grotesque.

"The Ladd Company wouldn't let me get out of the picture. I was ill. I had this flu that I couldn't shake. If you listen to the tape of *Divine Madness*, you'll hear this nasal quality in my voice. The movie wasn't a hit. I could see that this big thing that Aaron had helped me build was disappearing, evaporating, and there didn't seem to be anything I could do about it. There didn't seem to be any way I could prove myself.

"The final nail in the coffin came with *Jinxed*. In 1981, my agent sent me this script, and I thought half of it was pretty good. It seemed like a send-up of *Double Indemnity*, but I couldn't get anybody to admit it was a send-up. The people at United Artists couldn't figure out whether it was serious or a parody, so I sort of made up their minds for them. I said, 'Let's do it for real.' It seemed like it would be a good drama. The UA people were in the middle of their *Heaven's Gate* experience, and they needed product. They threw this project in my lap. So I, like a schmuck, picked up this piece of material that only existed as half a piece and decided I would make it into a whole piece. UA behaved as if I were the producer, they gave me the power to make decisions. I chose the director, Don Siegel, and the leading man, Ken Wahl.

"At the beginning of the movie there was a scene that was not working at all, and it was reshot twice. The UA people came to me and said, 'What are we going to do about the scene?' So I told them about a scene in an earlier draft that was good, and they said, 'Great.' Don Siegel, Ken Wahl, everyone was livid. I tried to be reasonable and tell them that the studio had asked me to do this and provided the money for the scene and found a place to reshoot. I went into Don Siegel's trailer to smooth out the situation. Siegel and Ken Wahl were in there, and I went in and sat down and they turned on me. They started calling me names and telling me what an asshole I was for doing this and making them do it, and who did I think I was? I got ready to haul off and hit Don Siegel. I really was so angry, I was getting ready to punch him. Then Siegel's wife, this huge, Amazonian woman, saw that I was going to hit him, and she came around behind me and held my arms. I just lost it. I went nuts. I was screaming. They were so hateful, so awful. My feeling about that whole experience is that I've had my revenge. What goes around comes around. I really believe that. It was only a matter of time before karma caught up with all of them. They put me through the mill, and I didn't deserve it. I really didn't.

"After *Jinxed,* I went into a very steep decline. I felt like I was having a nervous breakdown. I slept all day and cried all night. I couldn't get up. I couldn't face the world. I felt that everyone knew what they had said about me and that I had no recourse. I couldn't defend myself. I lost a lot of self-confidence. I lived with it for a couple of years and I tried to get back on my feet. I wrote *The Saga of Baby Divine* [a best-selling children's book] mostly on impulse. It was the only thing I had to hang on to, really. I was drinking to excess. I think I'm allergic to booze. There's someone who lives inside of me who never shows up unless I'm drunk, and that person is a really hateful person. I don't like that person, and no one else does, either. That demon, I just didn't want to see anymore — and the hangovers were so dreadful and the self-loathing so great — so I stopped drinking about three years ago. Anyway, I was truly miserable at the time. I didn't know what I was going to do with myself.

"When I was at my lowest point, Harry called me up out of the blue. We had met a couple of years earlier when I went with a group of people to see King Crimson. He told me he was a performance artist and that he would take me around if I wanted to see anybody. He never called me and I never called him. I got his name, but I didn't get his number that night. I used to look at his name in my address book sometimes and say, 'Boy, that guy was nice. I wonder what ever happened to him.' Two years after we first met, he called me. This was October of 1984. We were married two months later.

"Harry and I decided on a Monday to get married on a Saturday. And so we did. It was just like that. We drove to Las Vegas. It was snowing in the mountains. We got there very late at night. We went to get the license, but the line was too long, I mean, there must have been two hundred couples in line. So we went and checked into the wedding suite at Caesars Palace and changed clothes. I was wearing a grayish-blue, very pale chiffon dress that I had bought for our first formal date together, a movie premiere. It cost a fortune, but I really wanted to impress Harry. And when he asked me to marry him, I said, 'Well, you know, I just happen to have a dress.' And that's what I wore. My dress was very boom-boom—it had strings of beads hanging down—and I made a nice racket walking down the aisle. I wore silver shoes. And I carried a beautiful bouquet. It's dried now and hanging next to a picture of Harry in our bedroom. Yeah, we're sops. We're really soppy.

"By this time it was two o'clock in the morning, and we got our marriage license. We wound up at the Candlelight Wedding Chapel. We put on a sound-track tape of Fellini's *Juliet of the Spirits* and walked down the aisle. The fellow started reading us the service, and it was really quite moving. We both got teary-eyed at the part about the gold ring. At the end of the ceremony the guy said he liked my work—and did I know he was an Elvis impersonator? I said, no, I didn't know he was an Elvis impersonator. He told us he was very popular and had recorded some AC music. Harry didn't know what 'AC' was, and I explained that it was Adult Contemporary or Easy Listening, depending on which coast you were on. As we left the chapel the guy promised he would send us his single.

"We both were terribly nervous. I didn't know what the hell I was doing. I mean, I looked over at him and there he was. The enormity of it just hit me. I thought 'Oh, my God.' We hardly knew each other. It was quite a shock. The next day we drove home, and there he was in his house. And there I was in my house. We had never lived together. And do you know what happened two days later? It was around Christmastime, and I went to see my father in Hawaii and he went to see his in Germany. So we didn't really have a honeymoon. I was on Kauai and it was pouring cats and dogs and I really missed my husband. And he was really missing me too. I called him and said, 'Let's meet.' So we met in New York and had New Year's Eve there, and that was very, very sweet. Then we came back and he moved out of his house and into mine. It seemed like everything was different after that."

Midler's partner in domestic bliss has an unusual saga of his own. The fourth son of wealthy exiles from Nazism, Martin von Haselberg was born in Argentina in 1949. He grew up in Germany and England. At eighteen he apprenticed with a family-connected commodities-dealing firm in London, and became a trader in cocoa. By then, he had also joined the counterculture of the late sixties. He grew his hair and started wearing baggy suits from thrift stores. He made friends with artists and, although he had seen perhaps two plays in his life, enrolled in a suburban London drama school. There he met Brian Routh, and they became the Kipper Kids. In their act they are two incarnations of one Harry Kipper, a working-class lad with a big chin. The Kipper Kids left school before they were expelled. Brian got married. Martin sold all his belongings except a saxophone, lived on a commune in Hamburg, and traveled around Sweden on a stolen moped. The Kipper Kids met up again in 1971, moved to a garret in Paris, drank vast quantities of alcohol, smoked anything they could get, and wrote ideas for the Kipper Kids shows. They started touring and after about four years became well known in Europe as performance artists. In 1976, Harry and Harry hit America.

"The show is very scatological," von Haselberg says, "but in a very childish way. One of the things we do is our own version of *West Side Story*. We have on these very large T-shirts under which we have boards and four balloons that are filled with luminescent paints of different colors so it looks like we have four huge breasts. We usually just wear jockstraps. Our heads are shaved and we wear large false noses and false chins because the character has a very large chin where his energy is stored. Our faces are painted white with black dots, very obvious black dots for a beard, and a little Hitler mustache and dark rings around our eyes. We look pretty stupid and pretty sinister at the same time. We each have a bottle of Thunderbird. We whistle the tune 'Tonight' and we take swigs of this Thunderbird wine and then suddenly we grab the bottles by the neck, smash them, and start singing 'The Jets Song,' the knife-fight song. We lunge for each other with these broken Thunderbird bottles, stabbing each other and bursting these balloons. So our shirts are stained with these luminescent phosphorescent colors. Then we sing 'Maria,' except we call it 'Diarrhea,' and for that we have these little plastic bags with chocolate pudding hanging down our backs and we sort of follow each other around on stage slashing these bags of chocolate pudding, rubbing them over each other's asses. People love it. Once we did a show in Amsterdam, and someone in the audience kept asking quietly, 'What does it mean? Please, what does it mean?' The guy got terribly upset. It doesn't mean anything at all."

To make money a few years ago, von Haselberg started his own company that trades in commodity options. He has appeared as Harry Kipper only a few times in the last six years. Midler has never seen him as Harry, but then von Haselberg has never met the Divine Miss M. On their first date, he remembers, "It was just sort of instantaneous. We were meant for each other. It was like two people who had been looking for each other for a long, long time. I had never heard Bette Midler's music. I had always wondered what is it that she does, what is it that she is so famous for? Now I am beginning to learn. I did see *The Rose* and her Disney films. She won't let me see *Jinxed* or *Divine Madness*. I don't really know who the Divine Miss M is. That's my wife, isn't it?"

Since the baby was born, "Bette has become much more relaxed, much less frenetic," von Haselberg says. "Bette is an incredibly loving mother. She is a lot of fun with the baby. She does lots of voices and characters, and she becomes like a very sweet little girl herself. Bette is wonderful to live with. I never used to laugh as much as I do now. I really like it when she sings songs like Ethel Merman. I'll ask her to sing any song like Ethel Merman. It is very funny. And sometimes when there is a corny song on the radio, she will sing it like Vicki Eydie, in a sort of smooth, lounge-act style. Bette is never still around the house. She sings a lot, and when there is music, she often dances."

· · ·

"I warned Harry when I married him that I was a whiner," Midler says. "I would whine and say, 'Why can't I get a job? What's wrong with me? Why doesn't anybody want me in their pictures?' And he said, 'Well, what do you really want to do? How do you see yourself?' And I said, 'To tell you the truth, I think my best work has been my funny work, and if I could carve out a niche for myself, I'd like to be the funniest woman in the world.' He said, 'How do you do that?' And I said, 'Well, first you have to let people know you're funny.' And he said, 'How do you do that?' and I said, 'Well, you can do stand-up or make a comedy record or go to comedy clubs.' And he said, 'What about singing?' And I said, 'Well, I don't really care that much about singing anymore. Nobody seems to like my singing, but I know they like me when I'm funny. Maybe they'll like it if I'm really funny.' So he said, 'Go make a comedy album.' The very next week I called all my friends and said, 'I want to make a comedy record.' And they said, 'Okay.' And that was *Mud Will Be Flung Tonight.*

"Then, a year and a half ago, Paul Mazursky called me, and it was really like a call from the gods. You know, it really was someone who actually wanted, wanted me. My God, it's like *I'll Cry Tomorrow.* It's so Lillian Roth I can't stand it. But it was so nice. I didn't know him at all. I'd never met him. I had a picture of a tall man in tweeds, and he turned out to be a small man who had been a Borscht Belt comic. I relaxed immediately. I liked him tremendously from the very beginning. He wanted me to play the mother of a twenty-year-old in *Down and Out in Beverly Hills* and I was aghast. I think of myself as perennially twenty-eight. My soul feels twenty-eight, and I just never had to confront the fact that I could, at my age, have a twenty-year-old daughter. Once I read the script, I thought, well, if he wants me. I was so happy to get the work, terribly happy. The actual making of the film was one of the happiest experiences I've ever had anywhere. Richard Dreyfuss and Nick Nolte are both salt of the earth. Well, I'll tell you the truth. The truth is that all of us were on our uppers. Nick hadn't had a hit for a while. Richard had had certain drug problems. I had had such a bad time on *Jinxed* that I was practically out of the business. Paul Mazursky said we were like refugees from the Betty Ford Center. It was good for us, very healthy for us to be disciplined and to pay attention to what was going on and not let our personal demons get hold of us. Plus they gave me the underwear my character wore. The furniture was what really slayed me, but I didn't get that. I got the bras.

"The next movie was *Ruthless People*. It's like *Ruthless People in Beverly Hills—Outrageous, Ruthless People in Beverly Hills*. The titles all sound like that. Disney likes the rhythms of the titles they've chosen. We weren't allowed to see the dailies on *Ruthless People*. If I had seen the dailies, do you think I would have looked like that? I thought I looked the worst. I thought I looked absolutely grotty. I couldn't get over how I looked. I was just in shock, completely freaked. Not only that, but I didn't have a full-length mirror in my trailer, so I never saw the full effect of the fat suit I wore. My God, I mean, I was pretty shocked when I saw it. But it was funny. There was one scene, the first escape that I made, when I waddled out of the basement, and I saw the back of my butt. I saw myself waddling, and I got hysterical, completely hysterical. I just wished I had had a full-length mirror because then I really would have used the fat suit.

"In *Outrageous Fortune* I wasn't that pregnant. A little bit pregnant, as they say. I started the movie when I was two months' pregnant and finished when I was five months' pregnant. And I really didn't show. I was a little nervous, but not really. I didn't do very many of the stunts. They were really good to me, they filmed around me and worked very carefully so that I had very little to do. You know, I'm quite a healthy girl. I don't do drugs, I don't drink, I hardly ever have to go to the doctor. I had a nutritionist on the set who cooked for me to make sure I was eating really well but not gaining weight. I did not have one moment of morning sickness, not one minute, not one second, of morning sickness. I think I was meant to be pregnant. Harry and I want more children. We're going to try again at the end of this year.

"My last three comedies, I think, have certainly indicated a direction to stay in. The three characters are all unselfconsciously funny. The lady in *Down and Out in Beverly Hills* was really trying terribly hard to be refined, but there was a real broad lurking underneath her refinement. All three characters are pretty broad and pretty brash and pretty noisy in their own fashion, and they want to be noticed. I would say that they're not shrinking violets by any means. I'm having a wonderful time, I'm really enjoying myself. And as long as I'm having fun, I don't see any reason to change direction. If the quality of the scripts gets worse, then I'll have to start having second thoughts. But the truth is that if the material is good, then I feel I'll be all right. The next Disney picture I'm making is a comedy called *Big Business*. Lily Tomlin and I play mismatched sets of identical twins. Someday I hope to make a film about Ina Ray Hutton, the forties bandleader, and a movie starring the Divine Miss M. The Divine Miss M hasn't surfaced in me recently. I kind of miss her. She's been coming in and out of my life for so many years now and everyone asks after her, how she's doing. She's still alive and kicking. She'll pop up again.

"I feel that I'm not using all my talent in these Disney films. But why should I care? I'm having such a good time. What's better? To sit and moan that I'm not using all my talent or to go out and do as much work as I can and hope that someday I'll have a piece of material that will be equal to my talent? I think it sounds really pompous to say I'm not using all my talents. The truth is that I'm not. But I'm working and I'm doing good work and I'm loving it. And people are enjoying the pictures. They're funny and they add, not that much, but a little something, to people's lives. I'm not going to sit and say, 'Woe is me.' I can't. I'm too happy that anybody noticed I had any talent at all. You know? I would make a wonderful Lady Macbeth. I completely understand her motives. So it's not impossible that I may someday play Lady Macbeth. I'll wear a pair of platform shoes or something.

"I was always defined as a pop-culture person. I didn't mind it. I enjoyed it tremendously. But pop has a way of fading. It's much more transitory than any kind of film or acting success, I think. I'm not an icon yet. Maybe when I'm in my Sophie Tucker years. It's true that when I met Aaron Russo and he said, 'What do you want to have done by the time you're on your deathbed?' I said, 'I want to be a legend.' I have regretted saying that because people think I have some nerve. And I guess I do. I have some nerve. But what's the point of trying to be something or do something if you're not going to be as good at it as you possibly can be? And being a legend is the reward of being as good as you can be. My best work has always been revelatory. I always thought if you were an artist, you could make people laugh and make them cry, be able to take the experience of the audience and change them. If you are a true artist, you are always true. You don't lie. There's so much lying all the time from everybody, from TV, the press. People want to see the truth, and when they see it, they know it. You cannot fool them. I've always believed that. I've always tried to tell the truth."

.　　　.　　　.

Midler and von Haselberg live in a Mediterranean-style house that is layered into a hillside off Coldwater Canyon above Beverly Hills. The huge living room is surrounded on three sides by a terra-cotta terrace. Three sets of French doors, with a curved cloud pattern beveled in the windows, open onto it. There are lemon and tangerine trees and red rosebushes. There is a black grand piano in the living room and a corner fireplace with a hearth tiled in swirls of pink, yellow, blue, green. The ceiling is sloped, and beams are painted the palest yellow. The couches, chairs, and footrests are slipcovered in flowered rose or gray-and-white striped chintz. Pastel borders are stenciled around the doors and windows and light-wood floors. There is a Chinese Art Deco rug. There are hand-painted side chairs and a table with a collection of baby shoes: moccasins, dancing slippers, patent-leather Mary Janes, satin booties. Everywhere are huge glazed pots filled with fresh flowers, roses, lilies, tulips of every color. "About a year ago Bette started doing flower arrangements," von Haselberg says. "She really enjoys it. We go and buy huge quantities of flowers and then spend hours arranging them. I sort of sit and watch, and we chat while she does it. I help her take the thorns off the roses."

Midler loves the house. She bought it in 1980 and has been redoing it ever since. It used to belong to *New Yorker* humorist Charles Cooke, who left many of his paintings and books in the house. "Working on the house is really the thing that makes me happiest in life, except for my family, of course," Midler says. "I like it. You go to museums and you see paintings of rooms and you say, 'God, I wish I lived there.' I look at books all the time and I say, 'How come I don't live like that? I want to live like that.' You see what van Gogh did with his little bedroom and you say, 'Gee, I would be so happy in that little room.' He had nothing, but it is so beautiful. All I can say is that the idea of living in beautiful rooms has always been part of my life. I didn't grow up in beautiful rooms. I grew up in not very pretty rooms. I have to say I grew up in ugly rooms, and a lot of my energy goes into making spaces attractive. Houses are like a canvas for me. Maybe I was a decorator in a past life, or some French fairy swooping around Versailles. I think this house is a very special place. There is a balcony upstairs with a swing, you know.

We sit there, my husband and I and the baby, and we just swing and swing, swing into a state of bliss. We're really happy, very, very happy."

February 1987

In her 1988 Christmas movie, Beaches, *Midler played a Broadway star and sang on film for the first time since* The Rose. *She shot* Stella, *a remake of the 1937 Barbara Stanwyck classic,* Stella Dallas, *in early 1989. Midler is continuing her successful collaboration with Disney; in August 1988 she signed an exclusive, four-picture deal. The Kipper Kids are kicking around again, on HBO and Cinemax. Sophie Frederica is growing up bilingual. Her father speaks to her only in German.*

OLIVER STONE GOES TO WAR

*O*liver Stone is a powerful, even overpowering, man, six feet tall, with huge shoulders, a gap-toothed smile, and extravagant vitality. At forty, his hair, though thinning, is black, as is the curly tangle in the V neck of his sweater. Posing for pictures on a fringed white hammock in his sunny Santa Monica backyard, Stone rolls his blond two-year-old son, over his stomach and nuzzles him sweetly. He seems friendly, charming, but he exudes sexuality, the threat of violence, the threat of great appetites. When he laughs, none of the tension surrounding him breaks. When he talks, for hours at a stretch, not moving from his seat on a couch, his eyes don't leave yours, and his intensity is hypnotizing. His words are fervent, a rushed incantation.

At one point, while talking about Vietnam, the writer and director of *Platoon* eagerly bends his head forward and shows the ugly, wedge-shaped scar on the back of his neck where a piece of Vietcong shrapnel sliced into him. The bowed head is the pose of one who sees himself as a sacrificial lamb, a martyr, a marked man whose movies must enlighten. He must plunge America into the waters of memory so that there will never be another Vietnam. "We're Cold War babies, and unless we get out of this Cold War context, we're all going to die," he says. "That in a nutshell is the mission I've got, to try to get us out of this Cold War."

These feelings dominate Stone's most successful movie, *Platoon*, a semiautobiographical account of his experiences as an infantryman in Vietnam. *Platoon* brings back the horrors of that war. People across America, not just veterans, are lining up at movie theaters to remember and honor and mourn. The graphic and brutal film drops us from a U.S. Army helicopter into the Vietnamese jungles of 1967 and turns us into terrified participants, dog-tired, sore, soaking wet, angry, fearing death from the darkness at the turn of every leaf. In *Platoon* the evil Sergeant Barnes (Tom Berenger) kills Sergeant Elias (Willem Dafoe), a Christ in fatigues. Young Chris (Charlie Sheen) murders Barnes. At the end of the film Chris's offscreen voice speaks Oliver Stone's words: "Those of us who did make it have an obligation to build again, to teach others what we know, and to try with what's left of our lives to find a goodness and a meaning to this life."

Stone has a dramatic bent and a gift for self-aggrandizement that reinforce the larger-than-life personality he aims at the world. He has always seen himself in rather grand terms. At nineteen, with Joseph Conrad's *Lord Jim* heating his mind, he joined the Merchant Marine in Southeast Asia. He has referred to himself in print as "Ishmael, the observer, caught between two giant forces. At first a watcher. Then forced to act—to take responsibility and a moral stand." Stone has also invoked Homer's *Iliad* when talking about *Platoon* by calling Barnes the "angry Achilles" and Elias the "conscience-stricken Hector fighting for a lost cause, two gods—two different views of the war." But mythology becomes Stone in a strange way, as do excessive metaphors. His spirit calls to mind both the hungry lion and the bleeding, torn antelope in a Rousseau jungle, so much like the jungle of Vietnam where Stone burned in the green flames.

"I volunteered for the draft in April of 1966," he says. "They wanted to make me an officer. I had a decent enough test result. I said no, I don't want to be an officer. I said the Vietnam War is going to be over, and I've got to get there right away. I knew Vietnam was going to be the war of my generation, and I didn't want to miss it. I knew it was the one, I just knew it. I knew it was going to be the only war I would ever get to unless I became a journalist. The fastest way to Vietnam was through basic and then infantry training. You'd be finished in sixteen weeks and on the plane over less than six months after you'd enlisted. I asked first of all for infantry, and then combat infantry. I was really worried they weren't going to send me, which is ironic because I arrived in Vietnam in time for the juiciest part of the war for the 25th Infantry. My timing was impeccable, I must say. In hindsight, I got there. They flew us over on September 14, 1967. I lost my twenty-first birthday in crossing the date line. I started smoking that day. I said, well, if I'm going to die, fuck it, I'm going to light up.

"My first day in Vietnam I realized, like the kid in the movie, that I had made a huge mistake. My first day cutting point, cutting a path in the bush, I realized that this was going to be a dreadful experience, much tougher than I'd thought. I'd overlooked the pain and the misery of jungles and humps and the calluses and the digging of foxholes and, to be honest, the utter indifference of the veterans to any kind of concern about my safety. It was sort of on-the-job training. Here you go, kid, learn. Here's your machete, you cut point. That was the way it was. You learn if you can, and if not, you're dead. It was a real dog-eat-dog mentality in the 25th Infantry.

"There were a lot of draftees. They hated the regular army guys, and the regular army guys didn't particularly care for the draftees. The draftees were not highly motivated. Nobody in 'Nam was motivated. The first day I got there I got the picture. I got 84 days left, I got 160 days left, I got 298 days left, how many you got? You're 365, you're just a lottery number, and your time comes around. So everybody was just counting their time. They weren't counting winning, thinking about the John Wayne picture, the big picture, the strategy, tactics, where the fuck we were, what mountain we were supposed to get, who the gooks were. Nobody gave a shit. They were just into getting out. Survival was the key. I got that picture right away, and it wasn't very romantic. It was very unromantic, and I said, my God, like the kid in the movie, I said I think I made a huge mistake.

"I was in three combat units in Vietnam, and every one divided into two basic groups, like in the movie. On the one hand there were the lifers, the juicers, and the moron white element—what we would call in many cases white trash. The white trash had racist and reactionary attitudes toward everything, including gooks and blacks. Guys like Barnes were in this group. On the other side was a very progressive, hippie, dope-smoking element made up of black guys, plus whites from the cities, guys like Elias, Indians, random characters from odd places. These people would generally leave gooks alone. They were basically out to survive and make it through this 'bummer' with a sense of humor to some degree, trying to keep their integrity, their souls intact, because the war was a tremendous drudgery in the field. There were exceptions in both categories.

"I was doing pot for the first time in my life. I had never smoked a joint. I had never heard black music or rock until I got to Vietnam. Here's this Yale boy who all of a sudden has nothing to do with Yale anymore. I'm talking this hip slang, black talk. And the blacks really mothered me in a sense. They were the only people I felt liked me. There was a sense of love and comradeship which I didn't have with a lot of the other guys, the beer drinkers.

"I went over to the side of hating the gooks at one point. I became a bit of a monster. I emptied my clip at the feet of an old man just like Charlie Sheen does to that retard in the movie. I just lost it. I just got pissed off. The gooks wouldn't come out of the holes. It was nerve-racking to look down those holes. You never knew what was going to fire back at you or come at you. We'd been yelling at them to get the fuck out of the holes, and they just didn't move. We didn't like them. As far as we were concerned, they were supplying the Vietcong. They didn't like GIs. I just wanted to kill this old guy. He wouldn't stop smiling. He kept smiling, you know, that gook smile. That was driving me nuts. So I guess it was like out of those cowboy movies, you know—you don't want to kill somebody but you want to bring them right to the edge. So I shot up the sand at his feet. In the movie one of the guys had his throat cut and then was hoisted up on a tree stump. I didn't see that, but I heard about another incident where two 25th Infantry guys were found with their balls stuffed in their mouths. There were a lot of horror stories out there. I used that incident to show the audience the rage we felt toward gooks in general. Just being in that environment, you either go crazy or else you are totally insensitive or callous to begin with, and you become even more callous. It's another level of reality.

"I did save two girls from getting killed. It was in some village. There were two girls running across a sandbank. They were obviously girls, and the guys in my patrol were just taking potshots at them, and I stopped them from doing that. Then there was another incident. A girl was being raped, and I think the guys would have killed her. I went over there and I broke it up. We killed a lot of innocents, not all at once but at random. It was always random. It was never like My Lai. It never got as bad as My Lai. You'd see a gook on a trail. You'd yell at her, get the fuck over here, and she wouldn't understand and she'd keep going. The guy wouldn't wait, he'd just fucking raise his rifle and plug her. He knew that she wasn't going to run away. It was just an excuse. A lot of the guys hated gooks. It was a very racist thing. They really hated them, hated them all. They didn't trust any of them. So there was a lot of that random killing.

"They put me in the bush right away. I was wounded less than ten days later, on my first night ambush. That was like the scene in the movie. I saw the enemy for the first time, and my heart stopped. I froze completely. That was the enemy. It was no longer an abstraction. I thought I'd be . . . I knew all the technique. I knew I should blow my claymore first and then go for the grenades and then go for my rifle, and I did none of the above. Thank God the guy in the next position saw them and opened up. The ensuing firefight was very messy, very confused. I was wounded. The wound was on the back of my neck. It was superficial, but if it had been one inch closer, I would be dead. The guy next to me had his arm blown off. We lost one man in another position. We killed three or four of them. After that I became a much better soldier.

"Sleep was the most important thing, and hot food if you could get it. And showers. We could sleep better at base camp, but you slept light once you got used to that bush. The tension level was very high. Your radar was always out there. You had to stay alert. Duration of trips out to the jungle varied. Anywhere from two days to twenty days. The longest time was twenty days. One time we got stuck up in a rainstorm in a mountain for eleven straight days. I'll never forget that. We had leeches crawling up our cocks, into our mouths, everything. We were putting tape on our anuses and the tips of our penises so that when we fell asleep, the leeches couldn't get in. It was that wet. That was horrible. Eleven days in the rain. The helicopter couldn't get in to get us out. And the gooks were supposed to be around. We were waiting for them on top of it. That was miserable.

"The battle at the end of the film was based on a battle that actually occurred less than a mile from the Cambodian border. We'd been in that area a lot, running into a lot of firefights. The North Vietnamese had been running regiments down into Saigon in anticipation of the Tet Offensive, and we were getting the early influx of it from Cambodia. They hit us. I don't know why. They hit us all out with about five thousand troops that night. It was an all-night battle. It was very scary, being only one of two men in a foxhole that night and knowing they were there and not knowing where. In actuality, I happened to be on the inner perimeter that night. My unit had taken a break and we didn't have to do the outer perimeter.

"In the course of the battle I did get to the outer perimeter and I experienced some of that fear I tried to translate in the film. The gooks did penetrate the outer perimeter, which was very scary. There was hand-to-hand fighting. Early on in the evening I remember a kid, a sergeant, coming up to me and saying they're inside the perimeter. It was very spooky. Our planes laid the bombs right on top of us. They told us to get in our holes. We dropped bombs right on them. We killed about five hundred of them. I saw the bodies the next day. There were bulldozers, just like in the movie. They killed twenty-five of us and wounded a hundred and seventy-five. That's a lot. That's about two hundred casualties out of approximately five or six hundred men. It was very, very scary. In the movie when Chris wakes up after the all-night battle he sees a deer. I experienced that. We were cleaning up the bodies in the morning. I walked into an area of the jungle just beyond the battlefield that was relatively untouched, and I saw a deer. It was so incongruous in that setting. A deer had survived all this bombing. That deer became for me a symbol of hope, like there was a fragment of beauty left.

"We went back into that same area two weeks later because the activity never stopped. We reconnaissanced the whole area and got hit by an ambush similar to the one in the movie when Elias is killed. They ambushed the shit out of us. We took about thirty casualties and I don't think we killed one gook. I was wounded the second time there. Some guy tripped a satchel charge and blew it, and I got hit in the buttocks and legs. I'll never forget that hospital scene. We had about thirty-five casualties. Another unit had gotten hit the same day, and they were coming in on choppers too. The doctors were completely confused. They were trying to sort out who was in the worst shape. They were just piling them on. My injuries were very minor compared to those of a lot of the others. I got shrapnel in my right leg. It went into the bone. They decided that if they operated on the leg, I'd have to spend more time recuperating. If they let it go into the bone, I could get back into the field faster. I spent about ten days in the hospital.

"I received the Bronze Star much later. It was in the First Cavalry Division in a firefight. I assaulted a guy with a machine gun in an enemy spider hole. I blew him up. I was very upset that day. Two people I knew in my platoon had been killed and I saw their bodies and they just hit me wrong and I was wired. I forget the reasons why I assaulted that spider hole. It was one of those moments when you get stupid. But I was very upset.

"I was disciplined for insubordination twice. After I got that second wound they put me into this stupid auxiliary military police battalion in Saigon. It was a soft, rear-echelon job. I had to guard the embassies and billets in Saigon from bomb attacks. It was really boring to be on guard duty all night watching for gooks in the streets. My attitude toward those rear-echelon guys was really bad. I thought they were a bunch of assholes. And the sergeant didn't care for me too much. I was too much of a cowboy, a bush rat, a boony rat. They called us boony rats. I was filthy. My boots were completely dirty. You had to shine your fucking boots every day. Everything was peacetime army. I hated those lifer guys. They were the worst. This scumbag sergeant was probably making an extra two or three thousand dollars a month selling beer to the Vietnamese. Anyway, he was on my case. I pissed him off. I think I told him to go fuck off or something, so he said, 'I'm going to Article Fifteen you.' That's a disciplinary measure. They were going to put me in jail, so I made a deal with them. I said, 'Drop the charges and I'll go back to the bush.' They said okay. They sent me back to the bush in the First Long Range Reconnaissance Patrol. I got disciplined there a second time. Same kind of problem, a run-in with a lifer. I was kicked out and sent to another unit, what they called motorized cavalry, but we were basically humping in the jungle.

"There was a tremendous hypocrisy to that whole war. It was disgusting. It was filthy. It was wrong, deeply wrong. It stank about that war. Not that the war was right, but if we were going to fight the fucking war, they should have sent fucking troops and kept everything offshore. Resupply from boats if you have to. You don't build these huge fucking camps like Cam Ranh Bay, the biggest submarine port in Southeast Asia, which the Russians have by now. We built all these tremendous bases, enormous airstrips which by now have gone to the other side. We brought in our PXs, which completely corrupted the economy. American officers were selling black-market goods to the gooks. It was totally corrupt. People were partying night and day in the enlisted men's clubs while we were fighting. They'd bring in Filipino rock groups, money was being passed. The sergeants were getting richer and richer off the war, living like kings. It wasn't war for them.

"I did manage to get out twice. A soldier away from home. I played a few numbers. I played AWOL. I went hooky. I disappeared a few times in civilian clothes. I took some kind of military bus to Saigon and partied for a few days. I couldn't get busted by the MPs because I had my old Merchant Marine card and I spoke French."

"My father was a colonel on Eisenhower's staff in World War II and actually picked up my mother on a street in Paris. She was bicycling and he was bicycling. He liked her looks, followed her, and crashed into her. She was engaged to another man, a Frenchman. Her parents were totally shocked that this outsider had appeared, this usurper. He was Jewish, and my mother was Catholic. He was an American, a colonel. He promised her a good life in America and she went with that. She broke off her engagement and married my father in December 1945. Her name is Jacqueline.

"I was born on September 15, 1946. I am an only child. I learned French as a baby. I learned French before I learned English. When I went to first grade, I had a tremendous problem expressing myself. It took a few years to get into the groove of things. I spent most of my summers in France with my grandparents. I was very close to them, always. I identified mostly with my grandmother in Paris, so she is the one I wrote letters to when I was in Vietnam. That's why Chris writes letters to his grandmother in *Platoon*. My grandfather was in the French army during World War I. He'd been very severely wounded, and his foot was gangrenous. I saw it as a small boy. He used to tell me stories about trench warfare, and it all sounded like *Paths of Glory* to me, which I loved.

"My father's family came to America from Germany and Russia in the nineteenth century. My father's father had been wealthy but lost all his money in the stock market crash of 1929. My father was about 5'10", handsome, a very strong-looking man. He was very intelligent and had a dark, sarcastic sense of humor. He had been to Yale, but he graduated at the height of the Depression in 1931, so he became a department-store floorwalker. Then he found his way to Wall Street and stayed there pretty much for the next fifty years of his life. He made more money for his clients than he ever did for himself. He ultimately wasn't very smart about his own personal finances. It's a paradox of his life. But he was living pretty well, living in a town house on East Sixty-fourth Street, spending everything he was making. I went to private schools, to Trinity in Manhattan up until the eighth grade and then to the Hill School in Pottstown, Pennsylvania. The Hill School was a tough school, four really tough years. Good discipline. The whole idea was to go to a good college.

"My father wrote a newsletter called the *Lou Stone Monthly Investment Letter*, which circulated among politicians and economists. It was to the right. My father was very much to the right. The letter, which was topical, philosophical, was very highly regarded in the fifties and sixties. My father taught me how to write. When I was seven or eight years old, he used to give me a quarter a week for a theme. He would make me write a theme, about anything. I didn't care about what—I just wanted the quarter to buy a Classic comic. That was very good training. My dad loved a great story. He was a big storyteller, always had a story. He wrote plays and books on the side but put them in a drawer. They were unproduced and unpublished. He was essentially a very reticent individual. He had that attitude—I guess it was born at Yale—that a man should be totally anonymous and not stand out in the crowd too much, should be very conformist, shouldn't seek too much attention or fame. I was very conformist when I was a kid. I didn't want to stand out at all. My father's attitude was that life is hard work, and the important thing is to make a living. Don't assume you're ever going to make much of a living, but just try to make one. He was enormously frightened. He was really ravaged by the Depression and pissed about it.

"My mother was totally the opposite of my father, one hundred and eighty degrees from him. She was very much an outgoing, social person, had thousands of friends. She was very French. She was pretty, brunette, about 5'7". She still has a very thick French accent. My mother loved movies, always wanted to know movie stars. Every Thursday when I was a boy she made me play hooky from school. She'd slip me a note for the school doctor saying I'd been sick, and we'd go to the movies, sometimes see two or three. I loved it. My parents were a dichotomy. I had the contradiction in me: the really French, outgoing, optimistic side of my mother and a very dark, pessimistic, sort of Jewish side of my father.

"My parents divorced when I was sixteen. They both went their separate ways in life, though they remained friends. My mother split her time from then on between Paris and New York. She moved in with her boyfriend. She had several boyfriends. She went through quite a different life-style. There was a lot of adultery going on. It was a very bizarre story, like out of a John Updike novel. The divorce came as a total shock to me. The headmaster at Hill was the one who first told me about it. The world sort of changed radically for me then. I had always been under the impression that my father was rich, because I went to good schools. But when they got the divorce, he basically gave me the facts of life. He told me that he was heavily in debt. My mother had broken him, so to speak. He said, 'I'll give you a college education, and then you're on your own. There's no money, literally no money.' I was very shocked.

"Then he got a major reversal. He owned a bunch of stock in the firm where he worked. The company went belly up, and when the stock became worthless, his life savings were lost. It was a terrible blow to him. He never recovered financially. I say this because I think it pushed me, made me more aggressive in leaving my sort of privileged childhood behind. I spent a year at Yale, but I couldn't face the prospect of four years in another Hill School type of environment. I saw myself becoming an East Coast socioeconomic product. I didn't know what was going to happen, but I sensed that I was on one of those automatic tracks. I just wanted to experience a different reality. I knew there was something out there other than this East Coast social world. I wanted to break out of that mold. I read *Lord Jim,* and that was a world completely opposite of the one I was in. It was exotic, lush, it had a tremendous allure for me. So while I was still at Yale I got myself a deal to teach English, mathematics, and history at a Chinese Catholic school in Cho Lon, a suburb of Saigon. I arrived there in June 1965.

"I woke up in Asia. I was nineteen years old. I lived in the Catholic church, received a salary. I was surrounded by eight hundred thousand Chinese. It was just a wonderful experience to be nineteen, on your own in Asia for the first time in your life. It was everything I thought it would be — the heat, the blood-red sunsets, the green seas. Asia became an orphan home for me. But I lasted only six months as a teacher. Frankly, I had my fill of it. I'd learned what I had to learn and I didn't want to repeat the courses a second time. While teaching, I had been snooping around the waterfront. I was very much living the life of the streets in Saigon. The Marines were there. The GIs from the First Infantry Division were just arriving. Saigon at that point was very much like Dodge City. Guys were walking around with pistols. No curfews. There were shoot-outs in the streets. It was just wild.

"I fell in love with Chinese and Vietnamese hookers by the dozens. Whorehouses, drinking. I was drinking heavily. Anything went. Free license. I was also looking for a job in the Merchant Marine. That was *Lord Jim* again. I finally got a job as a wiper on a boat. That is the lowest category on the ship. It is the man who cleans out the toilets and the engine rooms and blows out the steam-engine exhausts twice a day. It's very dangerous. Hot oil falls on you, there's a lot of pressure, a lot of steam. Finally I couldn't stand that boat anymore, so I signed on to a second one. We sailed from Saigon early in 1966, all the way to Oregon. It was hell. We ran into a hurricane and the main engine actually broke down in the middle of the ocean. We almost turned over. Staring at the ocean through those portholes — it was frightening. At the time I had never been that close to death. I got my Merchant Marine union card, but I never went back to sea.

"I ended up in Guadalajara, Mexico. I had some money I had saved, so I had some freedom. I didn't really know what I was doing. Mexico had always seemed attractive to me, and I think in the back of my mind I wanted to write. I holed up in a hotel in Guadalajara and I wrote about four hundred pages of a book. It was called *A Child's Night Dream.* I went back to New York and then Yale for half a semester in September of 1966. I continued to write the book, which became fourteen hundred pages, and then I dropped out of school a second time two months later. I flunked everything because I was writing. I got zeroes in all my courses. The dean called me in and he said, 'Look, this is serious. Unless you turn this around right away, we're going to have to fail you. Your exams are coming up. Do you really want to stay here?' I said 'No.'

"My father was furious. He lost the tuition money for that semester. That was his reaction. He was pissed off. It cost a lot of money. Plus I wanted to write a book, and he thought I was out of my gourd. 'A writer? Get out of here. You don't know what you're doing,' he said. I had never written anything outside the classroom except for my twenty-five-cent themes. I was interested in experience, pure experience. I had had these Jack London–type experiences I wanted to write about, but I adopted a Joycean style to do it. I was making up new words. It was really bizarre. The book covered everything. It covered being born. It went all over the world. It went back to my childhood, my memories of it. It also had some historical flights of fantasy. I imagined an older relative of mine had been in Custer's last stand, and I wrote a whole sequence about that. I went to Vietnam to a battle before I had actually experienced the battles there. There were a lot of Merchant Marine stories. The thread of it, as I remember, was a boy who was about to commit suicide and he was trying to explain why. It started out as a suicide note. There were scenes in the book in which the boy describes all the different ways he is going to kill himself.

"Not that I was going to commit suicide, but that's the way it was written. I certainly had heavy suicidal tendencies when I was eighteen, nineteen. I thought about it often. I was very depressed, very sad. But I thought my book was going to be the best thing since Rimbaud. I thought it was going to shock the world, and I was going to be a nineteen-year-old prodigy. I really thought so. The book was totally chaotic, totally wild and insane, with great passages of lyricism here and there. Then it was turned down by Simon and Schuster. I gave up. I took half the manuscript and threw it into the East River. I was pissed off. I only have half of it left. I was into Rimbaud, burning your work. I had a very violent reaction to the book getting turned down. I said fuck it. I'm no good as a writer. These people are right. My father is right. I am a bum, I'm drifting. All of a sudden I felt very guilty about it all. I had tried to be special, to stand out, and I felt guilty, felt horrible. I felt like the right solution was total anonymity. I had to atone.

"The Army offered the possibility of anonymity. They cut your hair—you'd be a number, you'd be a name. I think my wanting to enlist went beyond that, too, to be honest. I think I really had a bit of a death wish, that I wanted to be killed. I just threw in the whole kitchen sink. I think in the back of my mind I wanted to go back to Vietnam to experience even a lower level of existence than that of a wiper. I wanted to see where it really stopped, what the bottom line was, where reality really is. So I think I enlisted because I had a strong desire to be anonymous, to be killed, and to atone. I was also rebelling against my father, trying to prove to him that I was a man, no longer a boy, so you can't treat me like a boy. I'm not a bum. That too. Patriotism went hand in hand. I never questioned the American involvement in Vietnam. To me it was absolutely correct. We were fighting the communists. I was raised in the Cold War. I was a Cold War baby. We were on the side of Galahad fighting the evil knights of communism."

"I came back from Vietnam in December 1968. I got busted ten days later. I was doing some drugs, took acid in San Francisco, Santa Cruz, Los Angeles, everywhere. I moved down the coast. I just got completely alienated by American society. I couldn't stay in the country. I went to Mexico, got fucked up in Mexico, drinking, partying. I came back to the United States, and I stupidly had all this Vietnamese grass on me that I had brought back from Saigon. This fucking old guy, the guard, caught me at the border, and they hit me with a federal smuggling charge. The FBI came and got me, handcuffed me, the whole shit. It was a serious charge. It was an ounce of dope. The government was taking drugs seriously, like it was an invasion. They treated me like crap, put me in a fucking prison for three weeks. It was the San Diego county jail, but I was a federal prisoner. This jail built for three thousand people had twenty thousand inmates. They were all kids. It was insane. Twenty thousand kids in jail for six months waiting for a trial. The public defenders were going crazy.

"I called my dad after about two weeks in the can, and I said, 'Dad, I'm back.' And he said, 'Where have you been? I thought you were in Vietnam.' I said, 'The good news is that I'm out of Vietnam. The bad news is that I'm in jail, facing five to twenty.' He just said, 'Oh, shit.' We ended up paying off a public defender. He bribed somebody; that guy bribed somebody else. For twenty-five hundred bucks they dropped the charges. Dismissed. The file disappeared. That was my homecoming. I got the true picture of the States. I went back to New York and bummed around for a long time in the East Village.

"I hated America. It was like that Jimmy Morrison song, 'Five to one, One to five, No one here gets out alive.' I just felt like I was fucked. I was a radical. I was really getting to be an anarchist. I would have joined the Black Panthers if they had asked me. I was ready to kill. Coming back from the war in Vietnam to this country was a bit like being a Jew who got out of a concentration camp in 1940 and stumbled back into the West to try to tell other people what was going on and nobody would believe him. It was insane. I kind of lived like Travis Bickle in *Taxi Driver,* in the shadows, not really able to link with anybody. No vets were around. There was nobody to talk to. I had long hair, down to my shoulders. I used to wear all black with silver bracelets, boots. I was doing my rockstar trip then. Jimmy Morrison was the hero, right? I was doing drugs, pot, angel dust type stuff.

"I was still a bum to my father. We argued a lot. My father didn't understand Vietnam. He didn't understand what I'd been through, which really hurt me inside. He didn't want to get it. He just wanted to stick to that line—'We're right. Let's bomb Cambodia, let's bomb Hanoi, we're not fighting this war right.' But at the same time Vietnam was still just a police action to him. It was driving me nuts. So I said, 'I'm going to wake this dude up.' We were at a dinner party with about thirteen people in the Hamptons. I put some acid in my father's Scotch. He was a big Scotch drinker. I watched him drink it. He was playing chess, and all of a sudden the chess game got more and more intense. He said, 'What am I on?' He looked at me accusingly. He was looking at me and saying, 'It's crawling up my fucking feet. What did you do?' He had a hilarious trip. At one point he was basically hanging on to the tree in the garden asking for more milk and cookies. I was laughing like a lunatic. I was hoping I could break through some barrier, that he would wake up and have a sense of humor about this whole thing. He certainly remembered that trip the rest of his life, and he always used to kid me about it.

"It was a wild time. I was doing a lot of drugs. Grass and acid. I was into Timothy Leary, that whole ear. I know it sounds corny, but I was really saved by film school. I bumped into some people I knew in the Village and they said, 'Hey, man, I'm going to film school. You can go to college, study film, and get a degree. The GI Bill gives you money.' To be able to study movies in college, it was like a movie buff's dream. So it was the thing to do. It was cool. It was like studying to be an astronaut or something. I enrolled at New York University on the GI Bill in September 1969. Marty Scorsese was my first teacher. Marty really helped funnel those negative energies I had into something positive. He was like a lunatic himself. He was like a mad scientist. He had hair down to here. But I could relate to his madness. He was someone on an equal wave of nuttiness. If he could do it, that set a good example for me, showed me that maybe here was a place to put my energy. Making movies became a consuming passion for me. I made a picture for Marty's class called *Last Year in Vietnam*. It was about a guy, a vet, who walked around in the same sort of jacket Travis Bickle walked around in. When I saw *Taxi Driver*, I was stunned by it. It occurred to me that part of the character of Travis was based on me, but I don't know. I was even driving taxis at night at the time. Marty didn't write the movie; Paul Schrader did. I never was as out of it as Travis was. I never plotted an assassination, but I think I could have gone that way. Marty helped channel the rage in me.

"I graduated from film school in 1971. I got married to my first wife, an Arab who worked at the Moroccan mission to the United Nations. I did shit work like typing pools, xeroxing at Avon Products. I was writing two screenplays a year. I wrote eleven screenplays between 1969 and 1976. I was always productive, no matter how drugged out I'd get. But I was really getting nowhere. I wrote and directed a cheap feature in Canada called *Seizure* in 1973. It went nowhere. It was released on Forty-second Street, and died. I couldn't get a job. I couldn't get an agent. I couldn't get anybody to read the fucking scripts. But I got a break in 1975. Robert Bolt saw a treatment I wrote, and he liked it and helped me write a screenplay. It was called *The Coverup*, a very left-wing version of the Hearst kidnapping. The FBI were the bad guys. Nobody wanted to make it. But through Robert, who is a very kind man, I got an agent finally, William Morris, and they started to push my stuff.

"At least I started to have an outlet, but nothing got made, and I was really kind of fed up. By 1976, my marriage had been over for a year. I was broke, turning thirty, and going nowhere. I said, Well, I'm not sure if anyone is going to make this movie, but I am going to sit down and tell the truth about what I knew in Vietnam. And I tried to do that. I think a lot of things were coming together at that moment. It was the two hundredth birthday of the United States. The country was on a patriotic jag. I was sort of caught up in the excitement. Watergate had happened. The Pentagon Papers had come out. I had been able to realize that the Vietnam war had been a terrible mistake. I wrote *Platoon* very fast in that summer of 1976, when the tall ships were in New York Harbor. I wrote it in July and August, pretty much, in the heat, in an un-air-conditioned apartment above a store. It was a friend's place at Second Avenue and Fifty-fourth. It was kind of a dump. The script I wrote then is pretty much the movie I made ten years later. At the time no studio wanted to make *Platoon* because it was too depressing and too grim. They said, 'good script, good script.' But who cares? It's too tough, too real. So I buried it again, accepting that the truth of that war would never come out because America was blind, a trasher of history.

"My agent had really been pressing for me to come out to Los Angeles to meet people. I decided I'd take a shot, so I moved to L.A. The *Platoon* script got me a lot of attention. Columbia liked it a lot and sent me to London to work with Alan Parker and David Puttnam on *Midnight Express*. That developed into a real dark-horse success. It took everybody by surprise. Got me an Oscar. Which stunned me. It was tremendous, like being on a magic-carpet ride. It was a tremendous high. I was thirty-two years old. I was a bachelor in Hollywood with an Oscar. All of a sudden I went from being nobody for ten years, a total reject, to being wanted by everybody overnight. In many ways I wasn't ready for it. I had no experience in Hollywood politics. I didn't understand that the movie business is a collaboration between money and art. I was a green kid, and the same thing that had happened to me in Vietnam happened to me in Hollywood. I got wounded. I got blown up right away. I went from a very high point in 1979 to a very low point in 1980. After I won the Oscar I tried to get my *Born on the Fourth of July* script made. That was one of the best scripts I ever wrote, the Ron Kovic story, about a paralyzed vet. Al Pacino was set to star, but just when we were going to start shooting, the money wasn't there. Everything stopped. Nobody wanted it. I felt very bitter. I felt serious filmmaking was impossible in Hollywood, so I did *The Hand*.

"*The Hand* was a psychological horror story. Horror was very successful at that point, so it was something Orion was willing to let me direct. I couldn't get *Platoon* or *Born on the Fourth of July* done, so I did a horror film with an established actor, Michael Caine. I worked very hard on that picture, but it was all compromise. A lot of studio pressure. There were changes made I didn't think should be made. I was a young director, very impressionable. I wanted it to succeed. I wanted it to be a good film, so I bowed to the pressure. It was essentially a psychological movie turned into a horror film with special effects. The studio wanted more hand. We spent close to a million dollars on this series of fucking hands. There were forty or fifty hands. It was like you had to be a mechanic to make this movie. If you really want to torture yourself, go on a stage with a fucking hand and an actor like Michael Caine and direct them having a fight. It's better to work with a shark or a gorilla, because you have more space. But a fucking hand? The studio made me shoot more and more horror. The picture was released in about eight hundred theaters in 1981, but the audience never went from day one. I was pretty devastated. I'd felt enormous heat in Hollywood, and all of a sudden I was cold. People who wanted me two years, a year before, didn't want to talk. I felt like a pariah.

"*The Hand* kind of buried me. After that movie came out I was no longer a force to be reckoned with. I wasn't a threat any longer. I had wanted to make radical movies, and nobody wanted to make radical movies. So my wife and I—Elizabeth and I had gotten married in 1981 —decided it would really be healthy for both of us to get out of town. I really had had a ball in Hollywood. It was pretty wild. I partied hard. I really did the Hollywood scene. Bachelor and all that shit. I got into a lot of cocaine and mushrooms. Wild mushrooms. They were heavy in those days. Then there was all kinds of new shit. I'd try everything. Before I met my wife I was sexually wild too. But I always kept a sober side. I always was productive. I never had a year when I stopped writing. No matter how fucked up I would get at night, I would always discipline myself to write in the day. I felt Hemingway was right: The true test of a man is to work with a hangover.

"I wrote four or five scripts during that period, but I knew that I could do better. I think the drugs were hurting my writing. I think I was repeating myself. I wasn't growing. I was going stale. If you're not busy being born, you're busy dying. It just wasn't happening for me mentally or spiritually, so we decided to go to Paris. There were no drugs there. We cut all our ties in Hollywood. I cleaned up my act completely. We stopped drugs cold turkey. Didn't touch cocaine anymore. We had good food, good friends. It was cold. There was no heat in our apartment. It felt great. I wrote *Scarface* in Paris, basically as an adieu to cocaine. I thought it was a smart move because I had wasted so much money on cocaine and it had beaten the shit out of me. I got my revenge by writing about it. It would have been horrible to have done all that coke, gotten wasted, and done nothing with it.

"Before going to Paris I had done a lot of research on *Scarface*. I went to South America. I hung out with dealers. I was wild. I did some crazy stuff. I hung out in Ecuador, in Peru. I almost got killed in Bimini. I was with some heavy Colombian drug dealers. I picked up on these guys. Bimini is a heavy-duty smuggling area. It's totally corrupt. I hung out at the Hunt and Fish Club, an old Hemingway club, with these Colombian guys at the bar. We got to talking. My wife was with me. I was using her as a decoy. I told them I was a screenwriter, I'm doing a movie. They were interested in movies. So we party. They want to do coke. So we go back to their room with them. They start showing us their coke and their guns. They're talking. These Latin guys are into talking about it. They're macho. They're cowboys. It's about four in the morning and I'm ripped out of my head and I mention the wrong name. The fucking guys' faces drop. All of a sudden it's, 'Hey, who the fuck are you?' I had been talking about this guy in Miami, a defense attorney, who had given me some information. I mentioned his name. Apparently this guy had been a prosecutor a few years before, and he had put away two of these Colombians. So they thought I was an undercover cop. They really froze up. They went into the john. I thought, This is it, they're going to come out with guns and they're going to shoot me here, because they don't fuck around. My wife was scared shitless. So these two guys are in the fucking john and I'm sweating and looking at the door. Fuck, getting blown away in Bimini at four in the morning doing research on *Scarface*, my fucking life is running before me. Well, they come out of the john and they tell me to get the fuck out. We didn't sleep too well that night. You can hear the motorboats all night. They're stacking the grass in the motorboats right at the hotel and driving them across to Miami. All night it goes on, all these fucking Colombians. The hotel is like living in a smuggling port.

"*Scarface* was a good script. I thought it was fresh, new. It was really conceived in terms of an opera. A comic opera. Some of my friends call it *Scarfucci*. The story I was telling was the rise and fall of a gangster. I did model it on *Richard III*. There were some scenes at the end when the Pacino character sees ghosts, is talking to a ghost. But the director, Brian De Palma, didn't go along with that. On the whole I was very pleased with the movie. It's gotten me a lot of free champagne from gangsters all over the world who ask me how I knew all those things. Some critics said the film was excessive. I don't think we went far enough. The chainsaw murder actually occurred. The Colombian way of dealing death is extremely painful. They're into torture. There are cases of them cutting somebody's throat and pulling the tongue through. I think the movie struck a nerve with the public. Certainly it was reviled by the industry. Everybody got kind of moralistic about it, saying this kind of violence is an insult to Hollywood.

"Michael Cimino approached me to write the script for *Year of the Dragon* in about November 1983. That was a lousy book, I didn't like the book at all. But he said, 'Well, we've got to make it, got to start from the ground up.' So we threw out the book as much as we could. We did a lot of research. We went to a lot of banquets in Chinatown. The Chinese were much tougher to penetrate than the Spanish gangsters were. Much tougher. They don't talk to foreigners, to round-eyes. Cimino and I must have gone to talk to all of the Chinese associations—tongs—in Vancouver, Toronto, Amsterdam. Michael ended up in Hong Kong and Thailand. We were on to a big story. But we were warned off by elements in Chinatown. In some ways the Chinese make the Mafia look like the minor league.

"The reason I ended up writing *Dragon* was that Dino De Laurentiis promised me that if I wrote it, he would produce *Platoon* and I would direct it with Michael Cimino functioning as an intermediary. I accepted that arrangement and we signed deals. Dino was having this end-of-the-year holiday in France. He took us to this insane restaurant in Paris called the Crazy Horse Saloon on New Year's Eve. We were celebrating the deal. At midnight everybody threw plates and champagne glasses. There must have been about four hundred plates broken that night. It was a wonderful, insane trip. Life looked great. *Platoon* was going to get made. After writing *Dragon*, I started to scout locations for *Platoon* in Mexico and the Philippines. I cast the whole movie, virtually.

"Then problems started to develop. Dino could not get an American distribution deal, and he generally needs a guaranteed American commercial release of about $3 million to put all his European financing into place. No American distributor would touch *Platoon*. I believe Dino tried, but he backed out. I sued Dino. We got into a long, complicated lawsuit, but we settled finally. I got my property, *Platoon*, back, free and clear. Dino absorbed all the costs, like the location trips. He paid me something for writing *Dragon*, although I took a large pay cut as part of the settlement. I was in despair. I was really at ground zero. I had to start all over again.

"I decided to make a break from Hollywood. It was a conscious break. I knew I was not going to be able to function in the mainstream. Dino De Laurentiis is about as far out as you can get in Hollywood, and it didn't work out with him. Nothing was coming to me from the studios. I was cold. So I just cut away. I said, I am going to make *Salvador*. I am going to mortgage everything I've got and borrow as much money as I can. Richard Boyle, the journalist a lot of the film is based on, was a friend of mine from back in the *Born on the Fourth of July* days. Sometime about December 1984, on the way to the airport one day, he pulled some notes from the back of his grease-stained car. When we got to the airport, he thrust them into my hands and said, 'Here, you might like this.' On the plane I read this random series of sketches of his various trips to El Salvador and immediately my mind clicked in. I said, This is it. It's interesting. It's cheap. It's close, we can go down the road and shoot it.

"Boyle is a fascinating character. I wanted to do his story with him starring in it, sort of a cinema-verité, journalist-abroad kind of thing. He was a free-lancer in El Salvador. He'd always get gigs here and there. He was a hand-to-mouth journalist. I think in general he was regarded by the press community down there as slime. He was a heavy drinker. He lived in the Salvadoran countryside with a Salvadoran woman. He became a part of the landscape because it was cheap. And he got a very good up-front look at the death squads, which ended up chasing him. He was chased out of the country.

"In early 1985, Boyle and I worked on the script in Los Angeles for *Salvador*. We were going really fast. He was living with us, in the living room. We'd find him at six in the morning, the TV on, he'd be in a rocking chair surrounded by beer cans and bottles, totally passed out.

He never changed his clothes. My wife hated him. Six weeks writing the script were too much for her. He'd come in and sit at the breakfast table and she'd lose her appetite—the smell of whiskey wafted across the table. One night he was so drunk, he drank all the baby formula. He needs liquids. It was a madhouse script. Richard would be pacing up and down saying this happened and that happened, and I would say, 'Richard, we got to get this into a story here.' It was a marvelous anarchic time, and the script was written rough. We kept it rough and primitive and documentarylike.

"I videotaped Boyle for a screen test, and then we went down to El Salvador to try to get military cooperation to shoot the movie. The Duarte government said, 'Let's go, let's do the picture.' We also had the cooperation of some Mexican guerrillas. The idea was to shoot the government side of the picture in El Salvador and then move to Mexico and film the guerrilla side. We would have gotten a lot of equipment for nothing. It was like *Apocalypse Now* in El Salvador, there were so many American helicopters. We were right on the verge of shooting. Then, while I was on a visit to New York, I read in the *Times* that our chief adviser and supporter in the Salvadoran government had been assassinated on a tennis court. The situation basically had gotten very hairy. Terrorism had reared its head in the cities. Suddenly the government went cold on the film. So did the military. The Duarte government said they wanted to project a tourist image to the world.

"So we tried to restructure the film in Mexico. Meanwhile I had met an English producer in Mexico, and he gave the script to John Daly, the head of Hemdale, the British film company. John read the script and loved the idea of two gonzos going to Central America. He was committed to a picture that attacked U.S. policy. We made a deal in twenty-four hours, a dream deal. He said, 'I want to make this movie. This is a great movie.' But John wanted to use real actors. He said, 'I'll give you more money, but let's get some actors and go for a wider market.' The only problem with Richard as an actor is that his skin tone changes every day. One day he would be red and the next day green.

"*Salvador* is an anarchic picture and it was shot under anarchic conditions. We had no money. Big crowd scenes. We were shooting in downtown Mexico City with a thousand extras. I thought we were going to start a revolution because there were so many people watching us shoot this like 'stop the repression' film. For the battle of Santa Ana we took over the whole town and we blew it up for a week. Richard was there every day, screwing all the extras. He went through the extras like the Russian army through Poland. The Mexican government was there. They censored the film. They were on top of me all the time. We had to close down production on the forty-second day. We escaped across the Mexican border, leaving behind unpaid bills. We reopened shooting in the States. It was a wild ride. But I love *Salvador*. I love it. I loved doing it. It has enormous energy. I hadn't directed in four years. I was saving it up. I put everything I could into it.

"The producer of *Platoon*, Arnold Kopelson, was very involved with *Salvador*, selling it abroad basically. After the lawsuit with Dino De Laurentiis, Arnold came in and optioned *Platoon*. We ended up making it with Hemdale. Hemdale didn't hesitate. They believed in it fully. After finishing *Salvador*, we really didn't take a day's break. We took the same crew and went from Mexico to the Philippines to shoot *Platoon*. We shot from March to May in 1986 and came in at $6.5 million. I was tired shooting *Platoon* at first. The humidity was very high in the jungle. But after about three weeks I got into that Vietnam mentality of not sleeping, living on your nerves.

"*Platoon* is semiautobiographical. It is as close as I could come to what I experienced in Vietnam. I could have made the movie in a more documentarylike style and it probably would have been more realistic. But it would have been more boring. Most infantry experience is very boring. You're not fighting most of the time, you're really between fights. Combat is intense, sharp. It's a night here or twenty minutes there. It's indelible, it's forever, but it is very brief periods of time. So the film is condensed.

"I think I got a kick out of watching Charlie Sheen play me, watching a young man who resembled me somewhat relive an experience I had eighteen years ago. Charlie is the same archetype I was, I guess. He was shy, he was slightly out of it, he was naive. He went through all the phases from being a very poor soldier to a very good soldier to being a monster to rectifying it. He hit all those notes. We had many discussions, but the actual physical grace of it is something that cannot be taught. I could sense the difference as the weeks went on in his physical approach to the role. He looked dorky and awkward the first couple of weeks, and I was a little worried. But he changed. Little things started to get better and better. He handled his weapon better. He moved more easily with a pack. He became smooth and deerlike, very elegant. He got excellent. You saw him firing his weapons and he looked beautiful. He looked like he was really infantry. He mirrored I think what happened to me. I was a city boy. My first day out in the bush I was a mess on point, but by the end of my tour I was a woodsman. I was pretty good. I walked up on a deer once with my full pack on. I was cutting point. That's pretty quiet. I could smell and I could see and I could hear. All the senses were in tune. I was sleeping out every night, living with snakes and leeches and ants. You get to be one of them. There was an odd serenity, a Zen-like calmness, that came over all of us. When you're in the jungle at night, and you're alone with the stars, you're centered, very, very centered. I don't think I ever, even in peacetime, have had similar unity with the earth.

"Elias and Barnes both existed. I met Elias when he was twenty-three, in the Long Range Reconnaissance Patrol. He was incredibly handsome, with thick black hair, Apache blood. He was like a rock star to me, the Jimmy Morrison of that time to me, the Cary Grant of the trenches. Elias was this godhead, he was like 'The Man,' the leader of the pack. He was the electricity, the guy everybody liked. He was a hotdogger. He wore bracelets and chains. He had North Vietcong belts. His costumes were really together. He was really hip. He was a sergeant, an incredibly good soldier. He was a good man, and you would want to serve with him. You felt like he'd take care of you. He wouldn't do any harm to the innocents. I remember him doing a lot of grass and having a very devilish aspect. When I met him, it was his second or third tour in Vietnam. Those guys who came back a second time, they had a thing about Vietnam. I had a line in the film but cut it: ' 'Nam is pussy, man.' 'Nam was Elias's pussy. 'Nam was Barnes's pussy. Elias didn't fit in in the States. There were a lot of guys like that. They didn't like it back in the world, they just didn't dig it. The lames in the world never got it. To me, Elias was like Billy Budd, that character in Melville. He was a hero. I don't think I would have written about him unless he had been killed. He died on some hill in the A Shau. I had already left his unit. All I heard were stories about it. I heard he was blown up by one of his own grenades. But that didn't sound like Elias; he was too smart to get wasted like that. There were rumors, never confirmed, that he was offed by somebody. There were a lot of fraggings in that war, especially in the later stages when it was really getting to be hopeless and there was no morale left.

"Barnes existed. That was not his real name. As far as I know, he could still be alive. I left before he did. I used real names in the movie only when the people were dead, like Elias and Junior. I never really saw Barnes at the height of his powers in combat. I could imagine what he was like, though. I wish I had had him as a sergeant. I was his radio operator for a while. He had been shot in the face above his left eye. I gathered that the bullet went in above his eye and somehow it didn't kill him. It didn't go out the back. The whole bullet or fragments of it probably lodged in his head, I don't know. He spent a year in the hospital in Japan. Doctors obviously operated on him very delicately over a period of time. The scar ran the whole left side of his face from his eye to his lower jaw in a sickle-shaped pattern layered with grafted skin. It was a miraculous thing. He was a scary man. I was never comfortable around him. He conveyed to me the sense that a terrible distortion had happened to him, an enormous loss. He called up in me pity and fear. There was a certain catharsis in watching his face. I always felt that at the base of Barnes there was this great frustration and obsession, the same thing that drove Captain Ahab to get the white whale. Barnes also seemed to me to be out there, beyond anything that I knew, or that most human beings know. He'd reached another level in life because he had been shot in the head and survived. He'd seen death and walked back. That's what gave him his mysticism.

"Barnes had been in Vietnam several times. He kept coming back. He was wounded about six times. After he was shot in the head he asked to come back. He was an obsessed man, very taciturn, great soldier, good man in a firefight. He would get drunk, play a lot of poker. Vietnam was his pussy. He was clearly obsessed with getting back at the gooks, getting even. Whatever the reasons, he never discussed them. He smelled the gooks. It may be an illusion, but I think he smelled gooks at a distance. Once I was out with Barnes on a routine patrol. I was the radioman. There was a point man first, Barnes was second, and I was third. We were moving through some bush. Barnes stopped, signaled quiet. He moved forward slowly, quietly, past the point man, disappeared into the bush. There was some rifle fire. We came up to Barnes. Two gooks were dead, about twenty, thirty yards beyond him. It was about eight o'clock in the morning. There were teapots and bowls of steamed rice. I imagine the gooks were having breakfast. Barnes had nailed them both and was really happy about it. It was a good kill. I think he enjoyed killing.

"Elias and Barnes were the two figures I remember the cleanest from Vietnam. They existed, but they were larger than life. To me, these two men were essentially mythic. I never saw anybody kill anybody like Chris murders Barnes in the movie. I used dramatic license when I wrote that. But I started with the hypothesis: What if Elias and Barnes had been in the same unit? What if Barnes had killed Elias? What if Chris had inherited the mantle, so to speak, from Elias? Chris was faced at that point with an enormous responsibility. What do you do about evil? Do you just walk away from it or do you try to liquidate it, eradicate it? It seemed to me that is what growing up is about. You have to take responsibility. You have to fight evil if you are going to be a man, at least a good man. That's why Chris killed Barnes. Barnes deserved killing. I also wanted to show that Chris came out of the war stained and soiled. I think we all did, every vet. We came back to this country fucked. We went over young men, innocent men, and we came back both good and bad, all of us, everybody in combat. We were out of step with our own generation when we came back. They were clean. We were dirty. I want vets to face up to it and be proud they came back. They made it. So what if there was some bad in us? So what? That's the price you pay. I wanted to make a point. Chris pays a big price. He becomes a murderer.

"Vietnam was a cold war. Vietnam was a result of the Cold War, and it is the Cold War that is ruining America. That is in a nutshell the mission I've got: to try to get us out of this Cold War context. I think that's been thrust on Vietnam veterans. We basically need a renewal of moral integrity in America because we're totally corrupt. We're totally on the side of repression. We're the police force of the world, equal to the Russians. The two of us have become equally corrupt, equally repressive. *Salvador*'s about that. We support thugs and bandits all over the world. We have repressed the rights to revolution and self-determination of people all over the world. Vietnam was a forgotten pocket of time. It was just totally forgotten, ignored, omitted from the history books. I wanted to make a document of a time and place. Essentially what I wanted to say about Vietnam was, 'Remember, just remember what that war was. Remember what war is. Don't fool yourself with any illusions about what war might be like. This is it. Never again.' If we deal with Vietnam, we can begin to deal with Central America. And if we can begin to deal with Central America, maybe we could begin to deal with the issue of what communism is and whether or not it actually is a threat.

"My father died just before I shot *Salvador.* In his last years he became much less anticommunist. He changed. He said, 'You're right. The Russians have nuclear subs fifty miles off the coast. What difference does it make if they're in Nicaragua or not?' He said we should negotiate with communists. He had a wholly different approach to the Cold War, which was very moving to me. I think he finally acknowledged that Vietnam had been an enormous mistake and that we had suffered, that I had suffered. I think *Platoon* would have been very exciting to him. In some way, I think he has seen it up there.

"I was never a religious person, but I became religious in Vietnam. I always believed I have a special relationship to the good Lord. I certainly have faith that there's a reason. Combat is totally random. It has nothing to do with heroics. Cowardice and heroism are really the same emotion. They're both fear, just expressed differently. Combat is just so lucky, so random. A person gets killed and another person lives; they're standing two feet apart. It's really pure luck, pure chance. So you either accept the fact that the universe is pure chance or you say there is some element of faith or divinity attached, that somebody is saved for a reason. Possibly I was saved for a reason. To do some work. Make a movie about it. Write about it. I didn't feel that way at the time. I hoped at the time that I would make it. I hoped. At one point I thought I was going to die. Between the first and second times I was wounded, I thought I wasn't going to make it. I really just hoped, I had a ferocious hope, that I would be okay. I was always praying in a mental way, hoping. Hoping is prayer.

"The worst nightmare I ever had about Vietnam was that I had to go back. It was a couple of years ago. I woke up in a sweat, in total terror. They had shipped me back. Somehow at the age of thirty-eight I got sent back. It was horrible. I think, though, that I got what I went for. I saw combat at ground level. I saw people die. I saw what death was like. I killed. I was almost killed. I once looked into a hole full of mud for weapons or rice—I forget what it was—in some fucking village, and this snake was staring at me, and I'll never forget the eyes in that snake, they were so dark and evil. I felt like that was the whole face of the war, and the war had snake's eyes in the mud staring back at me."

January 1987

Platoon *won four Academy Awards, including Best Picture and Best Director. Oliver Stone's film* Wall Street *opened in December 1987.* Talk Radio, *about a provocative talk show host, was released at Christmas 1988. In January 1989 Stone finished shooting* Born on the Fourth of July *starring Tom Cruise as Vietnam veteran Ron Kovic.*

DE LAFOSSE/ORBAN/SCHACHMES / SYGMA

MICHAEL JACKSON IN NEVER-NEVER LAND

*A*t about six o'clock, Joseph Jackson, Michael's father, stands up and puts on a brown leather jacket. We get ready to leave his office after an interview. Jackson says, "You hungry? You like Chinese?" We drive down Hollywood Boulevard in a big blue Mercedes convertible. At a stoplight, girls in a car next to us giggle and point and wave. Jackson smiles and waves back. We go to his favorite Chinese restaurant, Ting Ho, in Hollywood. Two plainclothes policemen are frisking a white punk in the parking lot. We eat steaming platefuls of shrimp and chicken with Chinese pea-

253

pods. "No one cooks at home," he says. "I'm the only one who eats meat. The rest eat only vegetables."

Jackson is very shy. He is wearing black pants, a black short-sleeved shirt, a maroon tie decorated with the official Olympic seal. He is not quite six feet tall, with thin legs and a slight paunch. On one wrist is a gold watch, on the other a gold-chain bracelet with colored stones. He wears a gold-and-diamond ring on the fourth finger of his right hand. His hair is bowl-cut over his forehead and ears, the thin corkscrew curls shiny. His eyes are green, his mustache a pencil line over his lip. His nose looks as if it might have been broken once. There is a black mole the size of a nickel on his right cheek.

He has no idea what to talk about. "I want you to eat," he says, "like you're at home." "Enjoyin' it?" he asks. Walking back to the car, he says, "You cold?" He gets a black leather jacket out of the trunk. In the car I say I had hoped to meet his wife and the rest of his family. He says, "I don't know." He is quiet. "I don't know. We're going to New York tomorrow." What about tonight? And he says, "I don't know. I don't even know if anyone's home. If I call, they'll say no for sure." He laughs, then is quiet. "You game?" he asks.

On the freeway to Encino we talk about cars and boats and nothing. We take the Hayvenhurst exit, and Jackson says, "This is our neighborhood." We cross Ventura and almost immediately turn into a driveway with an iron gate that swings slowly open. A TV camera stares into the car. "Everybody knows who's comin' now," Jackson says. The gate shuts and we pass a guard station. A uniformed man nods his head to Jackson. We start down a driveway about a city block long lined with well-trimmed shrubs. At the end, on the right, stands a four-car, Tudor-style garage. Above the doors is the word WELCOME. An oversize clock with Roman numerals marks the center of the building. Opposite the garage is a huge mock-Tudor house. We walk in a back door through what Jackson calls the "game room." It is completely lined with arcade video games like Frogger, Space Invaders, and Pac-Man. Nothing else is in it. The next room is empty except for piles of boxes and floating heart-shaped balloons. Michael is going to build a miniature of the Disneyland ride Pirates of the Caribbean here. It is dark and difficult to see.

·   ·   ·

Michael Jackson is a secret being. He is as cloistered in his Encino mansion as Elvis Presley was behind the walls of Graceland. Jackson does not give interviews to the press. It is impossible to get near him. His friends, close business associates, and family are reluctant to talk about him. Immersed in show business since age five, a star at age ten, Michael had no childhood and thus is a perpetual child. To protect himself from the harsh demands of celebrity and the adult world, Michael has sought refuge in resolute silence and in the fortresslike home he helped design. He has surrounded himself with Disney cartoons, toys, old movies, music, a motor scooter, an electric car that looks like Mr. Joad's Wild Ride at Disneyland, and a menagerie of exotic pets. Every Sunday with the fervor of ritual he shuts himself up in a room with no mirrors and dances until he drops, or until, like Peter Pan, he flies. Michael has said that he is "just like a hemophiliac who can't afford to be scratched in any way." One close friend explains: "Michael tries very hard to insulate himself from the world. He really is kind of like the boy in the plastic bubble. We might think his bubble world is fantastical — like an E-ticket ride at Disneyland — but to him it's very real. My only fear is that he'll step out of it and catch some fatal virus and become like everybody else. He is too special the way he is. He is not immune to the common cold, so he has to stay in his own little world of glass and magic. If he steps out of that world, it might be his last time."

Michael's appeal cuts across barriers of race, sex, age, and style. His face, like his music, is both black and white; his thread of a voice is both an ethereal tenor and an erotic keening. Steven Spielberg has remarked that Jackson is a cross between childlike and magical E.T., earth's favorite extraterrestrial and Chauncey Gardiner, the TV-bedazzled innocent portrayed by Peter Sellers in *Being There*. Jane Fonda, another friend, says, "Michael has a voice that belongs to everyone. It's a man's voice, it's a woman's voice, a child's voice, an adult's voice. It's everybody's voice. The music is universal. It's energetic and it's sensual. You can dance to it, sing to it, work out to it, make love to it." Michael's popularity is enhanced by his masterful ability to craft and manipulate the images he presents to the world. "He sees himself through the eyes of the public more than he sees himself in his medicine chest mirror," a sympathetic acquaintance says. "He has innate instincts about what the public requires of him. He is smart about what he does next. It is a creative ability."

In December 1982, Epic Records released Jackson's *Thriller*. Fifteen months later that album has changed the music industry forever, and Michael Jackson is the biggest star in the world. On February 28, 1984, Michael won an unprecedented eight Grammy awards. *Thriller* has now sold eighteen million copies in the United States. Worldwide, the total has topped thirty million. Epic continues to sell the album at the heady rate of one million copies a week around the globe. There are nine songs on *Thriller*; the seven singles released from the album have gone Top Ten (the first time a solo artist has ever managed such a thing), and two of them, "Billie Jean" and "Beat It," have reached number one. *Thriller* has been the number-one album for thirty-three weeks. It is the best-selling album, of any kind, of all time. John Branca, Michael's lawyer for the past four years, says, "Michael manages his career as brilliantly as he writes songs and dances and performs. He is very informed and aware of what is going on in his life, to an amazing degree. He is astute and makes all his own business decisions, and he doesn't make them rashly. He does his homework. Michael is his own Rasputin."

Michael and four of his brothers made up the Jackson Five, one of the best-loved rhythm-and-blues bands of the 1970s. (Parents Joe and Katherine Jackson have nine children: Maureen ("Rebbie"), thirty-three; Jackie, thirty-one; Tito, twenty-nine; Jermaine, twenty-eight; LaToya, twenty-seven; Marlon, twenty-six; Michael, twenty-five; Randy, twenty-one; and Janet, seventeen.) But it was lead singer Michael who broke out of the pack forever in 1979, when he released his solo album *Off the Wall*, which yielded a record four Top Ten hits and sold an unheard-of eight million copies around the world. Now he has surpassed himself with *Thriller*. From his seclusion, Michael has brought pop culture to its knees with his music, his videos, his dancing, his magic. No horizon seems beyond the reach of his rhinestone-covered white glove.

Until the last minute, there is no assurance I will see Joe Jackson. He has not given an interview in five years and has not actually agreed to give one now. He has already changed the meeting place from his home in Encino, a wealthy Los Angeles suburb, to his office on the seventh floor of the Motown Building in Hollywood. At 1:30 P.M., my contact puts in a call to his secretary to remind him we are on our way. He isn't there. We wait and wait. Finally Jackson's office returns the call. We get there at around four o'clock. The office is unimpressive: regulation furniture, except for a rectangular brown marble desk that sits like a sarcophagus on a chrome stand. There is a glass-and-metal étagère with a stereo and records. An ink sketch of a lion's face with blue eyes hangs on the wall, and there is a small bronze lion on the desk. Jackson tells me he is a Leo. A picture of Michael on stage in a silvery costume hangs above a small table that holds two ivory elephant tusks carved into totems. Jackson, a former steelworker from Gary, Indiana, is nervous, wary. He talks softly.

"I remember when Michael was a little kid. He used to sing when he was very, very small. When he was only about five years old, he sang songs like *Tobacco Road* and *Cloud Nine* by the Temptations, some of the other songs from Motown. We had a record player and we had our records. We had to learn those types of songs to be able to go out on Saturday night and sing to people. We used to do personal appearances on Friday and Saturday nights. I'd take the children out all over the city and into other cities. Michael would get his allowance every week from the tours. I gave him twenty dollars, and he would buy a lot of candy. He would call all his friends in the neighborhood and they'd sit around and Michael would give them candy, and he would enjoy them eating candy. That was the main thing he liked to do, and he loved to sing and dance. Michael's got the gift, all right. It's in the record sales and it's in his voice. I've seen Michael sing a ballad so pretty, people would just start crying.

"When Michael was younger, he liked animals, and he still likes animals. At home now we have a llama, two fawns, though they're big ones now, and we have a ram and a boa constrictor. Michael has three parrots, two pairs of swans—one's a black pair, one's white. Sometimes those swans get to fighting out there, plopping around in the water out there, and it wakes you up. He has some peacocks. I like animals, too, but I can be tired of them after a while. Michael never gets tired of an animal. He is like a child. In other words, he is still growing up. He still looks for advice from Katherine and me, and we give it to him. He works very hard at what he does to try to perfect it. He is very shy. I say that he's shy around a few people, but onstage in front of thousands and thousands of people, that's when he really comes across. If he was here with you and me, he would be shy. He seems to be doing pretty well; he hasn't gone crazy over all his success. It's very hard. He's got a lot of people trying to get to him and bother him and he has to smile when he wants to cry. It can be rough sometimes. But that's showbiz. You either have to deal with it or get out of it.

"I guess we were able to protect him when he was little by reading the Bible and all that. Michael is religious, more so than his brothers. He is a devoted Jehovah's Witness. They were all brought up studying the Bible. They would have Bible studies when they were very small. My boys are very good. They're not into drugs. I'm not just saying it. Other people can tell you that too. The Jacksons are not into drugs. There's nothing wrong with having a little drink once in a while, but they don't even do that. They don't smoke. They're in good health. Michael is thin as a razor. He goes into that studio and he dances two hours without even stopping, and that tells me that he's in great shape. It's a habit with him. Michael always could dance, and he was good at choreography, makes his own steps up. Most of the choreography you see the Jacksons do, they have some input, but Michael does a lot of it.

"Michael is a vegetarian. I mean really a vegetarian. He's the type of vegetarian that hardly eats anything. No fish. No meat. Nuts and grapes and things of that sort and dishes that we have a cook come in to fix. For fun Michael sometimes plays with the llama he has and he invites all the relatives, the kids. He likes kids. He has a popcorn machine—you've seen those old-time popcorn wagons on wheels you can walk up to and pop corn. That's what he does. He pops the corn for the kids. He has an ice-cream machine that makes this frozen custard and he gives all the kids custard. He has all kinds of games, pinball and video arcade games. Michael has a little scooter he drives around. Michael likes to dress casual all the time. When you see Michael dress up, it's a statement for just that purpose.

"When I found out that my kids were interested in becoming enter-tainers, that's when I really went to work with them. It took all my time to rehearse them. I rehearsed them about three years before I turned them loose. That's practically every day for at least two or three hours. Their childhood was very strict. They went to school every day. I rehearsed them after school. When the other kids would be out on the street shooting marbles, playing games, my boys were in the house working—trying to learn how to be something in life. They got a little upset about the whole thing in the beginning because the other kids were out there having a good time and they had to be in every day at a rehearsal. I noticed, though, that they were getting better and better. Then I saw that after they became better they enjoyed it more. Then it was time to go out and do talent shows. We won the highest talent show in the state of Indiana, and then we went over to Illinois and won there. It got so we could play nightclubs in Chicago like the High Chaparral and the Guys and Gals Club. This was on the weekends. I had a Volkswagen bus and I bought a big luggage rack and put it on top and had everybody on the inside of the bus. One day I noticed when I was coming out of the yard that the instruments on top of the bus were taller than the bus. There was so much stuff up there, all over everywhere. It was a struggle sometimes. We had to sacrifice and not buy certain things because we weren't making money. In order to get good instruments we would really have to save for them.

"A lot of people like to take credit for bringing the Jacksons to Motown. Diana Ross had a TV special, and she put us on it. She opened the doors for us. Gladys Knight was the first one who tried to get me to come to Motown. But Joe Jackson brought the Jacksons to Motown. About two years before we actually got there, I sent Berry Gordy a tape. They kept it about three months and then sent it back. But I knew the kids had something.

"We had some hard times, really hard times. But it looks like to me it's gotten harder. They're number one all around the world and looks like everybody's taking potshots at them, or taking a piece of this from them or a piece of that. People are trying to break up the family, and I'm trying to hold it together. The greed for money is what it is. I'm not about that at all. I think if they are together, they are strongest. Divided is sort of weak. What I'm speaking about is different people coming in, outsiders, who see money possibilities and try to separate the boys for their own purposes. I'm not talking about each of the boys going off and making their own albums. Michael hasn't gone off. He just made an album that became very, very successful.

"People have called me a racist. I'm not a racist. If I were, I wouldn't be sitting here talking to you right now. If I were a racist, I wouldn't have hired a lot of people that aren't black to work for me. If I were a racist, I wouldn't be here, I would be somewhere else trying to start a lot of trouble. That's what racists are doing. They are out there trying to put blacks against whites and whites against blacks. I'm not that. The reason there haven't been any magazine stories before now about this is that I was afraid of being misquoted. Michael has been misquoted several times. Set my record straight. I am not a racist. I am just the opposite. I wasn't raised that way. I'm an American. I gave my children one hundred percent of my know-how, knowledge, and my time in trying to develop them to be what they are today, and it has paid off and is still paying off.

"The Jackson music is a type of music that the young kids like, and as you know, the older people like too. It's music to send a message to all the people whether they're black or white. It's music for rejoicing, whether you're black or white. It's music for everybody, not just for one person or one race. It's for the whole world. You can tell the music is for the whole world because the whole world is listening and the whole world buys and the whole world dances."

A few people agree to talk about Michael Jackson. Steven Spielberg met him about four years ago through record producer Quincy Jones. Michael narrated the children's album *E.T., the Extra-Terrestrial.* Spielberg says, "If E.T. hadn't come to Elliot, he would have come to Michael's house. I think Michael really is three million light-years from home and he's visiting earth for the next fifty or more years but he's got better places to go afterward. It's a nice place Michael comes from. I wish we could all spend time in Michael Jackson's world. We'd be a much healthier race. Michael identifies with E.T. very much. He has seen the movie *E.T.* many more times than I have. I arranged for a picture to be taken of E.T. and Michael together. Michael really wanted it for his wall. I watched the photographers shoot the session and it was phenomenal to sit back and watch Michael and E.T. talk and exchange gestures. On the stage when you see Michael trip the light fantastic, he's like a puppy dog with a bite. There is something about him that you want to embrace and protect. Yet there is a rage inside him that comes across only when he is performing live, dancing, singing, on stage. I never have seen the rage in Michael when I'm with him in person, he is so soft-spoken and dear-hearted. I think he can be hurt very easily. He's sort of like a fawn in a burning forest."

Jane Fonda has known Michael Jackson for about three and a half years. They met at a Halloween party. He walked up to her and asked her if she would talk about acting with him sometime. Fonda says, "I didn't hear from Michael for a while after that party. Then out of the blue, when I was making *On Golden Pond* in New Hampshire, he called and asked if he could come observe the shooting. He came for about a week. The two of us stayed in the house on the lake we had and we would talk all night about acting. He wanted to know how I prepared, how I worked, how I see other people work. We talked about life and about Africa and about issues. We talked and talked and talked. He's a very deep person. I found him to be intelligent. It's not intellectual intelligence. It's instinctual and emotional. He sees himself as a medium in some ways. One time I asked Michael where his songs came from and he said it was like he received them from a higher level, that they just came from a higher plane through him.

"Once Michael and I were driving together in New Hampshire. We were talking about how great it would be to do a movie together. I told him how much I would love to work with him. Suddenly I turned to him and I said, 'I know what it is. I'd love to make *Peter Pan* for you. You are Peter Pan.' He got this expression on his face and I said, 'What's the matter?' He said, 'You don't realize what you've just said. All over my walls at home are drawings of Peter Pan. I understand that story.' He reacted very emotionally.

"Michael's talent is so total, it is his whole life. There is almost nothing left over beyond creativity for him because it absorbs so much of him. I would sit and tell him how I had an emotional breakthrough with a character and I could see him receiving what I was telling him like a sponge. I think Michael receives everything, pain, pleasure, joy, more viscerally than most people. He responds to everything. His skin changes, his color changes. It's palpable. He's like a harp chord. It's right there.

"Most people allow themselves to have a few calluses around their heart. Not Michael. His whole life he has been wide open. He can't have a few calluses around his heart. His life is his creativity. On some level he knows that, so he creates around him a world that protects him, protects his creativity. It allows him always to reach greater heights. Michael is in awe of life. He is in awe of children and animals. He is in awe of things that are unfettered and free. Every person who is a creative genius, whether it's Picasso or Michael Jackson, is also very much a child. When you lose that childlikeness you lose a lot of the creative juices. Michael, on some level, I don't even know if it's conscious, knows that he has to stand off the demands of reality and protect himself."

Seth Riggs, Michael's voice teacher, worked with him two hours a day, five or six days a week, for a period of about two and a half months while Michael was recording *Thriller.* Riggs says, "Michael is a high tenor who has a three-and-a-half-octave range, which is unusual. The average person has about a two-octave range. Michael does not sing falsetto. He doesn't jump outside his natural range to sing those high notes. What I did was work with Michael to extend his natural range. People say Michael takes female hormones to keep his voice high. That is not true. I am his voice teacher. I would know that. He started out with a high voice and I've taken him even higher. Michael can sing low — down to one octave below middle C — but he prefers to sing as high as he does. A tenor can always get more mileage, can develop more style by staying up in the high ranges. He simply does not take drugs. As a matter of fact, his religion wouldn't allow it. He is a Jehovah's Witness. He doesn't even believe in blood transfusions. Michael is a very special man. He would come in for his lesson and sit down and we would have a prayer and then read the Bible and then have another prayer and start to work. That's the way he liked to begin his day. Can you imagine a performer as big as Michael Jackson turning around in a lesson and discussing how wonderful God has been to him and how much he loves God?

"During his vocal exercises, do you know that boy would hold an F or a G above high C, put his arms up in the air, and do those spins and dance turns that he does, right in the middle of the lesson? He'd just put his arms above his head and spin, practicing holding those high notes. Hell, I never saw that before. I thought, 'Well, gee, should I tell him to stop?' And I thought, 'No, better not.' Hell, if he can do it, why stop him? Why make him average? He's obviously not average.

"Everyone thinks Michael is gay, and I said to him one day, 'You know, Michael, a lot of people think you're gay.' Michael started to laugh. He said, 'I know. The other day a big, tall, blond, nice-looking fellow came up to me and said, "Gee, Michael, I think you're wonderful. I sure would like to go to bed with you." I looked at him and said, "When's the last time you read the Bible? You know you really should read it because there is some real information in there about homosexuality." The guy says, "I guess if I'd been a girl, it would have been different." And I said, "No, there are some very direct words on that in the Bible too."'

"One day Michael came in for a lesson and he asked me for a glass of water. He said, 'I don't feel good. I'm nauseous.' I brought him the glass of water and said, 'What's the matter? Do you feel sick?' It was the day after Michael had danced on the Motown 25th Anniversary Special. Michael said, 'I got a call this morning from a fellow who said, "I thought you were marvelous last night, Michael. I just ran the kinescope two times before breakfast and I wanted to call you up and tell you how wonderful you were." I said, "Thank you very much. Who is this?" And the guy said, "Fred Astaire." ' Michael said he was so excited, he got sick."

Astaire says of Michael, "My Lord, he is a wonderful mover. He makes these moves up himself and it is just great to watch. I think he just feels that way when he is singing those songs. He is inspired. I don't know how much more dancing he will take up, because singing and dancing at the same time is very difficult. But Michael is a dedicated artist. He dreams it, thinks of it all the time. You can see what the result is. When he was growing up, his family lived in my neighborhood in Los Angeles. I used to see Michael and his brothers and sisters when they were little kids, playing on their bicycles, and I'd wave at them. Some years ago Michael and I were on a Dinah Shore talk show together. He was doing some dancing on it, I wasn't. During rehearsals we talked about dancing. He said, 'Oh, I'd love to dance.' I'd say, 'You can do it, go ahead.' But even when he was five years old he was a pretty damn good dancer."

Veteran jazz artist, composer, and arranger Quincy Jones produced *Off the Wall, Thriller,* and the *E.T.* album. Jones says, "In three months Michael and I did *Thriller* and the *E.T.* album. It almost killed us, but we did it. We had two studios going at once. We would walk from one studio to another. Michael has incredible concentration, faith, determination, patience, and discipline. He dances every Sunday no matter what happens. Even when we were recording *Thriller,* at the height of our craziest crisis with the record, he would go into another room and dance for at least two hours. He is an absolute perfectionist, a workaholic.

"Emotionally Michael is very fragile. He allows himself to be vulnerable. When we were doing the *E.T.* album, there were many times during the narration when E.T.'s life was in danger. Michael cried every time. He just couldn't go on. He's very sensitive. I left the crying on the record. I couldn't get it any other way. I said, 'Well, let's leave it there because this is real. It's a real emotion.' The same thing happened a few years ago on the song "She's Out of My Life." At the end of the song the words are: 'It hurts like a knife/She's out of my life,' and Michael couldn't sing the last line because he kept crying, just falling apart. So I said, 'Let's do it later.' Two weeks later the same thing happened. I was curious about it because I couldn't understand what he was relating to. He's never been married. I didn't know why he was so upset or why he identified with the lyric. Michael said, 'I just feel what Tommy Bahler was feeling when he wrote the song.' That is one of Michael's gifts, that incredible osmosis, that chameleonlike perception that just pulls him right in the situation. That's why he reads lyrics so well. I remember when he first did *Off the Wall*. He was like an actor, like Brando reading the lines.

"He's also got an incredible sense of humor. We laugh a lot. I call Michael 'Smelly.' He doesn't swear at all because of his faith. Everyone else in the business says, 'That take was real funky.' It's a common slang expression. Michael won't say 'funky.' He says 'smelly jelly' instead. So we've been calling him 'Smelly' for four years.

"Michael loves kids. When he comes to my house, my two kids, a seven-year-old and a nine-year-old, think that he comes to see them. He is very childlike. He is very idealistic. He believes in and relishes the fantasy aspect of life. He feels it. He loves it. He identifies with it. I think—I'm just giving my opinion—that he identifies with the people in a fantasy, like an E.T. that has a finger that can help people. He likes to believe in that kind of thing. Michael is totally connected to truth. He lets truth lead him everywhere. He won't go against truth. I hear him tell people not to try to write songs but to just let the song tell the people, let the song communicate, let the music tell you what it means, rather than try to impose your own preconceived ideas on the song. Michael has definitely been here before if you believe in previous lives. He's definitely been here several times before. He has an accumulation of all this incredible wisdom and talent and understanding of what art is all about. He is this beautiful man-child combination that is so strong. He has the gift of the wisdom of age and the daring and adventurousness of youth. Michael is a very pure person. That's what comes through, and I'm sure that's why he has connected with every soul in the world."

Joe Jackson leads me into the kitchen. It is gleaming: white floors, chrome-and-black ovens, stove, and appliances. The counters are made of tiles painted with green and yellow flowers. The foyer of the house is lighted by a chandelier dangling from the ceiling two stories above. The floor is white marble, the circular staircase leading to the second floor is carpeted in green. Bronze statues people the room. A square gold-leaf table holds a vase with an armful of flowers. There is a grandfather clock in the corner, ornamented with gold filigree. Everything seems to have been splashed with gold.

The "trophy room," as Jackson puts it, is off the foyer. The walls are covered with gold and platinum albums and singles. Glass-topped mahogany cases, the kind museums use for displaying rare manuscripts, glint with gold and platinum. Jackson takes me into the theater. The walls and the curtain drawn across the screen are teal. The thirty-two seats are upholstered in red velvet. Nearby, in the den, is a sunken horseshoe-shaped viewing area, with an overstuffed couch facing a fireplace and a built-in television set. Another large clock with Roman numerals hangs above the mantelpiece. Off the den is a bar under a leaded stained-glass window with a knight in armor looking up at a black castle on a hill. The bar is really an old-fashioned soda fountain: You can have whatever you want—ice cream, milk shakes, sodas. There are five stools, each built on a mahogany pedestal sculpted into a fish with the tail flipped up, the head at the base facing out, mouth agape. The living room is like a garden, with hundreds of flowers strewn over the couches and rugs. The formal dining room has a long, dark wood table and ten chairs upholstered in a blue-green, geometric peacock pattern.

Jackson takes me outside to the back. The patio is made of perfectly planted brown bricks. A tree is strung with tiny white lights. We turn to look at the silhouette of the house in the darkness. It, too, is outlined with tiny white lights, which trace squares along the Tudor lines. "The Tivoli lights," says Jackson. In the back courtyard is the old-fashioned red popcorn cart, the kind you see at country fairs with pretty gold lettering on the sides. Jackson wants to show me the swimming pool.

Behind it, a wall with a large mosaic of a parrot has four fountainheads carved like bearded Neptunes spouting water from puckered lips. There is also a Jacuzzi. We walk along a brick path lined with clusters of flowers that leads to a bridge over a pond. The moonlight shines on the two pairs of swans gliding on the water. One of the black swans lifts its head and makes a long, low sound. Jackson imitates the sound and laughs, "It's like a little dog barking."

On the other side of the pond are a white gazebo and two large bird cages nestled in trees by the water. In one cage is a pair of peacocks, the female mud-colored, the male electric blue even in the dark. Jackson walks over to a stable and introduces me to a ram named Mr. Tibbs and a llama named Louie. They stick their heads out to nuzzle. Two deer stand in a pen close by. We go to the garage and climb the stairs to the second story. It is a portrait gallery. The walls and ceilings are papered with hundreds and hundreds of photographs of the Jackson family. The Jacksons grow up on these walls. A corner of the room is filled with boxes of the get-well cards and gifts Michael received after his hair caught on fire during the filming of a TV commercial.

We walk back to the house. Only Jackson's wife, two of his daughters, and Michael live at home. Jackson says, "Let's see if anyone is around." His wife, it turns out, is shopping. We go up the circular staircase; I am following Jackson. He walks down the green-carpeted hallway and knocks on a door. LaToya, a striking woman who looks like Michael, comes out of her bedroom. She is warm and friendly. Jackson knocks on another door. Janet, the youngest Jackson child, also friendly, but quiet, says hello.

We turn around and walk down the hallway again, but this time to the far end of the house. I am still following Jackson. He knocks on a closed door. "Michael, I have someone I want you to meet." I can't hear what Michael says. "Can I bring her into your room?" asks Joe. He opens the door. The only light comes from a television set. The light glistens off Michael's hair. He and a young man who looks about twenty are sitting on straight-backed chairs facing the television. Michael is watching it intently. I can't see what is on the TV. They stand up. Michael is wearing a blue jacket and dark pants. The friend is wearing a plain white shirt and black pants. The room is very dark. There seem to be outlines of figures against the far wall. Above the TV are shelves, and on the top one I can see what looks like dolls or mannequins about two feet tall.

Michael, in a very quiet voice, introduces his friend to his father, giving only one name. I cannot hear it. Jackson introduces me to Michael, saying that I am from *Time* magazine. He adds, "We just had a nice, long interview." Michael and I shake hands. His hand feels like a cloud. He barely says "Hi." His friend extends his hand, which is damp. He seems nervous. Michael stares with his almond eyes for a long minute and turns to the television. There is silence and I feel that Joe is uncomfortable. It is so dark I cannot see anything. We back out of the room and Joe shuts the door. We walk away and he says, "Michael has a friend over. He isn't about to give any interviews. You got pretty close, though."

I call a cab. We walk outside. Katherine Jackson pulls up in a car and gets out with several packages. We follow her in. She is about 5′4″ and is wearing a blue pantsuit and a red blouse with a tie at the neck. She walks with a slight limp (she had polio as a baby). Her black hair rolls to the shoulders. Her skin is smooth and creamy brown like Michael's. Jackson tells her it would be good for her to have an interview with me. She says, "Oh, Joe, I don't want to do an interview. You know you and Michael always get misquoted." Joe says, "She says we won't be." Katherine Jackson says, "Oh, not now. I don't like interviews. Well, what do you want to ask me?" I tell her and she says, "All right, let's go." The three of us walk into the living room. Katherine, a devout Jehovah's Witness, sits poised and serene. She talks about her life raising nine children as if she were taking a walk over a patch of ground for the thousandth time, familiar and at ease with every bump and flower. We talk while my cab waits.

"Ever since Michael was very young," she says, "he seemed different to me from the rest of the children. I don't know what it is, I really don't. He's just, he's just different. Sometimes I used to wonder. I don't believe in reincarnation, but . . . you know how babies move uncoordinated? He never moved that way. When he danced, it was like he was an older person. When the boys used to practice their songs and their dancing, they used to say, 'What are we going to do?' And when he was five years old, Michael would make all the moves for them. I couldn't believe that all this was coming from this little kid. He could harmonize. He could do everything. When the boys were singing around the house, Jermaine led them and the other kids just sang background or harmony, and I noticed that Michael would just fall in, and it would come natural to him.

He would just start harmonizing. He wasn't taught. I knew then that he had a pretty good voice. I spoke to Joe and told him I thought Michael should start leading some of the songs. So Joe tried him out and he was fine, so Michael was leading at six years old. He used to play the congas. We didn't have any drums at the time because we couldn't afford to buy them. Michael would play the congas and sing and dance.

"I'm not surprised by what's happened with Michael. I felt that he could do it, and he knew he could do it. When he made *Off the Wall*, he told me, 'The next album is going to be better than this one.' He has a driving ambition to be better and better in his music and his dancing. His music has such an appeal because he doesn't just stick to one kind of music, like country or rhythm and blues or deep soul. Michael used to say, when he wrote, he'd write for everyone, even though the music business would list it as rhythm and blues because of him being black. But it's not really that. Music has no language barrier.

"Michael is pretty stable. I think it's his raisin'. We used to talk to the boys about getting 'big heads.' We used to tell them not to get a swollen head and think they were so great. None of them is better than anyone else. It's just one might have a little more talent, but that doesn't make you better. You're just the same as anyone else. It's just a job. Other people might be doctors and lawyers, but Michael entertains because maybe that's what he can do best. That doesn't mean he's better. I think Michael's strong religious faith has something to do with his stability. We used to read the Bible together. We still do that. Michael has always been strongly religious. He's even stronger now. With his busy schedule and all, he goes to all the readings. We have four meetings a week at the Jehovah's Witness Kingdom Hall. Michael does field service with friends twice a week for an hour or two. He goes door to door with the *Watchtower* and *Wake* magazines, which have articles in them about the Bible. When Michael goes door to door, people haven't been recognizing him. He has tried to disguise himself, but it's kind of hard to do that. He says when he knocks on the door most of the time people say, 'I've seen you someplace. Don't I know you?' And a lot of them look at him and turn around and say, 'No, it can't be him.'

"When the kids were very small, Michael was about three—we had seven kids at the time—the television broke one day. You know children; if they don't have TV to watch, then they have to do other things. That's the way they started singing and dancing. They were entertaining themselves. Joe had a guitar, he used to be in a band called the Falcons, and Tito started to practice on it. He fumbled with it and then got pretty good with it. When the boys didn't have the TV, they listened to records a lot—the Temptations, mostly, and James Brown. And they would sing their songs and dance to the music. The dancing came natural to the children. We also used to sing folk songs like 'Old Cotton Fields Back Home.' At first the boys would just sing along with me, and then they started quartet singing. They loved it. One day I told Joe that I'd like him to listen to the boys because I thought they were pretty good. He didn't really believe me because they were just playing around and having fun, but then he listened and he thought they were really good, so he started rehearsing them. Joe always kept them rehearsed. I think that's what did it. The rehearsing made them successful. And they liked what they were doing."

The cab pulls out past a three-tiered white fountain at the front of the house. Michael's red-and-white scooter bike is leaning against a wall. All the windows in the house are leaded glass with beveled panes. We start out the open gate, when suddenly the guard in the security station runs and calls after us. We return to the house. Michael's parents are waiting in the foyer. Katherine Jackson calls me by name and says, "There have been a lot of rumors about Michael, that he has had operations to have his eyes widened and his cheeks changed and everything. Those things are simply not true. He had only one operation, on his nose. We were hoping you'd set the record straight and put a stop to the rumors. They also say Michael is gay. Michael isn't gay. It's against his religion. It's against God. The Bible speaks against it." Joe Jackson repeats, "Michael isn't gay."

This time the cab gets past the gate, which clicks closed behind us. On the street are two police cars and a group of teenage girls hanging out, hoping for a glimpse of Michael.

March 1984

Michael Jackson turned thirty in August 1988. His Thriller *follow-up,* Bad, *has sold more than seventeen million albums around the globe and produced five number-one singles. He says his* Bad *worldwide tour was his last. Michael's favorite new pet is his celebrated chimpanzee Bubbles. He has used a hyperbaric oxygen chamber to maintain his youth; he admits to plastic surgery on his nose twice, and once to add a cleft to his chin. In June 1987 Michael offered a million dollars to buy the skeletal remains of John Merrick, also known as the Elephant Man, from London Hospital Medical College. He was turned down. A feature-length movie based on Michael's best-selling autobiography,* Moonwalk, *was released in Europe and Japan in the fall of 1988. He bought a ranch in Santa Ynez, California. He plans to devote more time to film and is said to be working on an animated version of the Beatles' song "Strawberry Fields."*